THE POLITICS
OF LANGUAGE
1791-1819

THE POLITICS OF LANGUAGE 1791-1819

OLIVIA SMITH

CLARENDON PRESS · OXFORD

Oxford University Press, Walton Street, Oxford OX2 6DP
Oxford New York Toronto
Delhi Bombay Calcutta Madras Karachi
Petaling Jaya Singapore Hong Kong Tokyo
Nairobi Dar es Salaam Cape Town
Melbourne Auckland
and associated companies in
Beirut Berlin Ibadan Nicosia

Oxford is a trade mark of Oxford University Press

Published in the United States
by Oxford University Press, New York

British Library Cataloguing in Publication Data
Smith, Olivia
The politics of language, 1791-1819.
1. Sociolinguistics 2. Great Britain—
Politics and government—1760-1820
I. Title
320'.014   JN210
ISBN 0-19-812878-9

Typeset by Grestun Graphics, Abingdon, Oxon
Printed in Great Britain
at the University Printing House, Oxford
by David Stanford
Printer to the University

In Memory
of Virginia Shea
1947-1976

Preface

Many would acknowledge that ideas about language and literature were élitist in the last half of the eighteenth century. This study is largely an investigation of that truism and of the conflict which ensued when those ideas were challenged by the democratic movement. Élitist, however, is too vague and too descriptive a term to portray accurately the social and political presence of ideas about language. The concepts encoded in theories of language, dictionaries, and grammars were brought energetically to the fore when non-classically educated writers attempted to gain a place in 'civilization'. Ideas about language and ideas about suffrage shared the central concern of establishing which groups of people merited participation in public life. Civilization was largely a linguistic concept, establishing a terrain in which vocabulary and syntax distinguished the refined and the civilized from the vulgar and the savage. When suffrage was challenged in the 1790s, ideas about language were applied by courts of law and members of Parliament to justify repressive measures. Radicals had the difficult task of not only justifying the capabilities of the disenfranchised, but also of redefining the nature of language. The literary experimentation of Thomas Paine, William Cobbett, and less-known writers accompanied the writing of new theories of language and new grammars. These writers recognized the centrality of language to their political arguments. Thomas Spence, a self-educated writer often considered to be the first socialist, devised a phonetic alphabet and wrote a dictionary for his new variant of English. William Cobbett wrote a grammar to teach the self-educated how to participate in public life. William Hone, in his self-defence for blasphemous libel, argued with his judge about the nature of language. The experimentation of Wordsworth and Coleridge proves to be one of many and diverse experiments concerning the relation of language to class.

Extensive and extremely good work has been done on eighteenth-century theories of language, and I have no interest in slighting works which I have admired and benefited a great deal from. I would suggest, however, that late eighteenth-century theories of language were centrally and explicitly concerned with class division and that they cannot be entirely understood without their political component being taken into account. In order to understand the social context of ideas about language, various works and types of texts which do not often appear in studies of literature and language will appear on the subsequent pages. The works of such writers as Thomas Spence, which are insignificant when discussing literary tradition or the development of linguistic theory, gain significance when discussing the vulgar language. William Hone's trial will be discussed as a significant event in which ideas about language were contested, and also as a literary text which Hone wrote in conformity with the literary traditions of his class. Assumptions about language stated during political trials and sessions of Parliament will indicate the social effectiveness of ideas which were formally encoded in theoretical and literary texts. Admittedly there will be a relentless focusing on political questions. I do not mean to imply that these are the only means of evaluating literary or linguistic works but that such evaluations are not made frequently enough.

The book is composed of six essays that are somewhat distinct according to their titles and which yet need to be read together if any given part is to have an adequate grounding. The style of the *Rights of Man,* repressive legislation, John Horne Tooke's theory of language, advances in printing technology, William Hone's political trials, the *Biographia*, and Cobbett's *Grammar* are more related subjects, and related in more complex ways than one might at first imagine. I would like to apologize for any disjointedness in the argument that results from this attempt at inclusiveness. Other oddities of the book include its concentration on an audience that was on the fringes of the conventional reading public. I refer to these readers as 'the audience' because I am interested in them as a large public group which shared some common interests and which received a great deal of public attention. Other terms such as 'reader' or 'readership' tend to imply that reading is a private act performed by an aggregate of otherwise dissociated individuals. Despite objections and qualifications that one might want to make, Cobbett's and Coleridge's audiences had distinct political interests, a distinct relation to the state, and a political conflict between them which cannot be discussed in terms of 'the reader'. Unless otherwise specified, 'the audience' refers to readers who were generally considered to be incapable of participating in the body politic and who intended to gain more social and political standing. This non-refined and politically concerned reading audience was created by an increase in the number of readers during a time of considerable political conflict. It was the advent of this audience which challenged the concept of the vulgar language, prompting a reconsideration of assumptions about language that justified class division. The so-called vulgar are the main subject here. Rather than repeat cumbersome phrases such as 'the emerging audience', 'the lower-class audience', or 'the non-classically educated audience', it seemed more appropriate to let them be the audience. Traditional reading material of this audience such as ballads and broadsheets is discussed only in relation to contemporary writings and not as its own topic. While the audience read chap-books and ballads it was considered to have a distinct and subordinate province. Although such material might express ideas about political events, it was not regarded as an attempt to participate in public life. In its own day, the conflict described here was often characterized as one between the gentlemanly and the manly language. Radicals did not often raise the possibility of an adequate women's discourse. Excepting Thomas Spence's work, women were excluded from radical works which either directly discussed language, such as Cobbett's *Grammar,* or which indirectly extended the potentiality of informal language, such as the *Rights of Man.* An analysis of the relation of women's discourse to public life is not included here, although I would be pleased if the book encouraged such a study. Nor is the conflict between dialects and a national standardized accent considered in a book which is about the printed word. Altogether, there was too much material to include, of too many varying kinds.

The book is preoccupied with the achievement of an informal printed language capable of expressing political ideas, what I tend to call an intellectual vernacular language. As will become clearer, such a language was rarely acknowledged in conventional theories, grammars, and dictionaries written after 1750. A vulgar language was said to exist, a refined language was said to exist, and others were not recognized. Such extreme concepts dismissed everyone except the classically educated as an identifiable group characterized by their incapacity for refined thought and moral behaviour. Varieties of social class and modes of education were disregarded as diverse groups of people were reduced to one, most disreputable kind. What we might regard as different types or styles of language were discussed in the eighteenth century as if they were actually different languages, distinguished by etymology, syntax, and the mentality of the speakers. Arguments stressing that vulgar and refined English were the same language were invariably written by radical thinkers. As eighteenth-century theorists did, I refer to vulgar and refined language as if they were languages, because I am interested in the concept and its efficacy rather than in the actual qualities of language. I do not refer to the 'vulgar' except to mean the vulgar as they were defined in conventional theories of language or as they were regarded by those who believed in the concept of vulgarity. I employ the term to convey the attempt to contain subordinate classes by those who accepted or relied upon the category. The argument that eighteenth-century concepts of language were 'hegemonic' is basic to this study. Antonio Gramsci defined the term as a dominant system of ideas, held at both conscious and unconscious levels, that keep a society politically intact. Although Gramsci's application of the concept is relatively modern, by the 1790s radical writers began to study ideas about language in relation to political and social behaviour.

Finally, as an American writing about England, my approach to the topic differs from what an English writer's would be. My interest in the relation of ideas about language to social structure was prompted by witnessing the effects of the Black and women's movements in the United States.

Clearly, ideas about language and the writing of literary texts drastically altered as subordinate groups began to achieve some political power. Black-American, which had formerly been characterized as substandard English, began to be understood as a language which had its own grammar and syntax to which conventional standards of correctness were inappropriate. The American language itself is generally considered to be less formal, more robust, and some might say more vulgar than English. I know that my sense of the language derives partly from documents that have no English counterpart, such as the speeches of Martin Luther King, the Gettysburg Address, and the Declaration of Independence. Without living in a country that has an exceptionally vivid vernacular language or even without having heard the radical oratory of the 1960s, I doubt that I would have conceived of this project or approached it in the same way. I would be alarmed, however, if anyone thought of the book as a simplistic act of linguistic patriotism. Whatever hopes one might have had for powerful, demotic speech cannot remain simple when encountering such speakers as Margaret Thatcher and Ronald Reagan. I would object more mildly to the criticisms of applying modern standards to old texts. The availability of a printed vernacular language does not depend upon chronology, but upon the power of particular social groups and the means they have of asserting it. The vernacular language appears to have been more available for writers during the Civil War and the early eighteenth century than after 1750.

Without living in England, the process of writing the book would have been strangely detached from its origins. I was fortunate in having the opportunity of studying here and also of receiving especially astute encouragement and criticism. Mr E. P. Thompson, visiting Rutgers University to teach a course on poetry and politics of the 1790s, gave a jaded and somewhat confused graduate student an unfamiliar sense of possibility. Mr Thompson's work as both a teacher and a scholar is crucial to the existence of this book, as many will recognize. At the University of Birmingham, Professor

J. T. Boulton supervised the thesis from which this book originated. I was fortunate in having a supervisor who was demanding, responsible, and thorough. Mr Edward Thompson, Mrs Dorothy Thompson, and Mr Richard Johnson were also generous with their time and attention. The resources of the University of Birmingham enabled me to learn new methods and perspectives from not only the English Department but from the Centre for Contemporary Cultural Studies and the History Department as well. Seminars conducted by Mrs Dorothy Thompson and Professor David Lodge broke down the intellectual and social isolation of post-graduate work. As did many others, I greatly enjoyed debating ideas with the late Professor Geoffrey Shepherd.

Many people commented upon the thesis once it was completed. Professor Hans Aarsleff read several chapters and commented upon them extensively. The book has benefited from his criticisms, and I am grateful to him both for his correspondence and for his book, *The Study of Language in England 1780-1860*. Professor John Lucas examined the thesis and his comments were remembered as it was being rewritten. Mr John Barrell sent extensive comments, and his grasp of the project was a great encouragement in transforming the thesis into a book. Reading his chapter on language in *An Equal Wide Survey* helped me to reformulate my own argument more coherently even though I do not refer to his book in the main body of the text. Too often, I have referred to books only when I disagreed with particular ideas. I would not want these comments to be mistaken for evaluations or for a disregard of those books in the bibliography that are not mentioned elsewhere. Because the book draws upon different disciplines and different approaches within my own discipline, it depends exceptionally on previously written work. I would like to make amends for my neglect and to state my gratitude generally. Mrs Patricia Smith, Ms Susan Nash, Mr Sam Schulman, and Ms Carol Rose Livingston also read the thesis and made suggestions. Excepting readers at the press, no one has read the manuscript since its existence as a thesis. I hope that those who encouraged it during its youth will be pleased with it now. Readers, editors, and copy-editors have assisted me with great tact and goodwill. The staffs of the Birmingham University Library, the Birmingham Reference Library, the British Library, the Bodleian Library, the Mugar Memorial Library, and the Boston Public Library were always friendly and helpful. Mrs Anne Buckley did an exceptionally skilful and rapid job typing the manuscript.

To some of the same and to others, I owe debts of another kind. Having been a stranger makes one almost painfully conscious of hospitality. To Edward and Dorothy Thompson, I am again especially grateful, for they were the pivots around which a great deal turned. Veronica Ware once tracked down a distant reference, and her friendship did much towards making me at ease in this country. Rowena Clayton, Laxmi Jandagmi, and Carol Shloss, at various times, let me have rooms in their houses in which to write. Susan Nash has always watched over the book (and myself) with her benevolent eye. To Tom, Jonathan, Hester, and Hannah Storey, I am grateful for their generosity and their company. As for Mark Storey, I would not know where to begin or how to stop thanking him.

OLIVIA SMITH

Contents

Abbreviations

BL   British Library.

EL   English Linguistics 1500–1800 (a Collection of Facsimile Reprints), ed. R. C. Alston, Menston, 1967.

HO   Home Office papers.

MLC *Memoirs of the Life and Correspondence of Mrs. Hannah More*, ed. William Roberts, 3rd edn., 1835, 3 vols.

PD   Hansard's *Parliamentary Debates*. Initially edited by William Cobbett and continuing to the present.

PM   *Pig's Meat: A Lesson for the Swinish Multitude*, ed. Thomas Spence, 1793–6, 3 vols.

PP   *Politics for the People: or a Salmagunday for Swine* (1793–5), ed. Daniel Isaac Eaton, Greenwood Reprint Series, New York, 1968, 2 vols.

PR   *Political Register*, ed. William Cobbett, 1802–36, 89 vols.

ST   *State Trials: A Complete Collection of State Trials*, compiled by William Cobbett and later by T. B. Howells, 34 vols.

Chapter I

The Problem

In 1817, William Cobbett discussed the subject of grammar in two issues of his newspaper, the *Political Register*.[1] He had some practical reasons for doing so. The recent suspension of habeas corpus had caused him to flee to the United States in order to avoid a second imprisonment. On the wrong side of the Atlantic, he could no longer obtain information to write about current topics in England. In addition, Cobbett intended to publish his own grammar and wanted to alert his readers to the subject's importance. The urgency which is evident in these issues of the *Register* and the range of what Cobbett considered to be related topics cannot be entirely explained on these pragmatic grounds. His discussion of grammar quickly reaches out to the educational system, the status of the classical languages, the patronage of the 'boroughmongers' by the aristocracy, the entry requirements to the bar (£500, if one did not know the classical languages), a dinner given by the Prince Regent attended by Eton students, *'bawdy'* Greek plays enacted by Westminster students, and the charitable education of the poor. Cobbett considered grammar, in short, as an integral part of the class structure of England, and the act of learning grammar by one of his readers as an act of class warfare.

The division between those who knew grammar and those who did not, was, according to Cobbett, one of the primary means of class manipulation. As in Paineite rationalism's portrayal of traditional religion, in Cobbett's assessment of traditional learning ignorance, mystery, and authority reinforced each other to oppress the majority of the population. The knowledge of grammar was monopolized by the 'Boroughmongers', or rather 'the *knowing ones* amongst them' who confined its study to the grammar schools and the universities while excluding it from the education given

[1] The *Political Register*, xxxii (29 Nov. and 6 Dec. 1817), 1059-1120. The *Political Register* will be abbreviated as *PR*.

to the poor (pp. 1065-6, 1084). Only the wealthy, and those whom Cobbett called their 'supple dependents' learned how to write correctly (p. 1066). Because grammar schools were no longer admitting as many poor scholars, the few foundation students who were admitted became, in Cobbett's view, dependent and servile towards the upper classes. Cobbett thought these students particularly dangerous because they combined the 'pride of the noble with far more than all the meanness of his meanest domestic servant' (p. 1077). Moreover, grammar-school students were so extensively drilled that 'must it not be a sort of miracle, if a bold thought, an original idea, ever came from such a mind' (p. 1086). Those ignorant of the learned languages were hindered by the status granted to a false notion: 'The very use of this appellation ['*learned*'] is a cheat; a trick, intended to impose upon the mass of mankind, and to keep them in a state of unnecessary, and, therefore, unjust subjection' (pp. 1067-8). By writing a grammar for the self-educated Cobbett intended to forestall the intellectual intimidation deriving from the assumption that only those who knew the learned languages could write English accurately. Cobbett stressed that as well as interfering with the effectiveness of written documents, an ignorance of grammar interferes with the ability to think boldly and clearly: 'It creates a dependence, a diffidence; it cripples; it benumbs' (p. 1117).

The political and social effectiveness of ideas about language derived from the presupposition that language revealed the mind. To speak the vulgar language demonstrated that one belonged to the vulgar class; that is, that one was morally and intellectually unfit to participate in the culture. Only the refined language was capable of expressing intellectual ideas and worthy sentiments, while the vulgar language was limited to the expression of the sensations and the passions. Such a concept required making the refined as different from the vulgar language as possible while also requiring that certain types of thought and emotions be advocated to the detriment of others. This pattern was fundamental to the linguistic project of the last half of the century, when language was studied with unprecedented intensity. The study of universal grammar at that time stipulated that languages were fundamentally alike in that they represented the mind, and fundamentally different in the quality of mind and civilization that they represented. 'The vulgar and the refined', 'the particular and the general', 'the corrupt and the pure', 'the barbaric and the civilized', 'the primitive and the arbitrary' were socially pervasive terms that divided sensibility and culture according to linguistic categories. The baser forms of language were said to reveal the inability of the speaker to transcend the concerns of the present, an interest in material objects, and the dominance of the passions. Those who spoke the refined language were allegedly rational, moral, civilized, and capable of abstract thinking. By dividing the population into two extremes, ideas about language firmly distinguished those who were within the civilized world from those who were entirely outside it. The complexity of social life was drastically reduced by the denial of the possibility of a moral and intelligent vernacular speaker. Writers such as Thomas Paine, William Hone, and William Cobbett were not possible according to prevalent ideas about language. A few grammars and a few theorists considered language as singular, that is as an entity which could be defined according to all or most members of the population, but such works were neither numerous nor strong enough to threaten a hegemony of language which had been forming since at least 1750. The combination of practical texts, theoretical works, and concepts of style formed an intact and complete system that might be refuted in part but which had cohesive strength in its entirety. Between 1790 and 1819, the hegemony of language was severely challenged. Because ideas about language justified class division and even contributed to its formation by accentuating differences in language practice, they were sensitive to any political movement which threatened to disturb class boundaries.

Bishop Lowth, author of the first comprehensive grammar (1762), Samuel Johnson, author of the *Dictionary of the English Language* (1755), and James Harris, author of *Hermes* (1751), the major theorist of universal grammar in England, form something of a linguistic trinity. These three seminal works, appearing almost within a decade of each other, indicate the acceleration of the study of language, marking its initiation into a more prominent social role and simultaneously perpetuating the even greater role that it would have later. Although these writers did not entirely agree with each other, they none the less contributed to the hegemonic assessment of language by characterizing the literati as a class and formulating a language that was appropriate for it. Many ideas about language scattered in more minor grammatical works, in critical comments, in other dictionaries, and even in recorded political discussions, were initially codified in the grammar, the dictionary, and the theoretical work which held unrefuted sway until the end of the century. Their own identity was in part created by their relation to each other, to other texts, and to an ideology that was rapidly gaining in power during the 1750s and 1760s. The ideas of Lowth, Johnson, and Harris were mutually reinforcing in terms of their meaning and their authority. Their congruence, or lack of it, with each other's ideas about language and with those of more minor writers as well determined the contribution which they would make to ideas as they were publicly held. The idiosyncracy of these three authors' thought is not of primary concern here because their thought will be studied in relation to the political effectiveness of ideas about language. Their ideas will be studied in so far as they contributed to the hegemony of language, justifying and perpetuating class divisions.

Grammar books held an exceptionally important position, for they taught students the concept of the refined language as they were learning to write. In addition, such books were remarkably impervious to change. The authoritative status of Lowth's *A Short Introduction to English Grammar* was immediately proclaimed: 'The prescriptive grammar of Bishop Lowth was greeted as the counterpart of [Johnson's] Dictionary.'[2] Printed in twenty-two editions before 1795, it was by far the most widely studied grammar of the last half of the century. Because it offered the fullest explanation

---

[2] Ivan Poldauf, *On the History of Some Problems of English Grammar before 1800*, Prague Studies in English, Prague, 1948, p. 284.

of syntax, many other grammars were based on it or strongly influenced by it until as late as the 1840s. In 1795, Lindley Murray's grammar gained the prominent position of Lowth's, selling millions of copies throughout the nineteenth century. Because Murray's grammar was a work of compilation, as he acknowledges in his introduction, eighteenth-century attitudes towards language, and specific rules as well, lasted long after they had been discredited in their initial form and long after they had lost their philosophical basis. In this manner, rules of language which had resulted from the concept of universal grammar, and which confused English with the classical languages, were pervasive and long-lasting. As late as 1921, the Newbolt Commission of the *Teaching of English in England* recognized, with overdue surprise, that the language had to be reconsidered extensively if it were to be made available to people of all classes.[3]

By stipulating that the value of languages depended on the mind or sensibility that they represented, universal grammar justified ignoring the language as it was spoken in the attempt to make English resemble the more perfect languages, Latin and Greek. Lowth's prescriptive leanings thus had a philosophical basis. Appropriately, he calls James Harris's *Hermes*, '*the most beautiful and perfect example of Analysis that has been exhibited since the days of* Aristotle'.[4] The earlier scholars, Ivan Poldauf, Albert Baugh, and Sterling Leonard interpret the popularity of Lowth's text as a sign of the widespread desire to formalize the language and to distinguish it from spoken English.[5] More recently, Murray Cohen and Brian Hepworth have described Lowth's grammar

---

[3] Report of the Departmental Committee appointed by the President of the Board of Education, *The Teaching of English in England*, 1921, p. 264.

[4] Robert Lowth, *A Short Introduction to English Grammar*, 1762, English Linguistics 1500-1800 (a Collection of Facsimile Reprints), ed. R. C. Alston, Menston, 1967, no. 18, pp. xiv-xv. The English Linguistic series will subsequently be abbreviated as EL. Statements concerning the extent of publication of any work published in the series derive from Alston's introductory comments or from his bibliography, *A Bibliography of the English Language from the Invention of Printing to the Year 1800*, Leeds, 1965-71, 11 vols.

[5] Albert Baugh, *History of the English Language*, 1951, pp. 343-4. Sterling Leonard, *The Doctrine of Correctness in English Usage, 1700-1800*, University of Wisconsin Studies in Language and Literature, no. 25, Madison, Wisconsin, 1929, p. 14. Poldauf, p. 135.

as a text designed for all social classes and have praised him for his disregard of universal grammar. Murray Cohen thus discounts Lowth's strong praise of Harris's *Hermes* as a remark which contradicts Lowth's own approach.[6] Lowth's regard for universal grammar is evident in other remarks, however, and also in his method. The high priority given to Latin is evident throughout. The title imitates that of Lily's Latin grammar, a citation from Cicero (without a translation) appears on the title-page, Lowth conjugates the same verb as Lily, and the tenses are the same in name and number. Lowth's use of Latin terms and definitions to explain the English verb system is peculiar because he states that the structure of English verbs derives from the Anglo-Saxon (p. 67). Several of Lowth's other explanations, rather than focusing on English, prepare the student for Latin: 'the Participle with a Preposition before it, and still retaining its Government, answers to what is called in Latin the Gerund' (p. 111); 'Hypothetical, Conditional, Concessive, and Exceptive Conjunctions seem to require properly the Subjunctive Mode after them' (pp. 140-1). Even Lowth's definition of the verb, the famous 'to be, to do or to suffer' applies more to Latin than to English.[7] Although Lowth objected strongly to the neglect of the English language, he was not primarily interested in codifying it as a distinct area of study. His main intention – to make the practice of English more uniform – was partially achieved as no other grammar had a comparable authority over such a long period. But this intention is contradicted by his other two: to aid in the study of universal grammar and to simplify the study of Latin.

The uniformity which the text did supply was a limited one, for the book was designed to serve a class that was already well educated. Lowth maintains that the only means available to learn correct English were to be knowledgeable in the classical languages, to frequent polite society, and to have read 'ancient authors' extensively (p. viii). His grammar

[6] *Sensible Words; Linguistic Practice in England, 1640–1785,* Baltimore, 1977, p. 86.
[7] Ian Michael, *English Grammatical Categories and the Tradition to 1800,* Cambridge, 1970, p. 372.

was designed to augment these means which he regarded as insufficient. Instead of regularizing the language, Lowth formalized it for an extensively educated class and by doing so increased the distinction between spoken and written English. Lowth exemplifies Albert Baugh's assessment of the eighteenth-century grammarians:

They approached most questions in the belief that they could be solved by logic and that the solutions could be imposed upon the world by authoritative decree. Hence the constant attempt to legislate one construction into use and another out of use . . . Thus, as Noah Webster pointed out, every time they refused to base their statements on the facts of current usage they were also refusing to preserve an agreement between books and practice and were contributing 'very much to create and perpetuate differences between the written and spoken language'. (pp. 353–4)

Far from intending the book for the 'poor and unlearned' or for 'ostlers, dairymaids, country school mistresses, foreigners and apprentices, not to mention school children', Lowth intended it to be taught by tutors to private students, what he means by 'private and domestic use' (p. xiii).[8] When Lowth states that he designed the book for a 'Learner even of the lowest class', he is not referring to social status, a meaning of the word 'class' that was not current in 1762. The phrase refers to the student's level of knowledge, as the context makes clear. His following remark suggests that more advanced students read *Hermes* (p. xiv).

Some self-educated people none the less learned from Lowth's grammar, including Thomas Holcroft and William Cobbett. Not many would have been willing to expend the effort that Cobbett did, who studied the book while posted by the army in Canada. 'The pains I took cannot be described: I wrote the whole grammar out two or three times; I got it by heart; I repeated it every morning and every evening, and, when on guard, I imposed upon myself the task of saying it all over once every time I was posted sentinel.'[9]

[8] Cohen, p. 84, and Brian Hepworth, *Robert Lowth*, Twayne's English Author Series, Boston, 1978, p. 139.

[9] *Memoirs of the Late Thomas Holcroft written by himself*, ed. William Hazlitt, 1816, 3 vols., i. 252. William Cobbett, 'The Life and Adventures of Peter Porcupine' (1796), *Porcupine's Works*, 1801, 12 vols., iv. 45.

Lowth's explanations did not help him because Cobbett studied the book without a tutor and with only considerable experience of reading and writing English. Lowth's definition of the verb confused Cobbett because he took it to mean exactly what it said: 'I really thought, that any word which was descriptive of *pain*, or *suffering*, of any sort, was a verb, such as *toothache, fever, ague, rheumatism, gout*' (*PR*, xxxiv. 260). Lowth's use of such undefined terms as 'conceptive' and 'excessive' presumably added to Cobbett's confusion. Rather than its suitability, the frequency with which the book was printed and its comprehensiveness, led to its circulation beyond the boundaries of its intended audience. Moreover, many simpler grammars were based on Lowth's study. Cobbett, for one, made effective use of the difficulties he had with the book by writing a grammar specifically for the self-educated. He had learned what to avoid.

The formality of the language in both Lowth's and Murray's grammars would have been unfamiliar to students who were not already considerably educated. Such students were confronted with the confusion of having to learn a new type of language as they were learning how to write: 'The Irregulars of the Third Class form the Past Tense by changing the vowel or diphthong of the Present, and the Participle perfect and passive, by adding the termination en' (Lowth, p. 71). Such a style implies that the vernacular is inadequate, an implication that is confirmed elsewhere in the text and that often has a moral edge. Students are sometimes explicitly told that ordinary language is bad. Lowth objects to placing a preposition at the end of a sentence because it is too much like 'common conversation' and not sufficiently 'grand and solemn' (pp. 127-8). To varying degrees — Murray more relentlessly than Lowth — the two grammarians associate formal language and grammatical skills with moral virtue. Lowth claims that language is the gift of God, and correctness within such a framework connotes using language as God intended it to be used. The following sentence which Lowth asks his students to parse combines an exercise in grammar with a lesson in morality: 'The power of speech is a faculty peculiar to man, and bestowed upon him by his beneficent Creator for the greatest and most excellent uses;

but alas! how often do we pervert it to the worst of purposes' (p. 9). In Murray's text, examples of bad grammar are sentences which portray sins, warnings, or temptations: 'What signifies good opinions, when our practice is bad?' and 'The Normans, under which general term is comprehended the Danes, Norwegians, and Swedes, were a people accustomed to slaughter and rapine'.[10] Correct grammar conversely is usually illustrated by sentences which portray socially prescribed behaviour: 'Virtue, honour, nay even self-interest, *conspire* to recommend the measure'; 'Patriotism, morality, every public and private consideration, *demand* our submission to lawful government' (p. 93). This characteristic of Murray's text was praised by one critic for appropriately combining 'religious and moral behaviour with the elements of scientific knowledge'[11] and scorned by William Cobbett for its attempt to 'inculcate passive obedience and softly promote the cause of corruption' (*PR*, xxxiv. 226).

The basic vocabulary of language study — such terms as 'elegant', 'refined', 'pure', 'proper', and 'vulgar' — conveyed the assumption that correct usage belonged to the upper classes and that a developed sensibility and an understanding of moral virtue accompanied it. Grammar, virtue, and class were so interconnected that rules were justified or explained not in terms of how language was used but in terms of reflecting a desired type of behaviour, thought process, or social status. James Buchanan, for instance, argues that the English verb system must be complex because the English people are wise and respectable. For grammarians to maintain that the English verb system might be simple 'is manifestly affirming, that the English Language is nothing superior to that of the Hottentots; and that the wisest and most respectable Body of People upon the Face of the Globe, own a Language which is incapable of ascertaining their Ideas, or of exhibiting the Soul, and its various Affections.'[12] Certain rules were established precisely because they would

---

[10] Lindley Murray, *An English Grammar*, 1795, EL no. 106, p. 88.
[11] Cited from the *Guardian of Education*, ed. Sarah Trimmer, July 1803, in the duodecimo edition of Murray's *An English Grammar*, 1808, ii. 520.
[12] *British Grammar*, 1762, EL no. 97, p. 105.

differentiate written from spoken English. Priestley argues for making the preterite differ from the past participle 'if possible' because the variation would make English more like an inflected language.[13] Bishop Lowth deplores the practice of numerous writers who do not distinguish the preterite and the past participle as in 'I have spoke', Addison, Milton, and Dryden among them. Elsewhere, Lowth again disagrees with the practice of English writers because it does not agree with that of 'our best ancient writers' (p. 52). Perhaps taking the cue from James Harris, Lowth confuses the definite and the indefinite tenses, a confusion which makes the English language more like Latin. Lowth explains the phrase 'I have written' as describing a definite point of action while 'I wrote' as describing an indefinite one (Poldauf, p. 284). The confusion of the two seems to have altered habits of speech. Writing approximately sixty years later, in his grammar of 1817, Cobbett described the use of 'I have written' to indicate the simple past as an identifying characteristic of the 'language of corruption'.[14]

Texts whose purpose it was to teach English often describe it as an inadequate language which needed to be propped up by the sticks of classical vocabulary and syntax. Joseph Priestley, famous as a scientist, educator, philosopher, and radical, criticizes other grammars for their disregard of 'spoken and written' English (p. x). None the less, he was not entirely free of the prevailing disregard of the vernacular language. In his grammar, he condemns 'mere native English' as he calls it, for being incapable of sufficient cadence and sufficient intellectual precision. He recommends that his students make their own styles as classical as possible because

Such writers, moreover, are in less danger of debasing their style, by vulgar words and phrases, or such as have long been associated with, and, in a manner, appropriated to, vulgar and mean ideas; than which, nothing can be more unworthy of the mind, much more the compositions, of a gentleman, or a person of liberal education . . . (p. 56)

---

[13] Joseph Priestley, *On the Rudiments of the English Grammar*, 1761, EL no. 210, pp. 16–17.
[14] *A Grammar of the English Language in a Series of Letters* (1818), 2nd edn., 1819, p. 136.

(Priestley omitted his discussion of style from subsequent editions.) Other grammars also identify and exclude vernacular speech. James Buchanan, who paraphrases passages from *Hermes* to incorporate them into his grammar book, argues that instead of translating Greek and Latin writings, students could learn an elegant style by 'reducing the Language of our best Writers into a meaner Style to be rendered back into pure Diction' (xxvi). The distinction between vulgar and refined language was not so much an idea that was explained to students as one that was subsumed in the definition of language and in the process of learning it.

Although a considerable variety of grammar books existed in the last half of the century, those which did not accord with the dominant assessment of language were unconfirmed by the presence of similar ideas about language either in other texts or in everyday life. Anne Fisher's *A New Grammar* (1750) and John Ash's *Grammatical Institutes* (1760) were reprinted often during the century, thirty-three times and forty times respectively compared to Bishop Lowth's of forty-three. Anne Fisher's offered the unusual service of teaching the language without teaching the inadequacy of vernacular English. Although John Ash's similarly teaches informal English, he specifies that he intends it for students who will not be engaged in public life. It was written 'not only for Ladies, but for young Gentlemen designed merely for Trade'.[15] Other, less dominant ideologies inform John Wesley's and John Fell's grammars. Wesley's ten-page chap-book grammar, *A Short English Grammar* (Bristol, 1748), encourages its own set of beliefs when it conjugates the verb 'I fear'. John Fell's, *An Essay towards an English Grammar* (unsigned, 1784), associates pure English with English liberty and attempts to include the findings of the theorist John Horne Tooke, as does William Hazlitt's grammar of 1811. Because these texts were not supported by an array of theoretical works, critical comments, and dictionaries and because they were not taught to the dominant classes, they did not interfere significantly with the concept of refined English or with its capacity to augment the distance between classes.

[15] *Grammatical Institutes,* 1760, EL no. 9, p. iii.

In schools as well as grammars, a distinction was made between those who learned to write 'for Trade' and those who learned to participate in public life. Cobbett's accusation that writing was a restricted skill was hardly exaggerated. Students in dame schools, the most inexpensive form of fee-paying school, rarely learned to write more than the alphabet. Sunday Schools were jealous of how much they taught to whom. A free form of education which had spread rapidly since the 1780s, such schools taught students how to read in order for them to learn their duty. Thomas Laqueur in *Religion and Respectability* (1979), argues that by 1820, Sunday Schools had become autonomous working-class organizations that no longer restricted learning skills, an argument which some would question. During the 1780s and 1790s, Sarah Trimmer, Hannah More, and Jonas Hanway, the most famous exponents of education for the poor, stress political quietude and religious learning as reasons for teaching the poor. In fact, they perceive little distinction: 'The better *Christians* they are, the better subjects they will make.'[16] Educational policy considered the problem of keeping students obediently in their social place despite their receiving the advantage of an education. Sarah Trimmer argues in favour of 'making such learning as general as possible, for then it ceases to give pre-eminence or to be a distinction'.[17] That is, students should be taught morality rather than ideas or information which might make them proud. (The transition from 'general' to 'useful' knowledge encompassed a significant shift, indeed.) Hannah More, famous as a former bluestocking and latter-day propagandist, similarly forbade any pride of achievement which might have made her students socially restless. As she told them in a speech, 'You are now furnished with Bibles; You have been taught to read and to understand them; so that, if you now fall into sin, you will no longer have the former excuse to plead.'[18] Such students, whom Hanway calls the 'lowest of

[16] Jonas Hanway, *A Comprehensive View of Sunday Schools*, 2 pts, 1786, p. xii.
[17] *Reflections upon the Education of Children in Charity Schools*, 1792, p. 4.
[18] Cited from a speech given to her students on the closing of the school at Blagdon, 16 Nov. 1800 in Henry Thompson, *The Life of Hannah More with notices of her sisters*, 1838, p. 186.

the reasonable world', were not encouraged to engage in an act which would make their ideas known (p. 6). Students were carefully taught enough writing to be shopkeepers or servants. According to Sarah Trimmer, they learned a handwriting that was limited to the 'common purposes of life', a hand which apparently only they themselves could read. Only students chosen to be teachers were to learn 'a fine hand' (pp. 21, 23). Thus, as Richard S. Tompson points out, an extensive gap existed between rudimentary forms of education and an extensive education based on learning the classical languages.[19]

A statement by Samuel Johnson from the Preface to his *Dictionary*, yet another text which disparages the language while it teaches it, exemplifies the extreme connotations of the difference between the vernacular and classically-based English. In the following passage, the word 'illiterate' means ignorant of Latin and Greek: 'Illiterate writers, will at one time or another, by public infatuation, rise into renown, who, not knowing the original import of words, will use them with colloquial licentiousness, confound distinction, and forget propriety.'[20] The political nature of Johnson's remark is evident in his choice of words which by their resonance associate an ignorance of the classical languages with sexual immorality and the breaking down of class division: 'public infatuation', 'colloquial licentiousness', and 'confound distinction'. The statement implies that writers of vernacular English become famous only because the public is irrational. As the compiler of the *Dictionary*, founder of literary criticism, and author of a prose style that was avidly read and imitated, Johnson was a uniquely important popularizer of ideas which emphasized the distinction between refined and vulgar English. His rhetorical sweep brought vividness and range to concepts which might otherwise have had neither. No other writer concerned with language, such as Ben Jonson or Jonathan Swift, had such an extensive and tenacious appeal to the public.

[19] *Classics or Charity?: The Dilemma of Eighteenth Century Grammar Schools*, Manchester, 1971, p. 23.
[20] 'The Preface to the Dictionary of the English Language', *Samuel Johnson: Selected Poetry and Prose*, ed. Frank Brady and W. K. Wimsatt, 1977, p. 295.

The *Dictionary* commanded an authority that lasted well into the nineteenth century, as Becky Sharp's temper and more scholarly sources reveal.[21] The Preface, in itself, disseminated conservative assumptions about language and its relation to class. There, Johnson maintains a clearly drawn distinction between the language of books and the language of the living; what was considered to be the distinction between a genuine and a corrupt language:

Of the laborious and mercantile part of the people, the diction is in a great measure casual and mutable; many of their terms are formed for some temporary or local convenience, and though current at certain times and places are in others utterly unknown. This fugitive cant, which is always in a state of increase or decay, cannot be regarded as any of the durable materials of a language, and therefore must be suffered to perish with other things unworthy of preservation. (p. 293)

Contemporary critics pointed out that Johnson's evaluation of 'cant' was biased by his knowledge of the classical languages and his ignorance of Teutonic ones; words which he perceived as having no history were evaluated as 'cant'. The individual instances of such mistaken identifications matter less than the evaluation of the language which they contributed to and which Johnson presents here. Johnson's characterization of the language of the lower and middle classes as predominantly cant, presupposes that the language of different classes is essentially different. The passage, in a rhetorical high point of the Preface, memorably condemns the language of all but the extensively educated. Late eighteenth-century dismissals of colloquial language frequently provoke such rhetorical excitement, moments of élitist efflorescence.

The influence of Johnson's political sensibility on certain definitions is well known. His awareness of political corruption is well represented by such words as 'pension': 'In England it is understood to mean pay given to a state hireling for treason to his country.' But Johnson also omitted well-established political definitions of certain words. His definitions of the words 'equal', 'rights', and 'liberty' are

[21] See James H. Sledd and Gwin J. Kolb, *Dr. Johnson's Dictionary: Essays in the Biography of a Book*, Chicago, 1955.

apolitical. The only meanings which they have, both in the definitions and the accompanying sentences, are abstract, hierarchical, or paternalistic. He defines 'liberty' with the stark definitions 'opposed to slavery' and 'opposed to necessity' but not as opposed to arbitrary power. The sentence which portrays the definition is also apolitical: 'Liberty is the power in any agent to do, or forbear, any particular actions, according to the determination or thought of the mind, whereby either of them is preferred to the other.' This sentence treats liberty as the characteristic of an individual will and not, as in its political sense, in relation to exterior control. Johnson's definitions of 'equal' also exclude the word's political significance. The first definition 'Like another in any quality . . . that admits comparison', is explained by a citation from Ecclesiastes: 'If thou be among great men, make not thyself *equal* among them.' The first sentence to explain the definition of 'right' as meaning 'Justice, not wrong' also describes a hierarchical order: 'persons of noble blood are less envied in their rising, for it seemeth but *right* done to their birth'. Throughout the remaining definitions the examples are mostly negative, and the sentences portray mistaken assumptions of power. The Pope backed by the sword, tyrants, Judas, and Agrippa are the characters who assert their rights. Johnson's last definition of the word, to mean 'Immunity or privilege', includes the possibility of citizens having rights in its example: 'Their only thoughts and hope was to defend their own *rights* and liberties, due to them by the law.' But the definition is a peculiar one for immunity and privilege are granted by someone else or by circumstances, as by the law in this example. His definition excludes the possibility of citizens having rights according to their own authority or status, a definition of considerable standing since at least 1689: 'It may be declared and enacted, that all and singular rights and liberties asserted and claimed in the said declaration are the true and ancient and indubitable rights and liberties of the people of this Kingdom.' (Bill of Rights.)

The *Dictionary*, by its long-lasting and extensive distribution, gave to the conservative ideology of the 1750s an enduring and influential life. The evasion of the political, the belief that language pertains more to literary texts than to speech, and the demarcation of pure and corrupt usage along class lines became more commonly held assumptions due to their currency in Johnson's *Dictionary*. The Preface and his definitions betray his political position, both his anger at corruption and his distrust of expanding political power beyond traditional boundaries. In the 1790s, conservative pamphleteers did not admit that the words 'equality', 'liberty', and 'rights' had any political meaning. Johnson's *Dictionary* might well have authorized their insistence that 'liberty' meant nothing more than the absence of restraint and 'equality' nothing more than the denial of people's varying degrees of talent.

At a more specific moment, the *Dictionary* played a role in augmenting class division. In 1805 the governing body of Leeds Grammar School, which had been founded in 1552 'for the free teaching of all young scholars, youths and children who should resort to it', petitioned to include arithmetic and modern languages in its syllabus, as well as Latin and Greek.[22] At first, the petition was granted, but then the decision was overruled by Lord Eldon, a judge who vehemently defended the established order throughout his long career. Adamson describes the ruling: 'In Eldon's opinion a free school meant a free grammar school, and a grammar school as defined in Johnson's *Dictionary* was a school for teaching the learned languages. The governors therefore could not lawfully use the endowment for teaching anything else.' (p. 43.) By 1805 grammar schools were already becoming non-local and élitist; Rugby had made the transition by the 1780s. Eldon's ruling authorized a transition that was already taking place, and made it legally impossible to prevent it. After the ruling Greek and Latin were the only subjects which could be lawfully taught without charge. Poor students stopped attending the grammar schools because the education available to them was inappropriate. In 1810, when the directors of Harrow were brought to court for not fulfilling the obligations of their trust, they won their case by arguing that Harrow was a

[22] Cited by John William Adamson, *English Education, 1789–1902,* Cambridge, 1930, p. 43.

grammar school and 'not now adapted generally for persons of low condition, but better suited to those of a high class' (cited by Adamson, pp. 63-4).

The role of the *Dictionary* in Eldon's ruling is both arbitrary and appropriate. Arbitrary, in that any definition of a grammar school would have served, once Eldon decided that a free school meant a grammar school, which it did not. Appropriate, in that scholars such as Johnson who had received a classical education without having the social status which usually accompanied it, played a major role in fixing usages of language as a means of class distinction, as Raymond Williams has pointed out.[23] The increasing demarcation of class division in the late eighteenth century is brought out sharply in this instance. Here a one-time foundation student of a grammar school writes a dictionary which, a generation later, a court of law applies in a manner that justifies the exclusion of students like himself from the grammar schools.

The influence of Johnson's style and aesthetic theory appears to have run a similar course. Concepts which he initially encouraged gained momentum until they became burdensome, restricting creativity to a degree which Johnson would probably not have supported. The concept of the pure or the general language narrowed the possibility of metaphor and the range of diction by characterizing concrete terms as vulgar. Johnson, however, was comparatively unrestricted by the standards which he encouraged:

Language is the dress of thought; and as the noblest mien, or most graceful action, would be degraded and obscured by a garb which was appropriated to the gross employments of rustics or mechanics, so the most heroic sentiments will lose their efficacy, and the most splendid ideas drop their magnificence, if they are conveyed by words used commonly upon low and trivial occasions, debased by vulgar mouths, and contaminated by inelegant applications.[24]

By late eighteenth-century standards, Johnson's style does not advocate what he recommends. Such phrases as 'the dress

[23] *The Long Revolution*, 1965, p. 250.
[24] 'Lives of the Poets: Abraham Cowley', *Samuel Johnson: Selected Poetry and Prose*, p. 380.

of thought', and 'drop their magnificence' became less
allowable as purity of diction became a more rigid concept.
Philosophers, as well as writers such as Wordsworth, Blake,
and Coleridge, protested against the bad effects of too great a
concern with pure diction. Dugald Stewart and George
Campbell stated that English prose was enervated by too
great a concern with delicacy, while also warning their
readers against vulgar diction.[25] James Gilchrist protested
that philosophers no longer had the freedom of Plato who
mentioned crocks and pitchers in his teachings.[26] When
Edmund Burke wrote *Reflections on the Revolution in
France*, reviewers chastised him for his imprecise grammar,
the broad range of his vocabulary, his extravagant metaphors,
and the inelegance of his emotions, what were generally
considered to be the characteristics of vulgar prose. Carefully,
the critic discusses Burke's style with the circumlocutions
appropriate to his status: 'The language possesses much more
of the periphrastic verbosity of Cicero, than of his neatness,
his correctness or his elegance; much more of the warmth and
vehemence of Demosthenes, than of his force and energy'.[27]
In the following citation, William Godwin dismisses earlier
writers such as Addison, Shakespeare, and Fielding for
writing in too colloquial a style. According to Godwin, all
writers before Johnson 'were prone to tell their story or
unfold their argument in a relaxed and disjointed style, more
resembling the illiterate effusions of the nurse or rustic, than
those of a man of delicate perception and classical culti-
vation, who watched with nice attention the choice of his
words and the arrangement of his phrases.'[28] In the second
edition of the *Enquirer* (1823), Godwin rewrote his essay
on literature in order to account for his greater appreciation
of earlier writers. This new edition reflects the persuasive
force of radical critiques of language in the Preface to *Lyrical
Ballads* and the *Diversions of Purley*.

[25] 'On the Tendency of Some Late Philological Speculations', *The Collected
Works of Dugald Stewart*, ed. Sir William Hamilton, Edinburgh, 1835, 10 vols.,
v. 187. *The Philosophy of Rhetoric*, a new edition, New York, 1855, p. 186.
[26] *Philosophical Etymology or a Rational Grammar*, 1816, p. 229.
[27] *Monthly Review*, 2nd series, iii (1790), 314.
[28] 'On English Style', *The Enquirer: Reflections of Education, Manners, and
Literature*, 1797, p. 373.'

Aspects of Johnson's style that embodied hegemonic assessments of language were those which were developed and imitated. Johnson's adroit use of concrete vocabulary, his occasional elegant simplicity, and the emotional intensity of such works as the Preface to his *Dictionary* were rarely noticed as the features of his style that were being imitated. In 1787 Robert Burrowes, a member of the Royal Irish Academy, wrote an essay in the hope of curtailing the number of Johnson's imitators. He protested against the frequency of writers who attempted to duplicate Johnson's disregard for common diction, simple syntax, and the 'particular'. He claims that imitators did not have Johnson's ability to be universal while keeping the specific case in the reader's mind. 'His sentences, deprived of those feeble ties, which restrained them to individual cases and circumstances, seem so many detached aphorisms'.[29] The *Rambler*, which contains Johnson's most formal prose, appears to have been the work usually chosen as a model for style. In his short-lived paper, the *Porcupine* (1801), Cobbett published a series of articles about the *Rambler* which were written to consider the 'undecided question' of 'how far our language is indebted to him [Johnson] for its elegance, perspicuity and energy, or to what degree of refinement he has advanced it'.[30] Others had fewer doubts. John Walker and Anna Seward testify to the continuing and beneficial effect of Johnson's influence. John Walker dedicates his *Rhetorical Grammar* (1785) to Samuel Johnson and praises him for alerting the public to the importance of language and for demonstrating to them 'a thousand improvements'.[31] Writing in 1795, Anna Seward praises Johnson for the reformation of English prose: 'To [his prose compositions] may be fairly imputed the immense improvement in English prose-writing within the last half-century; by Latinizing our language, he has expanded its

[29] Robert Burrowes, 'Essay on the Style of Doctor Samuel Johnson' (1786), *Johnson: The Critical Heritage*, ed. James T. Boulton, 1971, pp. 334-7.

[30] 'A Short Enquiry into the Moral Writings of Samuel Johnson', *The Porcupine*, 2 Oct. 1801, signed Atticus and also published as a pamphlet in 1802, *A Critical Enquiry into the Moral Writings of Samuel Johnson*.

[31] *Rhetorical Grammar*, 1785, EL no. 266, p. iii.

powers, and harmonized its sounds'.[32] What she expresses as praise, from the perspective of this study, raises the problem of how a dominant, Latinized style — and Johnson's seems to have dominated a particular period as none has before or since — might have hindered the articulacy of less learned writers. To the achievements of an authoritative dictionary and an authoritative grammar, Johnson contributed an authoritative style that was recognizably suited for gentlemen. Although Johnson's application of that style is admirable in itself, it is less attractive when seen within the context of language theory and the class interests which that theory served. Johnson's literary skills advertised concepts of language more gloriously than they otherwise could have been, and the prodigious influence of his style was in part due to its manifestation of a hegemonic theory of language.

While Samuel Johnson's style popularized hegemonic concepts, they were initially given credence by theories which defined the nature of language. James Harris's *Hermes*, published in 1751, was an exceptionally influential text because it defined language at a time when linguistic hegemony was in the process of forming. *Hermes* and other theories are of interest because they make the notion of vulgarity explicit, revealing its depth and its scope. From numerous angles, *Hermes* incorporated conservative ideology within a philosophy of language and presented it as scientific theory. It assigned politics to the realm of sensation; it justified social hierarchy with the rules of grammar; it argued that language was designed by God for the purposes of classical scholars; it argued strongly against observation as an adequate means of knowledge; it advocated a type of language that was intrinsically apolitical; and it encouraged a complex system of rules which made language unnecessarily difficult to learn. Grammar books, dictionaries, and literary critics later extended ideas which were 'proved' in *Hermes* and other conservative theories. Thus *Hermes* gave initial strength to the alignment of ideas about language with class by providing them with an allegedly scientific base. *Hermes* would be refuted philosophically by the turn of the century

---

[32] 'Anna Seward's general estimate of Johnson' (1795), *Johnson: The Critical Heritage*, p. 413.

but despite an effective refutation at that level, the ideas and assumptions which it formerly developed had already gained their own momentum. *Hermes* encouraged the growth of ideas about language that began to be held increasingly as common knowledge and which continued to be politically efficacious in that form long after the book which sent them bravely out into the world.

The belief that the self and language coexisted in a simple and direct relation was the foundation of theories of universal grammar, as it was studied in the last half of the century. Language was universal because it manifested the nature of the mind or spirit. Comments such as Hugh Blair's are commonplace: 'if speech be the vehicle or interpreter of the conceptions of our minds, an examination of its structure and progress cannot but unfold many things concerning the nature and progress of our conceptions themselves, and the operations of our faculties.'[33] Once any disjunction between the speaker and what is spoken is disallowed, the implications of the level of language use are unbounded. Language was generally understood to be a transparent manifestation of value, and theories of language established criteria to measure the soul and civilization. The categories were crude, a matter of barbaric or civilized, vulgar or refined, particular or general, and primitive or artificial without admitting any intermediary status. And they were overwhelmingly significant. The dichotomies of language theory were methods of analysis, essential concepts around which an understanding of language, knowledge, and society were constituted. Refined language demonstrated that one's mind was substantially, almost constitutionally, different from the mass of mankind's. Language revealed how one perceived, which in turn revealed one's worth and social status. Thus what now reads as a paradox originally made some sort of sense: 'And thus for the honour of CULTURE *and* GOOD LEARNING, *they are able to render a man, if he will take the pains, intrinsically more excellent than his natural Superiors*'.[34] The powers

---

[33] *Lectures on Rhetoric and Belles Lettres* (1780), Edinburgh, 1820, 2 vols., i. 121.

[34] James Harris, *Hermes; or a Philosophical Inquiry concerning Language and Universal Grammar*, 1751, EL no. 55, p. 425.

of language could transcend those of nature, class, and identity.

James Harris and other universal grammarians portray the mind as performing two basic functions, that of reflection and sensation, and maintain that a linguistic difference separates those who think from those who sense. Language is designed for the purpose of reflection, which means to express ideas which are not determined by either time or place. Although words can express ideas which refer to the material world, that world is not its essential concern: 'the Sum of all is, that WORDS ARE THE SYMBOLS OF IDEAS BOTH GENERAL AND PARTICULAR; YET OF THE GENERAL, PRIMARILY, ESSENTIALLY, AND IMMEDIATELY; OF THE PARTICULAR, ONLY SECONDARILY, ACCIDENTALLY AND MEDIATELY' (pp. 347–8). (Harris and most other philosophers of the time do not distinguish between the general and the abstract or between the particular and the concrete.) Fellow grammarian and friend of Harris's, Lord Monboddo, similarly aligns linguistic, intellectual, and moral categories, but he extends Harris's work by considering it in relation to a theory of society. The 'general' language is now discussed as 'arbitrary' or 'artificial'. Such a language was created by philosophers and artists to express 'perfect ideas', ideas which are entirely divested of the aspects of time, place, and matter. The artificial language 'could not have been produced by mere *people*, but must have been the work of *artists,* and men of superior abilities'.[35] In contrast, the languages of children, savages, and the vulgar, are *'imbruted'* in the material world (i. 130).

This extreme denunciation of concrete language was written into the language, that is Harris defines and evaluates the parts of speech according to their distance from materiality. Pronouns are despicable because 'LANGUAGE, tho' in itself only significant of *general Ideas*, is brought down to denote *that infinitude of Particulars*, which are for ever arising, and ceasing to be' (p. 77). Abstract words are admirable because they result from an energetic act of the mind which is one of the mind's greatest achievements:

[35] James Burnett [Lord Monboddo], *Of the Origin and Progress of Language,* 1774–92, EL no. 48, 6 vols., ii. 6.

'By a *more refin'd operation of our Mind* alone, we *abstract any Attribute* from its necessary subject, and consider it *apart,* devoid of its dependence.' (p. 37.) Prepositions, conjunctions, and connective adverbs, known collectively as the 'particles', were generally considered to be entirely pure. According to Harris, particles are completely without meaning and indicate universal relations. Their syntactical function of establishing relations between words reflects the relations which order the universe. Certain conjunctions exist because of the 'Principle of UNION diffused throughout all things, by which THIS WHOLE is kept together and preserved from Dissipation' (p. 250). Monboddo, Blair, and Beattie each praise the particles as the greatest achievement of language: 'This part of speech is the most artificial and complex of any, and is justly esteemed the glory of the grammatical art.' (Monboddo, ii. 117.) Hugh Blair explains why:

The more that any nation is improved by science, and the more perfect their language becomes, we may naturally expect, that it will abound more with connective particles; expressing relations of things, and transitions of thought, which had escaped a grosser view. Accordingly, no tongue is so full of them as the Greek, in consequence of the acute and subtle genius of that refined people.[36]

To use many particles indicates that one's mind is not bound by the material world and that it engages with 'pure' reason. The concept of pure reason depended largely on the definition of the particles, for it was their existence which proved that the mind could act without referring to either time or place.

According to these standards of language, English is corrupt, primitive, and vulgar. Monboddo describes it with the phrase, 'our northern dialect' (iii. 49). English is a corrupt form of Anglo-Saxon, which in turn is a corrupt form of Gothic. Gothic was a more perfect language, according to Monboddo, because, like Ancient Greek, it maintained the advanced characteristics of inflections and terminations (ii. 485). James Harris argues that any language with less than five moods and twelve tenses, the number of those in Greek, is necessarily corrupt (pp. 122-3, 147-8). Other comparisons

---

[36] Blair, i. 121; James Beattie, *Theory of Language*, 1788, EL no. 88, p. 360.

of English with Greek or Latin reveal the limitations of the native tongue. It has too many harsh sounds and an inadequate supply of connective particles. It is overly concrete, too monosyllabic, incapable of syntactical variation, and deficient in abstract terms and inflections. Many blamed the faults of English on the barbarian's conquest of Rome (Beattie, p. 200; Priestley, p. v). According to Monboddo, English was incapable of purity because the origins of its vocabulary were 'scattered through different languages' (ii. 185). Universal truth, achieved by reading classical literature, is the only valuable method of knowledge within Harris's theory of language. Reading Ancient Greek enables people to learn about permanent ideas whose value is proved by those ideas remaining static throughout the centuries. Harris's discussion of verbs conforms to these values. The indicative mode 'exhibits the Soul in her purest Energies, superior to the Imperfection of Desires and Wants . . . [and] serves Philosophy and The Sciences, by just Demonstrations to establish *necessary Truth*; THAT TRUTH . . . which knows no distinctions either of Past or Future, but is everywhere and always invariably one' (pp. 159–60). To concentrate on the present, in contrast, is to engage in the most degraded form of knowledge because it is 'necessarily common to all *animal* Beings, and reaching even to Zoophytes, as far as they possess *Sensation*' (p. 113). Monboddo argues similarly. Those who do not have the benefit of the artificial language are extremely inferior to those who do. Incapable of expressing anything other than needs and opinions, the vulgar language is 'degraded and debased by its necessary connection with flesh and blood' (i. 47).

Within Harris' scheme, political language with its necessary grounding in specific times and places, becomes both a sloppy intellectual habit and a slightly immoral exercise. Writers such as Alexander Pope who think about contemporary life are not only intellectually misguided but they distort the very purpose of language: 'to those who tell us, with an air of seeming wisdom, that *'tis Men*, and *not Books* we must study to become knowing; this I have always remarked from repeated experience, to be the common consolation and language of Dunces' (p. 425). Harris's definition of words as

U73689

the signs of 'COMPREHENSIVE and PERMANENT IDEAS, THE
GENUINE PERCEPTIONS OF PURE MIND' attributes qualities to
vocabulary that are in themselves arguments against reform
(p. 372). Words when used for the purpose for which they
were designed do not refer to what is contemporary. Such
words as 'King' or 'constitution' alter their significance
considerably if they are conceived of as forms of eternal
ideas, valuable in that they are common to all people, times,
and places; and not as historical entities, a product of and
amenable to change. As we shall see, the nature of abstraction was a crucial matter of debate between conservatives and
radicals. If the primary world of ideas and relations is a
source of meaning and order in itself, which is represented by
language, then language can become a metaphysical pun.
Prepositions represent the universal relations of place:
'Hence, we transfer OVER and UNDER to *Dominion* and
Obedience; of a King we say, *he ruled* OVER *his People*'
(p. 268). The stasis of one confirms the stasis of the other,
and the validity of social institutions reflects the awesome
powers of language. Finally, Harris advocates political stasis
by demonstrating that only an intellectual élite deserve the
privilege of public participation. It is one which Harris had:
he was Chancellor of the Exchequer and Secretary to Queen
Charlotte. His theory of language is, in some respects, an
overbearing act of self-congratulation, for it proves that
people like himself are closer to God because they know
about the permanent ideas which are the expressions of God,
unhindered by time, place, and matter. Others have significantly different types of thought and a significantly different
language. The vulgar, according to Harris and others, demonstrate their unworthiness every time they employ language by
the nature of the language that they speak. In order to
vindicate the character of any but a ruling and highly
educated élite, language and even the parts of speech would
have to be redefined.

No matter how they might have disagreed with Harris at
significant points, other theorists and rhetoricians continued
to divide language into two major categories which reflected
a wide gap in the moral and intellectual capabilities of
people. Lord Monboddo, for instance, has recently been

praised for writing an exceptionally modern theory, for recognizing the centrality of syntax, and even for being proto-Marxist in that he recognized that social life determined language practice.[37] Such assessments do not mention the very frequent presence of ideas about class in Monboddo's theory, either those that are implied or are stunningly clear: 'men, not properly educated, are by nature destined to be slaves and drudges, or else to be miserable' (iii. 450). At the time, 'properly educated' men were scarce. Monboddo's fascination with the difference between animals and humans and even his interest in syntax are, to a considerable extent, motivated by an impulse to differentiate some men from the animal nature of the majority. Despite his alleged modernity, Monboddo's theory conforms to a basic pattern. Nor did the Scottish philosophers of the common-sense school threaten the concept of refinement. Although they disagreed with some aspects of Harris's theory, they were engaged in a similar project. Whereas Harris and Monboddo employed ideas about language to counter the primacy of sensation and experience in Locke's philosophy, Thomas Reid, James Beattie, and George Campbell rely on it to refute Hume's scepticism. Despite the democratic air of their title, the common-sense school maintained rigid social divisions according to linguistic practice. George Campbell's *Philosophy of Rhetoric* stresses that the standard for language use should be what is 'reputable, national and present' by which he means the written practice of an intellectual élite (p. 173). The diction of the vulgar, he describes as 'counterfeit money, though common, not valued' (p. 165). Again, the spoken language is discounted as a respectable form, and the vulgar language is condemned as the manifestation of a stunted mentality (p. 166).

At first glance, primitivists such as Bishop Lowth, Hugh Blair, and Thomas Percy appear to be in substantial disagreement with hegemonic assessments of language. But rather than challenge the basic construct of ideas about language,

---

[37] Stephen K. Land, 'Lord Monboddo and the Theory of Syntax in the Late Eighteenth Century, *Journal of the History of Ideas*, xxxvii (1976), 423–40. L. Formigari, 'Language and Society in the Late Eighteenth Century', *Journal of the History of Ideas*, xxxv (1974), 275–93.

primitivists maintain it while arguing that primitive languages are of more value than was generally recognized. The characteristics of primitive languages and their essential difference from civilized language are not challenged. Concrete terms, emotional expressions, syntactical simplicity, an abundance of metaphors, and a paucity of terms are the distinguishing features of primitive language. Some writers appreciate such language as long as it is confined to the discourse of primitive literature. In his *Lectures on the Sacred Poetry of the Hebrews*, a text written in part to refute charges of the Bible's vulgarity, Robert Lowth argues that the passionate language of Hebrew poetry is not governed by normal laws of discourse. In a statement which Lowth allows to stand in order to reveal the persuasiveness of concepts which he was arguing against, he maintains that Hebrew poetry 'abounds with phrases totally unsuited to prose composition and which frequently appear to us harsh and unusual, I had almost said unnatural and barbarous'.[38] Lowth wants his readers to admire primitive language but not to imitate it or to consider it as similar to refined speech. He warns his audience against using metaphors from 'common life' as the Hebrew poets did because biblical language is essentially different from the modern language of reason. Hugh Blair evaluates primitive language much as Lowth does. Although he admires the emotional intensity and metaphorical character of primitive literature, he considers such traits as a necessary sacrifice to the advance of reason, the grammatical march of civilization (i. 82). In his introduction to the *Reliques of Ancient English Poetry*, Thomas Percy describes his embarrassment at publishing 'a parcel of Old Ballads': 'As most of them are of great simplicity, and seem to have been merely written for the people, he was long in doubt, whether, in the present state of improved Literature, they could be deemed worthy the attention of the public'.[39] The *Diversions of Purley* and the poems and the Preface of *Lyrical Ballads*, especially the 'Rime of the Ancyent Marinere', first placed primitive and civilized languages on an equal footing, as will be discussed in chapter six. Until then, a limited admiration of primitive

[38] Trans. G. Gregory, 2 vols. 1787, p. 321.
[39] 6th edn., 1823, 4 vols., pp. 9–10.

language co-existed readily with an assessment of language that stressed the necessity of refinement for public discourse and the essential difference between speakers of different types of language. Primitivists such as Blair, Lowth, and Percy kept open certain options which would be more fully developed later, but neither they nor the Scottish philosophers challenged the supremacy of the refined language.

The hegemonic understanding of language was efficiently self-protecting. By defining a theory of the mind according to a theory of language, both needed to be disproved in order for the one to be discredited. Joseph Priestley wanted to refute the work of conservative theorists by reinstating Hartley's philosophy. His work of aesthetics, *A Course of Lectures on Oratory and Criticism* (1777), attempts to align Hartley's theory of the mind with aesthetic theory, an interesting precursor to the Preface to *Lyrical Ballads*.[40] Although Kames preceeded him in the attempt — Priestley acknowledges his debt — Priestley was out on an intellectual limb without an appropriate analysis of language to demonstrate his philosophy of the mind or to disprove such theories as Harris's and Monboddo's. One could say the same of his *Course of Lectures on the Theory of Language and Universal Grammar* (1762), where Priestley considers language in relation to history and not to the mind or civilization. The vulgarity of terms does not indicate a particular mentality but is merely an 'accidental association' of a word with a particular social class.[41] Thomas Sheridan, whose work will be discussed in chapter three, discusses language as the single entity of a unified culture, but again his work is isolated, a rarity among congruences. Another radical theorist, John Horne Tooke, described the difficulty of discrediting a theory which had appropriated language: the means of expressing the refutation apparently disagreed with its content.[42] To challenge effectively the relation of language to the mind, one would have to redefine the parts of speech. Tooke achieved this, and simultaneously threw the nature of the mind and civilization into doubt. But his refutation of

[40] EL no. 126, pp. i–iii.
[41] EL no. 235, p. 233.
[42] *Diversions of Purley*, 1798–1805, EL no. 127, 2 vols., i. 15.

conservative philosophers did not totally alter ideas about language as they were publicly held nor as they were maintained by books which taught the language and which had a larger audience: Blair's *Lectures*, Campbell's *Rhetoric*, Murray's *Grammar*, and Johnson's *Dictionary*.

Such books had a double edge. They established grounds for dismissing any writings addressed to or originating from the vulgar audience, while making a language considered adequate for public discourse more difficult to learn. Monboddo, Harris, Beattie, and Blair, each dismiss simple language in terms which evaluate the minds of the authors according to their style. By such formulations, it would be impossible to write in a vernacular without declaring the inadequacy of one's self and one's audience. According to Harris and Monboddo, vulgarity meant a language excluded from God's order. And according to Priestley (in the first edition of his grammar), Blair, and Beattie, the milder terms of barbaric and primitive have similar connotations: certain types of language: 'mere native English' or 'our northern dialect' are opposed to civilization. Indignation, a common characteristic of political writing, is primitive in Blair's terms. Anger, vehemence, a non-abstract vocabulary, and an abundance of metaphor could be dismissed according to Blair and others as primitive both morally and intellectually. In spite of the individual disagreements of these writers, in spite of the forty years spanned by their writings, these authors agree on one fundamental point: that there were two types of language which were intrinsically related both to class distinction and to qualities of mind.

Conservative concepts of language were perpetuated not only by texts, but by the political conflict which they would be called upon to contain. Ideas about language soon became more widely known as they were applied by the state and its supporters to protect themselves from criticism. Trials for sedition, discussions in Parliament, comments in newspapers, and responses to petitions relied on the notion of vulgarity to argue against the concept of extended or universal male suffrage. Because both suffrage and ideas about language depended on the question of who was considered to be capable of participating in public life, the two were vitally connected. The ability to define simultaneously a class, its moral worth, and its language presented a formidable stumbling block to the possibility of discussion between classes. If one's language is condemned, no means exist of refuting the charge. Employed vehemently and often enough, ideas about language became in themselves a source of antagonism, as Cobbett's articles and numerous political confrontations reveal.

Petitions to Parliament favouring extended or universal male suffrage provoked responses which relied on assumptions about language. Between 1793 and 1818 (and later as well), Parliament dismissively refused to admit petitions because of the language in which they were written. As Parliament's refusal remained the same no matter what the petitions' style, the pitch of the argument grew increasingly intense. In 1793, 1810, and 1817 such petitions were presented from various social groups. The few that were accepted were ordered to lie on the table and not referred to Committee. Except for an occasional remark such as Thomas Sheridan's — 'he suspected that the objection to the roughness of the language was not the real cause why this petition was opposed' — political arguments were contained and then dismissed within the context of ideas about language.[43] The size of the majority rejecting petitions on this ground was substantial: the figure of 109 to 21 is representative (xxx. 784). In 1793, petitions such as those from Nottingham and Sheffield stated explicitly the class of petitioners. Wilberforce, Dundas, and Ryder objected to the following 'highly indecent and disrespectful language' (xxx. 784):

> Your petitioners are lovers of peace, of liberty, and justice. They are in general tradesmen and artificers, unpossessed of freehold land, and consequently have no voice in choosing members to sit in parliament; — but though they may not be freeholders, they are men, and do not think themselves fairly used in being excluded the rights of citizens. (xxx. 776)

[43] Hansard's *Parliamentary Debates*, xxx. 784. Subsequently abbreviated as *PD*.

Comments dismissing such language did not require much elucidation. Wilberforce argued more fully to counter the protest that the language of petitioners could not be described as 'indecent' when it was the same which members of Parliament used to address each other and their constituents: 'Liberty of speech and freedom of discussion in that House, formed an essential part of the constitution; but it was necessary that persons coming forward as petitioners, should address the House in decent and respectful language.' (xxx. 779.) The necessity of writing in a 'decent and respectful language' was a new requirement for petitions. Arguments that pointed out that it took a considerable degree of education to write in formal language were discounted. Those who favoured accepting the petition also mentioned an earlier one from Nottingham (1783) which had advocated universal suffrage. Although it had been 'much bolder and more irregular in its language' (xxx. 464), it had been accepted. The rejection of the Sheffield and Nottingham petitions was tremendously important for it established a precedent for rejecting petitions for the reason of language alone.

Once the criterion of language was allowed it proved difficult to evade. In 1810 other petitions were presented. During the discussion of these, social respectability was used as an argument to disprove the predictable allegation of insulting language. Signers of 'the most respectful description and of considerable property and influence' (xvii. 114) were presumably incapable of writing indecent language. A petition from Reading was accepted which had been signed by twelve freeholders representing a larger public meeting: 'the language of this, though firm as it ought to be, was respectful' (xvi. 949):

The petitioners cannot conceive it possible that his Majesty's present incapable and arbitrary ministers should be still permitted to carry on the government of the country, after having wasted our resources in fruitless expeditions, and having shewn no vigour but in support of antiquated prejudices, and in attacks upon the liberties of the subject. (xvi. 955)

The fine but crucial distinction between firm and indecent

language apparently depended on who was speaking. The petition from Reading was as strong as the petition from Sheffield, despite its more formal language. It appears to have been more acceptable because of the social status and the small number of the signers.

Political perspective, as well as class, could affect the standards of propriety. Major John Cartwright, who had advocated universal suffrage since the 1780s, submitted a petition which was not protected by either his social status or his self-conscious attempt to write in a decent language. In the citation which follows, he discusses an event of the previous year. Castlereagh and Percival had been excused by the House from the charge of manipulating elections because such practices were common:

Although there be not in human speech words by which the thoughts of the petitioner on this the decision of the House can be expressed, he cannot dismiss the subject without saying, but disclaiming any idea of being indecorous, that such treatment of the people is beyond endurance. (xvi. 1022)

Those who objected to the petition maintained that the inaccurately remembered expression '"past all endurance", [was] fully sufficient to warrant the rejection of the petition' (xvi. 1031).

In 1817, a large number of petitions were addressed to Parliament by the disenfranchised, such as the following from Yorkshire:

The petitioners have a full and immovable conviction, a conviction which they believe to be universal throughout the kingdom, that the House doth not, in any constitutional or rational sense, represent the nation; that, when the people have ceased to be represented, the constitution is subverted; that taxation without representation is slavery . . . (xxxv. 81–2)

Discussion of this petition reached a new pitch of excitement. To Canning, 'if such language were tolerated, there was an end of the House of Commons, and of the present system of government' (xxxv. 85–6), to which Romilly replied, he 'carried his refinement too far' (xxxv. 90). Whereas the rough language of the petitions of 1793 was grounds for dismissal, the more literary quality of the Yorkshire petition made it less acceptable.

When he [C. Grant] perceived no want of literary talent, no deficiency of knowledge, in that document, and when he saw that if it was intended to insult the House, it would be impossible to select any language more appropriate for such a purpose, he confessed he knew not what other inference could be drawn from it. (xxxv. 90)

When the same petition was presented from another county, the Chancellor of the Exchequer argued that the language was evidently not 'the genuine authentic language of the petitioners' but the 'dictation of certain factious demagogues' (xxv. 91). The county of Berkshire resubmitted the same petition with the objectionable passages amended, but it was again rejected: 'He [Castlereagh] did not know what words had been left out of the petition, but he imagined that there could not be any more objectionable than those which remained.' (xxxv. 873.)

Sir Francis Burdett submitted over five hundred petitions allegedly containing almost a million signatures. These were all rejected either because they were printed or because they were the same as petitions which had already been rejected. He argued: 'it was of the utmost importance to the country that they should come to some decision, in order that the people might know in what language the House would be inclined to lend their ears to grievances.' (xxxv. 993.) His suggestion was not taken up because if rules were formulated the House would then be unable to protect itself sufficiently: 'It would only give these persons an opportunity of choosing words by which any such rule might be evaded, and then they would come to the House with language as offensive, or more so, and say that it was not within the rule.' (xxxv. 994.) If rules were to match the flexibility with which ideas about language were used by the House, they would necessarily have to be distressingly clear. Either stricter rules would have to be formulated for radicals and the disenfranchised or the freedom of other petitioners would also have to be curtailed. Subject-matter would also have to be applied as a criterion. Various members recognized that stricter requirements of delicacy and precision were applied against petitions in favour of universal suffrage and annual elections. Such standards would be difficult to clarify without provoking further disagreement.

Relying on language to subsume political ideas, however, is not an innocuous gesture. Rejection of the petitions implied that the disenfranchised could not write in a language which merited attention. Petitioners, such as those from Sheffield, did not respond gladly to the charge: 'We shall trouble them no longer with our coarse and unmannerly language.'[44] While the new demand for a decorous language protected the state from criticism, it also rigidified the distance between the House and the disenfranchised. If the vulgar did not formerly know of the assessment of their language in theories of language and literary works, responses to their writings in the House, in courts of law, and in conservative publications would soon make it clear.

[44] Cited from 'The Proceedings of the Public Meeting held at Sheffield . . . on the 7th of April 1794', in the 'Second Report of the Committee of Secrecy respecting Seditious Practices', *PD*, xxxi. 737.

Chapter II
Rights of Man and its Aftermath

John Simple, speaking of his wife's stay-maker to Mr
Worthy: 'He is one of the prettiest-spoken men in the
world'.[1]

The publication of *Rights of Man* demonstrated that a
language could be neither vulgar nor refined, neither primitive nor civilized. Such dichotomies of theory did not
account for the possibility of an intellectual vernacular
speaker, nor did literary values account for the possibility
of an intellectual vernacular prose. Even a writer as bold and
as experienced as Thomas Paine was somewhat constrained
by conventions of language. Describing the reason for the
interval between the two parts of his book, he states: 'I
wished to know the manner in which a work, written in
a style of thinking and expression different to what had been
customary in England, would be received before I proceeded
further.'[2] Other factors besides Paine's talent contributed
to the possibility of his writing such a uniquely audacious
book. Paine was not denounced as a vulgar author until he
had written *Rights of Man*. The respect of such people as
Edmund Burke and the Duke of Portland might well have
increased his ability to disregard conventional standards.
Also, Paine began writing in revolutionary America, a time
and place where English concepts of language lacked a strong
ideological hold. That he hesitated at all indicates the
tenacity of concepts of language and suggests the greater
difficulty of writers who remained in England.

Thomas Paine was hindered by literary convention but not
by living within social relations which imposed limits to his
abilities and interests, as were his English counterparts.
Francis Place, for instance, described the financial necessity

---

[1] Unsigned, *A Dialogue between Mr. Worthy and John Simple*, 1792, p. 4.
[2] 'The Rights of Man', *The Writings of Thomas Paine*, ed. Maurice D. Conway,
1894-6, 4 vols., ii. 394. Conway's edition differs considerably from P. S. Foner's.

of disguising his inappropriate tendency to read. He carefully kept his library hidden because he lost valuable customers when they discovered he was 'bookish': 'Had these persons been told that I never read a book, that I was ignorant of every thing except my business, that I sotted in a public house, they would not have made the least objection to me.'[3] The most devastating aspect of eighteenth-century assessment of language was its philosophic justification of this notion of vulgarity. While criticizing the stultification resulting from a rigid class society, Paine simultaneously demonstrated that the limits it imposed were fictitious. He stressed the intellectual and moral capability of his audience and wrote in a language that was alleged not to exist, an intellectual vernacular prose.

Thomas Paine wrote the *Rights of Man* in reply to Edmund Burke's *Reflections on the Revolution in France,* and the two books stand in a curious relation. Generally, the *Reflections* was received with gratitude by the radical movement for bringing greater definitiveness to political ideas. John Thelwall (principal orator of the London Corresponding Society) claimed that he did not consciously hold a political position until he read the *Reflections*. Only then did he realize that he had previously believed in the frequently reiterated phrase 'the glorious and happy constitution' and that he believed in it no longer. Others, he reports, responded similarly to the book. Burke

wrote the most raving and fantastical, sublime, and scurrilous, paltry and magnificent, and in every way most astonishing book ever sent into the world. A book, I will venture to say, which has made more democrats, among the thinking part of mankind, than all the works ever written in answer to it.[4]

Radical democratic clubs, such as the Norwich Society, praised Burke for initiating the great debate 'by which he

---

[3] *Autobiography of Francis Place*, ed. Mary Thrale, Cambridge, 1972, p. 223.
[4] John Thelwall, *The Tribune*, 1795-6, 3 vols., ii. 220.

has opened unto us the dawn of a glorious day'.[5] Fully describing a conservative viewpoint, Burke established a background which enabled others to recognize their own thought. Ideas which had previously been unformulated were now held consciously or disowned.

By writing about politics in an unusual manner, Burke made the radical position more capable of being articulated. Making political thought more conscious, in itself, makes it more expressible. This is the usual benefit of good discussion and both Thelwall and the Norwich Society were grateful for it. Also, Burke disregarded various literary conventions in the *Reflections* which hindered the development of an intellectual vernacular. He wrote in a manner that was recognized as both refined and vulgar. Philip Francis, who read the *Reflections* before publication, advised Burke not to publish it. It was too emotive, the language was too wide-ranging, it would serve the radical cause, and it would initiate a pamphlet war.[6] Reviews of the book concur with Francis's initial assessment. The *Monthly Review*, which has also been cited in the first chapter, was both awed and offended by the book. Burke's writing drew on an unfamiliarly wide range of metaphors, 'sublime and grovelling, gross and refined'.[7] Its vehemence, its disorder, and its disregard of elegance were the characteristics of his prose that did not accord with prevalent appraisals of the refined language. While reading the published and expanded version of the book, Francis sent further criticism to Burke:

Once for all, I wish you would let me teach you to write English. To me, who am to read every thing you write, it would be a great comfort, and to you no sort of disparagement. Why will you not allow Yourself to be persuaded, that polish is material to preservation?

(*The Correspondence*, p. 151)

Francis's confident tone derives from an authority that was fully supported by an intact and well-known literary code.

[5] 'Resolutions of the United Constitutional Societies of Norwich', cited during the trial of Thomas Hardy, in *A Complete Collection of State Trials*, initially compiled by William Cobbett and later by T. B. Howells, 34 vols., xxiv. 292. The *State Trials* will be abbreviated as *ST*.

[6] *The Correspondence of Edmund Burke*; vol. vi, ed. Alfred Cobban and Robert A. Smith, Cambridge, 1967, pp. 85-7.

[7] *Monthly Review*, 2nd series, iii (1791), 314.

Burke held various ideas which disagreed with the basic tenets of language theory. He did not believe that the rationalism of Greek and Roman civilization constituted the most valuable strain of European culture. The inclusion of feeling in feudal modes of behaviour and government makes it superior to Greek and Roman forms:

It is this ['the mixed system of sentiment and opinion'] which has given its character to modern Europe. It is this which has distinguished it under all its forms of government, and distinguished it to its advantage, from the states of Asia, and possibly from those states which flourished in the most brilliant periods of the antique world.[8]

Burke's idiosyncratic admiration of chivalry included a criticism of the late eighteenth-century's assessment of reason. By arguing against the Dissenters, Burke argued against an ideology which had a radical form, and which also held pervasive sway. The political stance of the *Reflections*, as Conor Cruise O'Brien explains it, was of a peculiar kind: 'These writings — which appear at first sight to be an integral defence of the established order — constitute in one of their aspects . . . a heavy blow against the established order in the country of Burke's birth, and against the dominant system of ideas in England itself' (Introduction to the *Reflections*, pp. 34-5). Burke's style is one means by which he both attacks and defends the established order. The frequency of such phrases as 'influenced by the inborn feelings of my nature' (p. 168), indicate the extent of Burke's disagreement with theorists who had isolated reason as an autonomous faculty. Burke's willingness to rely on experience, his assumption that emotions are not transitory and irrational but a valid component of thought, and his unwillingness to detach himself from the ordinary world by his diction are the eccentric characteristics of his prose. Burke attacked the Dissenters with a charge that, in fact, does not belong specifically to them but to anyone who concurred with the dominant theory of language: 'They despise experience as the wisdom of unlettered men' (p. 148).

Paradoxically, Burke disregarded literary conventions in

[8] *Reflections on the Revolution in France*, ed. Conor Cruise O'Brien, 1969, p. 170.

order to maintain the status quo. Vulgar language appears in his book with full consciousness of its vulgarity, usually portraying the minimal sensibility that would prevail if the radicals were successful: 'The state ought not to be considered as nothing better than a partnership agreement in a trade of pepper and coffee, callico or tobacco, or some other such low concern' (p. 194). Such uses of language are effective because their recognizably vulgar vocabulary condemns the minds and morals of those who think in such terms. The alignment of intellectual and spiritual values with class affected by theorists of language allows Burke to insult the radicals by his choice of diction. What is unusual here, however, is Burke's distinctive notion of vulgarity. He employs vulgar terms to portray sensibility that relies only on reason — what was usually considered to be the greatest achievement of the refined languages. Burke's use of vulgar terms does not portray a plebeian and irrational mind, but the brutality of a mind that performs with only one faculty. Elsewhere Burke uses vulgar terms without the pointedness of his comment here. Whereas Philip Francis sarcastically apologizes for the 'elegant' phrase 'I *vow to God*' in his letter to Burke (*The Correspondence*, p. 87), Burke adopts the language of workers to convey his meaning more precisely. To do this without apology is extremely unusual: 'A politician, to do great things, looks for a *power*, what our workmen call a *purchase*' (p. 267). With a style that was recognizably deviant, Burke brought vulgar terms, arguments based on experience, and impassioned speech into political discourse. For Paine to break the same conventions for the purpose of disrupting traditional class alignments might have been more difficult to achieve without the unsettling of literary conventions performed by the *Reflections*.

Other contributing factors should be considered before we return to Burke. Paine's reading of French authors and his experience of revolutionary America provided him with a range of conventions that was foreign to English literature and English concepts of language. This externality was essential to his becoming an author and to his becoming the type of author he became. Although he was admired as a debater and had written an unpublished pamphlet while in

England, his arrival in the United States brought aimless talents sharply into focus: 'It was the cause of America that made me an author'.[9] By the time of writing *Rights of Man*, Thomas Paine had already contributed to the development of an intellectual vernacular in the United States. Eric Foner points out that Paine's achievement with *Common Sense* is analogous to his achievement in England with the *Rights of Man*. With that pamphlet also he was the first pamphleteer to address a broadly-based audience with colloquial language and to articulate political ideas that had remained unexpressed.[10]

Paine's experience of a culture which was considering the political implications of a range of questions, including language, undoubtedly gave him a greater freedom from the restrictions on language use than was possible in England. The revolutionary movement was quick to recognize the importance of language. By 1789, Noah Webster had developed a critique of the class bias of English theories and practice of language. He argued that language had been distorted in the grammar texts in order to make it more closely resemble Latin and Greek, that the model of grammar should be the spoken tongue, and that English usage had been artificially constructed to maintain and perpetuate class distinctions. According to Webster, the cumulative effect of the works of Johnson, Lowth, Sheridan, and others was to hinder the process of speaking and writing:

The general practice of a nation is not easily changed, and the only effect that an attempt to reform it can produce, is, to make *many* people doubtful, cautious, and consequently uneasy; to render a *few* ridiculous and pedantic by following nice criticism in the face of customary propriety; and to introduce a distinction between the learned and unlearned, which serves only to create difficulties for both.[11]

Although English ideas and concepts of language were present in America (Lindley Murray was American), they did not have the monolithic status which they had in

---

[9] Thomas Paine, 'The Crisis', no. 14, *The Writings of Thomas Paine*, i. 375.
[10] Eric Foner, *Tom Paine in Revolutionary America*, 1976, p. 79.
[11] *Dissertations on the English Language*, 1789, EL no. 54, p. 205.

England. There is no need to establish that Paine had read Webster's theory of language. His own writings had helped to create an intellectual vernacular, and his associates in the United States, Franklin and Jefferson for example, were skilled writers of vernacular prose. The literary training of William Cobbett and Joel Barlow in the States, as well as Thomas Paine, is not coincidental. One of the achievements of the radical movement in England, the extension of literature to an increasingly large portion of the population, was greatly furthered by the more flexible literary and linguistic traditions of the United States.

Paine recognized, however, that *Rights of Man* was a different type of project from *Common Sense* or *The Crisis*. These earlier works were shorter pieces written to argue specific positions. *Rights of Man* portrays a class structure and analyses its contribution to the survival of the English form of government. Paine's task in writing his book was to portray his full sense of that class structure, while also equalling the skills of Edmund Burke, who had an extensive education and was a respected member of the literati. The stylistic combat is an exciting component of the *Rights of Man* because Paine's ability represents the possible achievements of any member of his audience. In any situation, one of the pleasures of reading exceptionally good prose lies in discovering that the language can achieve more than one had imagined. To the early readers of Paine's book, this pleasure must have been especially strong due to the alleged incapacity of the language in which he wrote. Other replies to Burke, such as James Mackintosh's, refuted Burke's ideas, but they did not challenge the scope of the debate or alter the extent of possibilities. Thomas Paine, with more political acumen, understood that the problem presented by the *Reflections* lay equally in Burke's style and his definition of the audience. Thus, Paine had not only to write a political vernacular prose, as he had already done, but to write in a manner that would refute the political implications of the literary skills represented by Edmund Burke.

There is more fulness to Paine's writing in *Rights of Man* than that of *Common Sense* or *The Crisis*, and that may have been encouraged by the *Reflections*. A greater use of metaphor, a more vividly present narrator, and a keener awareness of his audience are the characteristics of Paine's prose that match Burke's use of himself as a narrative device, his broad range of images, and the frequent attention he pays to his readers. Paine seems to have augmented his own skills in the combined gesture of learning and retaliation. Although Burke's style is allusive and literary, and although he distrusted the vulgar populace intensely, he does not write in a language that scorns the vernacular. The *Reflections* was adapted for the emerging audience simply by the process of omitting certain passages.[12] Such writings as Mackintosh's *Vindiciae Gallicae* or Godwin's *Enquiry concerning Political Justice* could not be adapted without being extensively rewritten. If the book had been written by an author with a more conventional sense of the gentlemanly language, Paine could not have augmented his own skills in the process of rebuttal while also developing an intellectual vernacular. By disregarding restrictions on prose style, Burke enabled Paine both to meet Burke on his own ground and to write in a manner that was, in spite of the glimmering precedent, revolutionary.

Burke and Paine employ a personal narrator in distinct ways, but both of them convey to their readers a full sense of their personalities and rely on their skill in conveying themselves as the fundamental proof of their argument. Burke had accused the French and English radicals of being unfeeling, and he relied on portraying his sensitivity to support his argument. This accusation pervades Burke's writing sufficiently to require an answer. The balance Paine achieves between a response that is called for by the content of the *Reflections* and one that is called for by his democratic politics reveals how fully Paine had appraised his opponent and how consciously he employs his own style. To answer the charge of insensibility, Paine chooses to portray himself as a sensitive writer whose reasoning and emotions are unexceptional. By diminishing himself, Paine eventually builds up a clear and powerful portrayal of

---

[12] James T. Boulton, *The Language of Politics in the Age of Wilkes and Burke*, Westport, Connecticut, 1975, p. 261. The chapter is generally indebted to this book.

ordinary men. The Preface and the opening pages of the book contain the most explicit contrast between Paine and Burke. Paine's experience of the French Revolution and of having known Edmund Burke accord Paine some status, but he does not make so much of them that his political thought is portrayed as a result of his unusual life. Paine recognized the necessity of contrasting himself with Burke while concurrently not calling much attention to himself, for such a ploy would undermine the basic assumption of the prose style, that everyone's thought is adequate for political participation. Paine's narrative stance manages both to define himself clearly and to pay an unusual amount of attention to his readers. As a narrator, Paine is both intensely present and unusually self-abnegating. One of the means which enables Paine to manage such a paradoxical position, is to define himself not by direct portrayal, but by leaving readers to recognize the contrast between his characterization of Burke and the image Paine creates of himself by the style of his prose.

In *The Language of Politics*, J. T. Boulton describes the contrapuntal relationship of the two: 'If Burke "confounds everything" by failing to make distinctions and refusing to define his terms, Paine should work by definition and clarity; if Burke's book is a "pathless wilderness of rhapsodies" then Paine's should be well ordered and comprehensible.' (p. 146.) The difference exists in the formulation of Paine's sentences, as well as in the book's overall organization. The spaciousness and clarity of Paine's writing depend on the syntactical emphasis on the nouns and verbs. There are few adjectives and adverbs in Paine's prose. This conveys the sense that Paine's efforts are concentrated on fundamental issues. Setting a paragraph of the *Reflections* against the *Rights of Man* will clarify several of these points.

Always acting as if in the presence of canonized forefathers, the spirit of freedom, leading in itself to misrule and excess, is tempered with an awful gravity. This idea of a liberal descent inspires us with a sense of habitual native dignity, which prevents that upstart insolence almost inevitably adhering to and disgracing those who are the first acquirers of any distinction. By this means our liberty becomes a noble freedom.

It carries an imposing and majestic aspect. It has a pedigree and illus-
trating ancestors. It has its bearings and its ensigns armorial. (p. 121)

Burke's tendency to couple nouns and adjectives presents the
impression that there is one way in which we are compelled
to respond to things. It emphasizes appearance because our
response is determined by publicly manifested attributes
which are uncontestable. Verbs are hardly noticeable in this
passage. They serve to augment the power of objects while
they do not acknowledge the possibility of choice or action.
In Paine's prose, nouns and verbs are rarely modified. In the
passage below, Paine employs an unusual number of adjectives and adverbs while he describes Burke's concept of
the crown. He presents his own view with a simpler sentence
organization. Such a style places great emphasis on the nature
of things and the consequences that follow.

Mr Burke talks about what he calls an hereditary crown, as if it were
some production of Nature; or as if, like Time, it had a power to
operate, not only independently, but in spite of man; or as if it were a
thing or a subject universally consented to. Alas! it has none of those
properties, but is the reverse of them all. It is a thing in imagination,
the propriety of which is more than doubted, and the legality of which
in a few years will be denied. (ii. 363)

Such phrases as 'what he calls the hereditary crown' remind
readers that the power of certain terms depends on the
credence given to them and not on qualities inherent in the
object itself. Paine treats monarchy, titles, aristocracy, mixed
government, and the church and state as the products of
social organization. Terms are defined, not according to an
immutable identity, but according to how they came to exist
and the bearing they have on 'the sphere of man's felicity'
(ii. 320).

During Paine's trial for writing Part Two, the Attorney-
General objected to Paine's discussion of the constitution,
not only because Paine scorned the thing itself, but also
because he thought of the word with too much historical
specificity. While Paine discussed the constitution as an
identifiable object which had been shaped by the historical
process and the needs of various social groups, the Attorney-
General presented it as an autonomous idea. The sense he

conveyed of it, as changing according to its own life rather than human interference, was common to conservative pamphlets of the time. It 'has been growing, — not as Mr Paine would have you believe, from the Norman Conquest — but from time almost eternal, — impossible to trace' (*ST*, xxii. 384). Behind their contrary interpretations lies an alteration in the word which had resulted from the American Revolution. In John Adams's *Answer to Pain's Rights of Man* (the Attorney-General relies on this work later in the trial), Adams also considers Paine's use of the word. To Paine's argument that England had no constitution, he replies:

Of course there never was a people that had a constitution, previous to the year 1776. But the word with an idea affixed to it, had been in use, and commonly understood, for centuries before that period, and therefore Mr Pain must, to suit his purpose, alter its acceptations, and in the warmth of his zeal for revolutions, endeavour to bring about a revolution in language also.[13]

As well as reflecting a change in the word due to the American Revolution, the disagreement between Paine and the Attorney-General also pertains to their differing concepts of signification. Adams's sense that Paine's use of 'constitution' indicates a 'revolution in language also' was borne out by a recently published work on language. John Horne Tooke, an associate of Paine's and a fellow member of the London Constitutional Society, wrote the *Diversions of Purley*, a work which would refute conventional notions of abstract vocabulary (see chapter four). To consider 'constitution' as the Attorney-General does here, is to consider it within the framework of the late eighteenth century's concept of abstract ideas. 'Monarchy' and 'constitution' within such a scheme, had an eternal existence whose value was confirmed by their status as ideas 'COMMON TO MANY INDIVIDUALS; not only to Individuals which exist now, but which existed in ages past, and will exist in ages future' (Harris, p. 341). Paine had a sense of such terms as magical because their power as words disguised their historical

---

[13] 1793, p. 10. Misspelling Paine's name was a frequent device of authors who disagreed with his politics. The American edition which the Attorney-General refers to appeared earlier than the London edition.

identities. To give them credence is to be 'immured in the Bastille of a word' (ii. 320). By treating them as concrete nouns, Paine transforms them from permanently fixed ideas to objects which could be produced, altered or removed:

A constitution is not a thing in name only, but in fact. It has not an ideal, but a real existence; and wherever it cannot be produced in a visible form, there is none. (ii. 309)

By engendering the church with the state, a sort of mule-animal, capable only of destroying, and not of breeding up, is produced, called *the Church established by Law*. (ii. 327)

The shift in perspective that Paine performs in the *Rights of Man* made a tremendous difference. Words which had protected political institutions by the manner in which those words were considered were made vulnerable to 'a style of thinking and expression different to what had been customary'. More than any other discrete facet of his work, this one 'destroyed with one book century-old taboos'.[14]

Whereas Burke's diction and metaphors define his class allegiance and his aesthetic sensibility (in the passage cited, for example, Burke transforms the 'spirit of liberty' into 'bearings and ensigns armorial'), Paine's is non-individuating. His literary allusions refer to works that were generally read, such as *Pilgrim's Progress*, the Bible and *Don Quixote* (Boulton, *Language of Politics*, p. 141), and his vocabulary does not contain unusual words or words used idiosyncratically. Although Paine considers such words as 'monarchy' in an unusual way, he considers them with a strictly ordinary vocabulary. This gives readers the impression that his words derive from his ideas and not from an eccentric sensibility. Paradoxically, it confirms their faith in the independence of his thought, while confirming also that he is not very distinct from themselves.

Because Paine does not choose to discuss himself directly, his style of writing is the primary ground for substantiating the author's identity. To refute Burke's charge that radicals are unfeeling, Paine describes Burke as a man without compassion who is struck by his own aesthetic vision and not

14 E. P. Thompson, *The Making of the English Working Class*, New York, 1966, p. 92.

the actual event of human suffering. The portrayal of Burke's reasoning as 'strange and marvellous' (ii. 276) culminates in several pages wherein Paine attacks him with a metaphorical onslaught. The culmination of Paine's portrait of Burke is resounding — one of the moments in the text when Paine's words strike readers with the energy of a sudden and new idea of their own:

It is painful to behold a man employing his talents to corrupt himself. Nature has been kinder to Mr Burke than he is to her. He is not affected by the reality of distress touching his heart, but by the showy resemblance of it striking his imagination. He pities the plumage, but forgets the dying bird. (ii. 288)

Here, Paine's portrayal of himself implied in his criticism of another and the confirmation of this portrayal in his language, are well co-ordinated. Paine presents his response to Burke as if everyone would have the discernment and the kindness to respond in the same way. His reaction is grounded in general truth, and his compassion, by the parallel construction of the first two sentences, shares in the qualities and scope of nature's kindness.

The structured appearance of these sentences is a general feature of Paine's prose. Two sentences of equal length are followed by a sentence twice as long divided into two equal parts. The three sentences are summarized by a short sentence divided into two unusually short phrases. The symmetry is pleasing in itself, and, at its best, the expanding and contracting syntax provides for a changing rhythm that marks the pace of Paine's thought. In this instance, the general statement and the specific case are of the same length. A sentence twice as long establishes the contrast between them, and the short phrases of the third appear with a quickness that is designed to imitate the imagination. In another instance, previously cited, a short phrase presents a fact, while the two following phrases, of approximately similar length, describe two results occurring at different times: 'It [the crown] is a thing in imagination, the propriety of which is more than doubted, and the legality of which in a few years will be denied.' The syntax implies that every thought is in its correct place, receiving due weight and completed to the end of its course. Paine's presentation of untraditional and disruptive ideas was muted by their appearance in a grammatical background of order and symmetry. The writer appears more as someone who is fulfilling the form of his sentences than as someone expressing extremely unusual opinions.

Further, the structured syntax heightens the vernacular rhythm of the prose. Paine, in an unusual manner, brings formality and colloquialism together to serve each other's purpose. The syntax conveys the informality of speech rhythm and the traditional eighteenth-century values of balance, order and logic:

> The circumstances of the world are continually changing, and the opinions of men change also; and as Government is for the living, and not for the dead, it is the living only that has any right to it. That which may be thought right and found convenient in one age may be thought wrong and found inconvenient in another. In such cases, Who is to decide, the living or the dead? (ii. 281)

The interplay of the vernacular diction and the formal syntax is more reminiscent of Augustan poetry ('Absalom and Achitophel' or *The Dunciad*, for example) than of late eighteenth-century prose, as are other characteristics of Paine's style; the brevity and self-containment of his sentences, a tendency to present ideas in two parts of similar length, and the accentuated rhythm. At times Paine comes strikingly close to the couplet form by concluding two parallel phrases with words, which although they do not rhyme are closely related to each other by their meaning: 'He pities the plumage, but forgets the dying bird'; 'Our enquiries find a resting place, and our reason finds a home' (ii. 304). To bring formal syntax and vernacular diction together as successfully as Paine does implies that the attributes of syntactical order are inherently compatible with the spoken language, when formal syntax was widely held to distinguish vulgar from refined usage.

To return to the 'dying bird' passage, the concluding image is all the more effective because it is contained within an extremely balanced framework. Syntactical expertise was an eighteenth-century skill. In the Preface to his *Dictionary,* the fullness of Johnson's emotions struggles against the confines of his syntax, and the tension between the two is moving. Here the order of the syntactical arrangement does not prepare the readers for the sudden extension of meaning. The tension lies between the intellectual excitement experienced by the readers and the denial of it by the syntax. Paine's ability to perceive beyond appearances is portrayed in an image that simultaneously confirms Burke's cruelty to nature. So much meaning in a four-word phrase provokes an experience of totality when the readers expect the addition of another part.

Paine's criticism of Burke for being a spectator of his own prose contrasts with the casualness of Paine's relation to his own images. As in the 'dying bird' passage, Paine usually disregards his own images while the readers are surprised by them. This is another facet of his self-abnegation as an author for it implies that such skills are unexceptional. It also confirms Paine's refusal to be distracted and his continuing with a steady pace to concentrate on fundamental issues. In one instance, however, Paine pulls back and responds to his own writing. After describing how the 'wondering cheated multitude' was duped by the fusion of the church and state he reacts to the phrase:

When I contemplate the natural dignity of man, when I feel (for Nature had not been kind enough to me to blunt my feelings) for the honour and happiness of its character, I become irritated at the attempt to govern mankind by force and fraud, as if they were all knaves and fools, and can scarcely avoid disgust at those who are thus imposed upon. (ii. 308)

Paine does not appear as a first-person narrator without special occasion. He usually does so to convey information that his readers would not share, such as his first-hand knowledge of events in France, or, as here, to portray his own reaction. The parenthetical phrase is one of the many instances when Paine can strike off repercussive ideas in the readers with a short and seemingly inadvertent phrase. In contrast to the imaginative basis of Burke's hysteria, Paine grounds his emotions in nature and contemplation. His feelings are shown to be a part of his thought, some of which he trusts and others of which he disciplines.

Paine makes the difference between his and Burke's style important by using them as a means of contrasting two political systems. Burke's style embodies methods of the state, for both he and tyrannical governments reduce the population to passive spectators of a theatrical show. Paine's theatre images are effective because they flexibly combine various components of his argument. His incorporation of a public audience points out that Burke ignored an essential factor of his own imagery — the audience, which is the body politic. Again, the extent of Burke's vision is shown to be near-sighted. By referring to less élitist forms of theatre, Paine's imagery is applicable to the experience of a larger reading audience (Boulton, *Language of Politics*, 143). Finally, Paine adapts an aesthetic image into a political one. Burke's theatre portrayed his response to events in France, especially as he compared the downfall of the Queen to viewing a Greek tragedy. Paine employs the same image to define the political relation between suppressive governments and the oppressed population: 'A vast mass of mankind are degradedly thrown into the back-ground of the human picture, to bring forward, with greater glare, the puppet-show of state and aristocracy' (ii. 296). Paine deflates the grandeur of Burke's scenario by altering Burke's image. By combining many aspects of his argument into an image — one which always contrasts with nature — their interrelation in the exposition also has an imaginative life. The theatre imagery provides a basis for Paine to manoeuvre, with great agility, around his portrait of the state.

Paine equates Burke's style and methods of the state both imaginatively and by discussing political variations in the customs of language use. Paine admires La Fayette's prose for directing attention to the living and for provoking thought with 'clear, concise, and soul-animating sentiments' (ii. 282). Elsewhere, he expresses admiration for Rousseau and Abbé Raynal for a 'loveliness of sentiment in favor of liberty, that excites respect, and elevates the human faculties' (ii. 334). The elected representatives of the National

Assembly speak in a style that reflects the dignity of their status as representatives:

They have not to hold out a language which they do not themselves believe, for the fraudulent purpose of making others believe it. Their station requires no artifice to support it, and can only be maintained by enlightening mankind. It is not their interest to cherish ignorance, but to dispel it. They are not in the case of a ministerial or an opposition party in England, who, though they are opposed, are still united to keep up the common mystery. (ii. 332)

The language of Parliament is corrupted both by its origins and by the manner of elections. Members of the House of Commons must ask the King's permission to speak, and the King refers to both Houses as 'my parliament' (ii. 330). Such a practice reflects the origin of the Houses in a grant from the crown. Paine maintains that English political language is a remnant of the Norman Conquest, for it reminds the speakers of their subjection.

That this vassalage idea and style of speaking was not got rid of even at the Revolution of 1688, is evident from the declaration of Parliament to William and Mary in these words: 'We do most humbly and faithfully *submit* ourselves, our heirs and posterities, for ever.' Submission is wholly a vassalage term, repugnant to the dignity of freedom, and an echo of the language used at the Conquest. (ii. 331)

Generally too much an internationalist to stress the belief that English liberty was based on the more democratic forms of Anglo-Saxon government, Paine apparently believed a linguistic version of the Norman yoke myth. A specific language was brought to England during the Conquest which supported alien and authoritative forms. Language usage is creative in Paine's view in the sense that it defines and perpetuates political relations. Changing the style of language is a means of political and moral reformation. The aim of Paine's writing is similar to his description of the task of the National Assembly: 'The National Assembly must throw open a magazine of light. It must show man the proper character of man; and the nearer it can bring him to that standard, the stronger the National Assembly becomes.' (ii. 332.)

Paine's narrative stance performs an analogous gesture:

while disregarding his own position as the author, Paine focuses an intense degree of attention on to his readers. His own thought — the actuality of having conceived and expressed his own ideas — is frequently denied. His thoughts appear in terms of speaking the obvious and the common-place or recognizing the impossible and the absurd:

There never did, there never will, and there never can, exist a Parliament, or any description of men, or any generation of men, in any country, possessed of the right or the power of binding and controuling posterity to the 'end of time'. (ii. 277)

A greater absurdity cannot present itself to the understanding of man than what Mr Burke offers to his readers. (ii. 279)

The weaker any cord is, the less it will bear to be stretched, and the worse is the policy to stretch it. (ii. 280)

Such presentations rapidly build up the readers' sense that there exists a public understanding that is intellectually adroit and competent to deal with political questions. The style of Paine's prose foregoes the necessity of having to establish this point by replacing a contentious idea with a self-evident assumption maintained by the manner of introducing other ideas. Surprisingly, Paine never explicitly states in the *Rights of Man* that people are generally intelligent enough to merit participating in government. A pamphlet of 1782, written by Sir William Jones, reveals the difficulty of politely convincing the populace that they are intelligent without inadvertently stressing the distance between social classes:

Peasant: Why should humble men, like me, sign or set marks to petitions of this nature? It is better for us peasants to mind our husbandry, and leave what we cannot comprehend to the King and Parliament.

Scholar: You can comprehend more than you imagine; and, as *a free member of a free state*, have higher things to mind than you may conceive.[15]

[15] *Principles of Government in a Dialogue between a Scholar and a Peasant*, 1782, p. 1.

(Sir William Jones, later to become the famous linguist, was a member of the London Constitutional Society, as were Thomas Paine and John Horne Tooke.) Paine's style is more gracious. He compels his readers to be aware that they are thinkers and that their ability to think is powerful:

We have now, in a few words, traced man from a natural individual to a member of society. (ii. 307)

In casting our eyes over the world, it is extremely easy to distinguish... (ii. 308)

By frequent use of rhetorical questions and frequent reference to an understanding shared between himself and the readers, Paine brings his readers into the book. 'I' and 'we' become two identities which share a relation and various activities. The signposts (as J. T. Boulton describes such statements as those cited above, p. 119) that indicate the progress of the argument serve more than the function of ordering Paine's ideas. They show Paine to be a skilled and conscious craftsman who knows what needs to be done at which point: 'To possess ourselves of a clear idea of what government is, or ought to be, we must trace its origin' (ii. 309). He reveals explicitly the progress of his argument in order to show how it is done and to remind readers of what has been accomplished. Tasks are designated and achieved with skilful ease. The signposts elucidate the process of thought and make thinking a conscious process by commenting upon the process as the readers are engaged in it. They give to the readers a keen, and at times exhilarating, sense of the 'mightiness of reason' (ii. 284).

The signposts convey a sense of progress and intimacy by disrupting the distinction between writers and readers. By using the present tense and the pronoun 'we', Paine presents the illusion that he and the readers share the activity of constructing an argument. At times, Paine dramatically breaks out of the standard relationship of an author and his audience: 'The instant we ask ourselves this question, reflection feels an answer' (ii. 296). This is an intense moment, when readers self-consciously share the thoughts and feelings of someone else. Elsewhere, Paine discusses his book as if it were a dialogue, and such discussions awaken the rhythm of the prose and the colloquialism of the language. Generally there is a sense that the writer and the readers are engaging in conversation at its best — free-ranging, intellectual, and vivid. This general tone becomes explicit and suddenly lively when Paine starts talking to his readers: 'What will Mr. Burke place against this? I will whisper his answer.' (ii. 315.)

Paine's images are also congenial. The following metaphor is a shared one, not only because it describes an ordinary event, but because Paine describes it in such a way as to make his past and the readers' present as synonymous as they can be:

I know a place in America called Point-no-Point, because as you proceed along the shore, gay and flowery as Mr Burke's language, it continually recedes and presents itself at a distance before you; but when you have got as far as you can go, there is no point at all. Just thus it is with Mr Burke's three hundred and sixty-six pages. (ii. 286)

Paine's presentation of an event in his own memory as a present experience of the readers eliminates the separation between the two. The metaphor performs the same trick again. Readers are told at the end of the sentence that there is 'no point at all'. Paine's comparison of the landscape to Burke's writing is irrefutable because readers are sensing the emptiness which Paine says describes the process of reading the *Reflections*. Again, the readers and the writer align. The credibility of the metaphor is enhanced also by Paine's use of Burke's language to describe the landscape. The passage concludes with an inversion of the tenor and vehicle. The landscape described by Burke's language turns into a description of the three hundred pages. The metaphor seems remarkably complete and has the thoroughness of a sound argument. The ability of the tenor and vehicle to change positions clenches the analogous nature of the two.

A similar process occurs on a larger scale throughout the book. Shared experience, the inversions of tenor and vehicle, and a convincing use of surprise distinguish Paine's use of metaphor. Paine skilfully controls the reader's experience by turning previous material into imaginative and descriptive language. Analogies between Burke and the state are not overtly stated, but are made by describing the two in similar terms. Readers are familiar with the various elements of the following passage, but reading it has a strong impact because the elements appear in a new configuration:

> It is not from his prejudices only, but from the disorderly cast of his genius, that he is unfitted for the subject he writes upon. Even his genius is without a constitution. It is a genius at random, and not a genius constituted. But he must say something. He has therefore mounted in the air like a balloon, to draw the eyes of the multitude from the ground they stand upon. (ii. 314)

The metaphors here condense an argument by recombining earlier descriptions of authoritative power. The image of Burke turning himself into a balloon carries with it previous descriptions of authoritative governments, false elevation, and inventions. Conquering governments had combined the church and state while 'the wondering cheated multitude worshipped the invention' (ii. 308). The English government had been criticized for being one which arose '*over* the people' (ii. 310). And the mob exists because 'it is by distortedly exalting some men, that others are distortedly debased, 'till the whole is out of nature' (ii. 296). The passage alludes to previously disparate moments in the book while it combines them into a single imaginative description. To the Attorney-General of Paine's trial, this interrelation of the text compounded its wickedness:

> to see the whole malignity of it, it is necessary to have a recollection of several preceding passages . . . extracts of it can be made to contain the whole marrow; and at the same time that each passage, taken by itself, will do mischief enough, any man reading them together, will see that mischief come out much clearer. (*ST*, xxii. 387)

Such words as 'constitution' and 'machine' stimulate a response that is not called for or acknowledged by the passage. Paine can forego the necessity of making an argument by relying on the ability of his diction to portray the analogy between Burke and authoritative governments.

While Paine's prose determines the impact of the images, it simultaneously, and, despite the contradiction, leaves the reader free to respond to the material with an independent imagination. In the *Pennsylvania Packet* Paine discusses briefly the inability of Gouverneur Morris to lead readers to an idea without explaining it to them in a dull fashion. (Morris later became the American ambassador to France. Against the wishes of the American government, he made little attempt to shorten Paine's imprisonment under Robespierre or to lessen the threat of his execution.) Although Paine is talking specifically about humour here, the passage is pertinent to Paine's ability to depend on readers to complete his thought:

He has yet to learn that affectation of language is incompatible with humour. Wit may be elegantly spoken, but humour requires a peculiar quaintness of expression, just sufficient to give birth to the conception, and leaving, at the same time, room enough for the fancy of a reader to work upon.[16]

Paine apparently believed that refined language was unsuitable to a prose style that granted the readers some independence of mind. Elegance emphasizes the position of the writer to the extent of excluding participation by the readers. In *Rights of Man* Paine leaves 'room enough' by relying on the ability of his diction to stimulate his readers' imagination, an imagination which the previous material has already shaped and guided. While Paine's skill lays the groundwork for such passages, readers suddenly perceive more implications to an argument, and the perception appears to be their own. Paine's type of imagery makes the readers aware of what their minds can do by urging them half-way to an idea and then leaving them to complete it. As he does by his narrative stance, Paine abnegates his own position to emphasize the intellectual activity of his readers.

One means Paine has of surprising his readers is to transform previous topics of discussion into images: 'Even his genius is without a constitution' (ii. 314); 'He has stormed it [the French Revolution] with a mob of ideas tumbling over and destroying one another' (ii. 357). Objects of analysis suddenly become part of the imaginative life. By turning what had previously been discussed into a means of description, the scope of an idea enlarges with a discernible sense of

---

[16] *Pennsylvania Packet; or, the General Advertiser* (16 March 1779), p. 1.

expansion. In *A Letter Addressed to the Abbé Raynal* Paine discusses the ability of an author to strike several faculties at once as one of the achievements of good prose. Writers must

combine warm passions with a cool temper, and the full expansion of the imagination with the natural and necessary gravity of judgement, so as to feel rightly balanced within themselves, and to make a reader feel, fancy, and understand justly at the same time. To call three powers of the mind into action at once, in a manner that neither shall interrupt, and that each shall aid and invigorate the other, is a talent very rarely possessed.[17]

Paine's prose can achieve this. Readers, at times, feel themselves reflecting a 'rightly balanced' author. Judgement, understanding, and the imagination can be simultaneously active. By using previous ideas as a source of imagery, Paine transforms ideas from an object the readers perceive into a means of perception. This is the inversion of tenor and vehicle on a large and repercussive scale. The transformation is exciting because the difference between the argument and the image is the difference between a discrete idea and consciousness.

To say that Thomas Paine animated his audience would be something of an understatement. His desire to enliven his readers, in the full sense that he used the term, was clearly fulfilled. New readers were brought into the reading public when the *Rights of Man* initiated a new type of reading material. By November 1792, it was claimed that *Rights of Man* 'is now made as much a standard book in this country as Robinson Crusoe and the *Pilgrim's Progress*'.[18] Accounts of the sale and distribution of it vary, but not to a great extent. Part One, at the price of three shillings, sold fifty thousand copies in 1791 (for the sake of contrast, Burke's *Reflections* sold thirty thousand copies in two years, and he believed the sales to be unprecedented). Part One was reprinted when Part Two was published in April 1792, both

---

[17] *Writings*, ii. 69–70.
[18] Benjamin Vaughan, 30 Nov. 1792, Home Office papers, 42.22, cited by E. P. Thompson, *The Making*, p. 108.

selling at the price of six pence. E. P. Thompson accepts the figure of two hundred thousand for Parts One and Two between 1791 and 1793, including the number of abridged versions distributed by the democratic clubs and the extensive circulation of the book in Ireland (p. 108). Richard Altick finds this less credible but accepts the figure of fifty thousand for the sale of Part One (and Part Two sold more, as he and others point out) 'in a few weeks'.[19] In 1802 Paine estimated the sale of both parts at four or five hundred thousand, and in 1809, at 1,500,000, a figure which includes foreign translations. Of this figure, everyone is doubtful, and accounts of the circulation of the *Rights of Man* conclude with suspecting the figure and then claiming a less huge, yet still vast extent of circulation.

The intriguing question behind such figures is the unknown numbers of those who began to read or write specifically because of the *Rights of Man* or because of the continuing political debate. There is sufficient evidence to demonstrate that such a phenomenon occurred. John Butler's *Brief Reflections on the Liberty of the British Subject*, was one of the many pamphlets which responded to Edmund Burke. Butler apologizes for his style by exerting his talents to portray the 'several disadvantages peculiar to men in servile stations':

I assure you, sir, that there is but little besides the present production to constitute me an author. Honours, titles, places or preferments, I have none. No study to cultivate reflection but a cold chamber, no hours of leisure but the hours destined to the refreshing slumber of soft repose; no assistance but the light of Reason, which lays grovelling under the disadvantages of a barren and uncultivated education.[20]

Similarly, *A Letter to William Paley from a Poor Labourer* (1793) replied to the misrepresentation of poverty in Paley's *Reasons for Contentment*. Although the *Reflections* and other works stimulated people who had not written before to write, contemporaries most frequently associated the extension of literacy with the *Rights of Man*: 'We no longer look for learned authors in the usual places, in the retreats

---

[19] *The English Common Reader: A Social History of the Mass Reading Public, 1800-1900*, Chicago, 1957, p. 70.
[20] Canterbury, undated, pp. 9-10.

of academic erudition, and in the seats of religion. Our peasantry now read the *Rights of Man* on mountains, and on moors, and by the wayside.'[21] The excitement of reading ideas presented as powerfully as Paine presents them, in a style that suddenly brought one's own language into the realm of the literary, must have been immense. Richard Carlile, a radical important in the early nineteenth century, describes the impact of the book on himself in terms that would have warmed Paine's heart. He felt the dissolution of an unnamed confusion and the intellectual awakening which Paine portrayed as the greatest value of political consciousness. Characterizing himself before he read Paine's works, he wrote 'I was a weed left to pursue its own course'.[22] William Cobbett, writing in 1805, described the impact of reading the *Rights of Man* in vivid terms, even though he was at that moment a conservative defending himself against the charge of former radicalism:

I explicitly stated, that, previous to my *seeing* what republicanism was, I had not only imbibed its principles, I had not only been a republican, but an admirer of the writings of PAINE. The fault, therefore, if there was any, was in the head, and not in the heart; and, I do not think, that even the head will be much blamed by those who duly reflect, that I was, when I took up PAINE's book, a novice in politics, that I was boiling with indignation at the abuses I had witnessed, and that, as to the power of the book itself, it required first a proclamation, then a law, and next the suspension of the *habeas-corpus* act, to counteract them. (*PR*, viii. 523)

For both Carlile and Cobbett, reading *Rights of Man* initiated politically active and literary careers. Cobbett wrote his first political pamphlet, *The Soldier's Friend* (1792) in the mood he describes here, buffeted by his experience of corruption in the army and encouraged by the exposition of corruption in the *Rights of Man.*[23] Richard Carlile did not read the book until the nineteenth century when the economic hardship of 1816 led him to consider political questions. Then he began

[21] T. J. Mathias, *Pursuits of Literature*, 2nd edn., 1797, p. 238.
[22] Guy A. Aldred, *Richard Carlile, Agitator; His Life and Times*, Glasgow, 1941, p. 20.
[23] My attributing the pamphlet to Cobbett will be discussed in the next chapter.

his long, stubborn and eventually successful attack on the legal limitations of freedom of speech by republishing Paine's works. The influence of the *Rights of Man* extended also to those who had less spectacular political careers.

Its history among the democratic societies further reveals the book's intellectual impact. Among the new political clubs the book was distributed, read out aloud, and debated. Francis Place describes the self-respect which resulted from discussions of such books:

The moral effects of the London Corresponding Society were considerable. It induced men to read books, instead of wasting their time in public houses, it taught them to respect themselves, and to desire to educate their children. It elevated them in their own opinions. (p. 198)

The Constitutional Information Society in Sheffield (founded in the late months of 1791) was the first political club to be founded by mechanics. In that year, it sent Thomas Paine a request for permission to publish two thousand copies of Part One 'for themselves'. Other localities similarly sent Paine requests to print a cheaper edition: '. . . from Rotherham, from Leicester, from Chester, from several towns in Scotland; and Sir James Mackintosh . . . brought me a request from Warwickshire, for leave to print ten thousand copies in that county. I had already sent a cheap edition to Scotland.'[24] The publication of the book led to increased activities and the founding of new societies. Paine provided them with both a political ideology and an heroic figure: 'All the leading members of the London Corresponding Society were republicans . . . This they were taught by the writings of Thomas Paine.'[25] During 1791, the London Constitutional Society, a more gentlemanly organization that had existed since the 1780s, was primarily concerned with distributing Part One. When Part Two appeared, various members left due to disagreements over Paine's discussion of the economy. The Society then stepped up its activities. Members, especially Horne Tooke, assisted

[24] 'Letter Addressed to the Addressers on the Late Proclamations', *Writings*, iii. 65.
[25] Cited from BL Add. MS 27812 fo. 64 by E. Foner, p. 234.

the new London Corresponding Society, communicated with groups outside London, began to liaise with the new French government, and distributed other radical pamphlets (E. P. Thompson, *The Making*, p. 111). The political activity of the 1790s (and this is equally true of the repression) was entangled until at least 1795 with the publication of the *Rights of Man*. Expressions of gratitude for the book from societies in Manchester, Norwich, and Sheffield (these are the societies mentioned in Thomas Hardy's trial for high treason: there were others as well), indicated the energy and hope which the book brought: 'To Mr. Thomas Paine our thanks are especially due for the First and Second parts of the *Rights of Man,* and we sincerely wish that he may live to see his labours crowned with success in the general diffusion of liberty and happiness among mankind.'[26] The book was instrumental to the democratic movement of the 1790s which 'marked the emergence of "lower and middling classes of society" into organised radical politics' (E. Foner, p. 220).

Thomas Paine taught members of the London Corresponding Society to accomplish the unfamiliar task of writing their ideas (E. Foner, p. 225). There is a metaphorical truth to the anecdote that is only rarely discernible. The extent to which Paine facilitated expression by writing in a vernacular language is the invisible extent of his influence. The accounts of Cobbett and Carlile suggest that in their cases, reading the *Rights of Man* was virtually a precondition to their writing. Conservative pamphlets frequently portray workers questioning squires or master workmen about the ideas in Paine's book or picking up the pen for the first time to join in the political debate (these will be discussed in the third chapter). Even those who did not want literacy to increase, regretfully gave accounts of the new and active literacy and associated it especially with the *Rights of Man*. A study which attempted to appraise its influence on the writers who did not have an accustomed position among the reading public would be worth doing. Richard Altick's assessment that the major impact of the book, in spite of the broadening of the literary territory, was in the repression and retaliation that followed,

---

[26] Cited from the 'Resolutions of the United Constitutional Societies of Norwich', *ST*, xxiv. 292.

must be appraised with an awareness that discussions in Parliament, accounts in provincial newspapers, King's proclamations, and the activities of Hannah More or the Association for preserving Liberty and Property are more ready to hand than accounts of the stimulation that would lead people to read or write (Altick, p. 72). The repression was widespread and thoroughgoing. Although the literary audience may well have shrunk back to its previous size when repression prohibited the publication of radical tracts in 1795, it reappeared with greater strength in the second decade of the nineteenth century. Thomas Paine's work was instrumental both to the repression of the 1790s and to the movement which countered that repression later in the nineteenth century.

The intellectual excitement released by the book was paralleled by a great deal of terror. Particularly at the end of 1792 and the first few months of 1793, Thomas Paine became a mythical figure, provoking a complex response of fear, vehemence, and glee. He was frequently burned in effigy, in one instance 'with a large Cabbage under one arm and an old pair of Stays under the other'.[27] In Littleton 'a wooden image of Paine was pounded to bits with a sledge hammer with such vigour that the executioner's hands ran with blood' (E. P. Thompson, *The Making*, p. 112). In January and February, the *Nottingham Journal* reported several events in which Paine was ritualistically killed. At a dinner and dance, ladies stoned Paine's effigy: 'It appeared an entertainment of sweet things, for there were no less than nineteen dozen of China oranges eat, and many of the young ladies fired thirty rounds each at Citizen Tom whose effigy was hung on the eastern arch of the old abbey.' (xlix (9 Feb. 1793), 3.) A week later the journal reported another adaptation of Thomas Paine into a form of entertainment. The following account of his arrest and execution occurs in a column of otherwise factual events.

He was sentenced to be Hanged on the arm of a large tree, near the above Village, which was accordingly done, amidst a great concourse

---

[27] *The Nottingham Journal*, xiviii (12 Jan. 1793), 3.

of people; he was left hanging on the tree a considerable time, after which the company retired to the Coffee-House for refreshment . . . Paineites had laid a plan to convey the remains of their Champion away from the Tree, which the LOYALISTS being aware of, fell on, routed, and put to flight; the whole GANG of them. (xlix, (16 Feb. 1793), 3)

By 1793 Paine was perceived half as a ghoulish figure and half as a more realistic danger because of his book's stimulus to new forms of political organization. These two ways of perceiving him were not entirely distinct. Even the King's Proclamation against Seditious Writings (May 1792), conjured a new character of Thomas Paine to suit the purpose of persecution. When members of the House objected that there was no need to hunt out secretive authors when authors were not disguising their identities, the Attorney General and Secretary Dundas replied that 'Paine' was a common name and might easily be a pseudonym for one author or a group of authors (*PD*, xxix. 1504, 1513). The information Paine supplies about himself, as well as his fame, must have made such an answer appear hollow.

Between 1792 and 1795, the circulation of Paine's work was one of the main reasons given for the passage of repressive legislation and one of the main reasons given for the arrests of those charged with high treason. From the King's Proclamation of 1792, to Paine's trial in December, to the Report of the Committee of Secrecy, to the Suspension of the Habeas Corpus Act, to the treason trials of 1794, and to the passage of the Treasonable Practices Act, Parliament debated and attempted to contain the political and intellectual energy released by Paine's writings. Throughout these procedures the *Rights of Man* and its circulation by the democratic societies were major topics of discussion. The combination of factors which the government recognized as threatening was accurate: the distribution of an inexpensive edition, the correspondence of societies from different parts of the United Kingdom, and the class composition of the societies. Speaking in 1794 in favour of the Habeas Corpus Suspension Bill, Lord Grenville described May 1792, when the London Constitutional Society began to distribute Part One, as initiating an ever-increasing fervour of treasonable activity:

Precisely at this period it was, that these societies came forward . . ; they began their operations by endeavouring to corrupt the minds of the lower classes of the public, by disseminating pamphlets, containing the whole of their system: they passed a resolution of the 18th of May, 1792, to distribute a cheap edition of a book intituled 'Rights of Man'. Here was the foundation of that system which had since ripened into treasonable practices by subsequent proceedings, which were followed up with incredible activity. (*PD*, xxxi. 576)

Until 1795 the government often asserted that the distribution of the *Rights of Man* initiated a profound and dangerous change.

During Paine's trial in December 1792, the prosecuting attorney stressed the alarming availability of Part Two: 'all industry was used . . . to obtrude and force this upon that part of the public whose minds cannot be supposed to be conversant with subjects of this sort' (*ST*, xxii. 381). Part One had not been prosecuted because the price of the book prevented those who could not argue against it from reading it: 'and when confined to the judicious reader, it appeared to me that such a man would refute it as he went along' (*ST*, xxii. 381). Price and style were the two means by which the government determined whether or not a work should be prosecuted. Until 1798, works confined to a small audience, such as Godwin's *Enquiry concerning Political Justice*, remained unhindered by prosecution. In a simplistic manner, the trials for sedition or libel estimated intellectual understanding by a financial scale. An inexpensive price was evidence of the author's malicious intent because it established that the books were addressed 'to the ignorant, to the credulous, to the desperate' (*ST*, xxii. 383). Also, Paine's style confirmed that the *Rights of Man* was not a work of reason. During his trial, the language of gentlemen was contrasted to Paine's 'phrase and manner' (*ST*, xxii. 383). As theories of language had established one type of reasoning, and identified it with a particular class, such comments did not require much argument. The style, the author, and the audience confirmed the identity of each other.

Conservatives seemed to have no means of identifying a non-upper-class movement except in terms of conspiracy and treason. If the political activity was not the spontaneous outburst of a section of society that was by definition un-disciplined, inarticulate and emotive, then it was necessarily disciplined by an externally imposed conspiratorial design. Discussing the Report of the Committee of Secrecy (1794), Pitt described these two possible alternatives:

> Such language as this, coming from people apparently so contemptible in talents, so mean in their description, and so circumscribed in their power, would, abstractedly considered, be supposed to deserve compassion, as the wildest workings of insanity; but the researches of the committee would tend to prove, that it had been the result of deep design, matured, moulded into shape, and fit for mischievous effect when opportunity should offer. (*PD*, xxxi. 502)

Treason and conspiracy were more admissible concepts than that of a politically aware vulgar population. Accordingly, Horne Tooke was tried for high treason in 1794 for being the detached conspiratorial genius of the democratic societies. As leader of the Constitutional Society who was a friend of Thomas Paine and who aided the London Corresponding Society, he provided a focal point for an alleged systematic network. The Attorney-General describes the societies as Horne Tooke's unsuspecting private army:

> It was by the strength of the Corresponding Society, consisting of some thousands — by the strength of all these societies, in different parts of the kingdom, that were to be affiliated and associated with this [Tooke's] society, that the objects of this society were to be carried into execution, without much of personal hazard to those who were the real authors of the plan that was in agitation, and was well nigh ripening. (*ST*, xxv. 538-9)

Such arguments denied the possibility that the movement for political reform was an intellectual choice performed by numerous members of the population. The charge of treason and the belief in a deep malevolent design classified the movement as evil and precluded the necessity of giving it serious attention. The trials of Thomas Hardy, John Thelwall, and John Horne Tooke were in effect, a trial of the demo-cratic societies generally. The inclusion of resolutions passed by other societies, the stress placed on the distribution of Paine's book, and the inclusion of the publications of various societies as evidence indicates that the trial was not of an individual but of a political movement.

The Attorney-General, in his opening argument, stakes the credibility of his case on proving that the principles of the democratic societies were those of Thomas Paine and were therefore necessarily treasonable:

> I claim no credit for the veracity with which I assert, that this conspiracy has existed, unless I show you by subsequent acts of this society, that at this moment they meant what Mr. Paine says, in principle and practice, is the only rational thing – a *representative government*; the direct contrary of the government which is established here. (*ST*, xxiv. 294)

As the government also intended to prove the existence of acts that were more obviously treasonable – that the democratic societies were manufacturing arms and that the convention in Scotland was an extra-parliamentary legislative body – a surprising amount of weight and attention was given to *Rights of Man*. The Attorney-General proceeded on the basis of an extravagant equation between the ideas of Paine's book and the alleged intentions of the society. Examining a cutler from Sheffield, he asked him:

> How do you understand the passage I have read to you, that 'monarchy would not have existed so many ages in the world, had it not been for the abuses it protects'? Did you understand that to be a recommendation, to the people of England, to protect and cultivate the monarchical principle, or to destroy it as soon as they could? (*ST*, xxiv. 1045)

This is an unconvincing assessment of the process of reading; if Thomas Paine says that monarchy is corrupt, his readers will directly proceed to violence. Because high treason was legally defined as the 'compassing of the death of the King', the Attorney-General emphasized the emotive and violent character of the book's readers in order to justify the charge.

The danger which originally justified the suspension of habeas corpus was disproved during these trials. Of the twelve who were arrested, Tooke, Hardy, and Thelwall were tried and acquitted, the remaining charges were dropped. Arguments to continue the suspension included further discussion of *Rights of Man* (*PD*, xxxi. 1159), and the suspension was reactivated yearly until 1801. The discrepancy of attempting to convict on the basis of physical danger to the throne when the danger lay in changing patterns of thought became obvious with the outcome of the trials: 'It was ridiculous in the extreme to have it high treason to kill the king, and not high treason to destroy the monarchy itself' (*PD*, xxxii. 247). Legislation passed in 1795 and 1798 established laws which were designed to curtail the possibility of certain intellectual exchanges. It reasserted the boundaries that had previously been maintained by the hegemonic status of literature and language.

Chapter III

The Pamphleteers: The Association, the Swinish Multitude, Eaton, More, and Spence

Patriot to a Courtier: 'To say the truth Sir, one
would imagine you had lived your days in courts, for
you are master of the language'.[1]

Thomas Paine was confident that the distribution of his
works would give the radicals an important advantage: 'As
we have got the stone to roll it must be kept going by cheap
publications. This will embarrass the Court gentry more than
anything else, because it is ground they are not used to.'[2]
The head start which he envisioned lasted only a short while.
In November 1792, the Association for Preserving Liberty
and Property against Republicans and Levellers (more simply,
the Association) was formed to imitate the techniques of
radical political groups. The cheap distribution of pamphlets
and the publication of resolutions encouraging other loyalist
clubs rapidly established a network which greatly surpassed
that of the London Corresponding Society. Although the
question of whether or not the government instigated the
Association is unresolved, it is clear that the Association's
activities were co-ordinated with government action, that its
ability to distribute pamphlets depended on the government's
assistance, and that its adherents in Parliament — Pitt, Burke,
Windham, and Grenville — enhanced its power. Aided by
an extensive education and armed with literary traditions
and conventions of language, conservatives had the advantage
over radicals, who were frequently less formally educated and
who were attempting to adapt literacy to a new and
unfamiliar purpose.

[1] *Politics for the People: or, a Salmagunday for Swine* (1793-5), ed. Daniel
Isaac Eaton, Greenwood Reprint Series, New York, 1968, 2 vols., i. 124. Later
abbreviated as PP.
[2] Cited from Blanchard Jerrold's *The Original*, 1874, by E. P. Thompson,
The Making, p. 111.

Each side, however, began from a contradictory position. Radicals needed to prove that they were not vulgar, but as the notion of vulgarity was a linguistic one, they could not write in 'mere native English' without demonstrating their vulgarity. Conservatives, who wished to forestall the growth of democratic ideas among the audience, did not want to extend either political awareness or literacy. Pamphlets produced locally could discourage literacy by employing a dialect form of English such as *A Wurd or 2 of good counsil to abowt hafe a duzzen diffrant sorts o fokes* (Birmingham, 1791). Such material did not grant its audience practice in reading which would contribute to their ability to understand other writings. Tracts intended for national distribution had to rely on other means — the simplest being to recommend that their readers not read. The *Liberty and Property* series, which was energetically distributed through the two thousand branches of the Association and through churches, taverns, coffee houses, factories, and barber shops, portrays employers advising their workers to concentrate on financial self-improvement and not to damage themselves by spending time with books: 'I seldom read anything except my Bible and my Ledger'.[3] The debate between the two parties had its own life, however, and in one aspect the opposing sides acted in unison. They responded quickly to each other's writings, and the audience gained in knowledge and numbers by the urgent need to answer the opposition.

The government and the church aided the Association both by intentional acts, such as distribution, and by the less formal co-operation of a group of people known to each other and working for the same cause. The Association's initial resolution was published in ministerial newspapers, including those in the provinces, 'evidently on government instructions for the editor of the *Sun* informed Reeves that he had been told to insert them by Evan Nepean, Under-Secretary to the Home Office'.[4] Nepean was also a close friend of John Reeves, the Association's founder. Reeves's

---

[3] *Liberty and Property preserved against Republicans and Levellers; A Collection of Tracts* [1793], no. 4, p. 8.

[4] Austin Mitchell, 'The Association Movement', *Historical Journal*, Cambridge, vi (1961), 60.

income depended on the continuing stability of the government, and he has been adequately described by Albert Goodwin as a 'monopolist, if ever there was one, of lucrative public offices'.[5] Hannah More's contribution to the tracts, 'Village Politics', found its way to the Association when the Bishop of London gave it to the Attorney-General, who in turn gave it the Association. Thousands of copies of her tract were distributed by the government in Scotland, Ireland, and Wales. William Paley, who contributed *Reasons for Contentment* to the *Liberty and Property* series, was rewarded for it with a prebend at St. Paul's by the Bishop of London.[6] Sermons were given recommending the Association's work, including one by Bishop Horsely to the House of Lords. William Cobbett, who dedicated the collection of his American writings to John Reeves, wrote a handbill in 1803 that was left on the pews of every church in England allegedly by the Association, which had dissolved in 1793.[7] Although the handbill states that it was printed by the Association, Cobbett later claimed that it was paid for and distributed by the government (*PR*, xv. 917).

The radical network could not match this combination of forces, especially as radical writers and publishers had to contend also with the intimidations and citizens' arrests which the Association did much to encourage. Between 1792 and 1795, Eaton was arrested six times and Spence four. Both Daniel Eaton in 1793 and Thomas Spence in 1792 were arrested on charges brought to the court by Association members, for selling works by Thomas Paine.[8] Spence was verbally abused and roughly handled by the runners sent by the Association to arrest him. On another occasion, he was expelled from his bookstall when a member warned his landlord that he would lose customers if Spence continued to rent the premises. Such activities were encouraged by the alarmism of the Association's propaganda and by its rec-

[5] *The Friends of Liberty; The English Democratic Movement in the Age of the French Revolution,* 1979, p. 264.

[6] *Memoirs of the Life and Correspondence of Mrs. Hannah More,* ed. William Roberts, 3rd edn., 1835, 3 vols., ii. 343, 341, and 427. Later abbreviated as *MLC.*

[7] *Important Considerations for the People of this Kingdom,* 1803.

[8] *The Trial of Daniel Isaac Eaton, July the tenth 1793* [1793]; *The Case of T. Spence* [1792].

ommendation to arrest those 'who appear to plot and contrive against the peace and good order of this happy country'.[9] The full extent of their publications is unknown, but its monthly series, *Liberty and Property preserved against Republicans and Levellers,* was by itself a formidable operation which stimulated fears of revolution. The Association combined and performed efficiently within the three domains of law, intimidation, and propaganda.

When considering their achievement at the end of 1793, the Association claimed that the Bull family letters, and especially 'One Penny-worth of Truth', were its most effective publications.[10] Radicals and reformers imitated the Bull family letters more frequently than other types of Association tracts, an occurrence which supports its claim. The relation between Thomas Bull and his less dignified brother John is of interest because it parallels the relation between the Association and its vision of its audience. The first letter contains the ideas and the techniques which the *Liberty and Property* series was to repeat relentlessly in the attempt to persuade its audience against thinking politically. It was not only radical ideas which the Association wanted to keep from its readers but also any type of political thinking. The tracts were designed to replace political awareness with racism, religion (of a kind), nationalism, sexual chauvinism, and, most emphatically, adherence to rigid class divisions.

It was essential for the tracts to persuade their audience that their subordination was necessary and desirable. The evident superiority of Thomas Bull to his brother John, and to those John represents, demonstrates that social position accords with different levels of intelligence and social worth. Simultaneously, fraternal concern portrays class differentiation as affectionate and sweet. The equality that exists between brothers contributes an aura of warmth to Thomas's argument against social and political equality. His frequent mention of his brother — 'It seems John, you and I', 'John, I'll tell thee plainly', 'Won't that be a *Loss*, John' — implies

[9] *Proceedings of the Association for preserving Liberty and Property against Republicans and Levellers* [1793], p. 12.
[10] *Association Papers addressed to all the Loyal Associations,* 1793, p. ii.

a persistent awareness of John's life and present dilemma.[11] Such a technique forestalls any potential condescension inherent in one person's telling another how to think. The author was evidently aware of such a danger: 'They have tried their skill upon me, and so they will upon you; but I write you this letter to give you warning, that you may look to yourself.' Thomas acknowledges the cerebral dizziness he sensed when he first encountered the vocabulary of radicalism: 'With talking about Right and Equality, and Constitution and Organization, and such like, they made my head turn round: but I see now pretty well what they mean.' (1. 1.) Thomas is thus portrayed as a person who has considered the questions raised by the democratic movement with considerable effort. By using rhetorical questions frequently and by demonstrating the process of his reasoning, Thomas includes John in his mind's careful activity.

One of the skills of the letter is to present emotional arguments as if they were rational — extremism is presented as a step-by-step process of thought and in a quiet tone. Distorting the meaning of vocabulary and events gives extravagant arguments a superficial air of sense. Equality never means representation in Parliament or equal status before the law. It usually means the disruption of sexual or class roles: 'They begin with telling us all *Mankind are equal;* but that's a lie, John; for the Children are not equal to the Mother, nor the Mother to the Father; unless where there is *Petticoat Government*; and such Families never go on well.' (1. 1-2.) The word 'Constitution' rarely means anything: 'When all Power is taken from those who are now entitled to it by Law, and put into the hands of the Mob armed with pikes and daggers, that's a *Constitution*, John.' (1. 2.) Contemporary events and figures are rarely mentioned or are referred to inaccurately. Thomas Paine, for instance, appears as a character in a joke about robbery (1. 3). This effort to distort and confuse information is one facet of the anti-intellectualism of the tracts, for they focus attention on rumour or conversation rather than on the declarations of the democratic societies or writings such as the *Rights of*

---

[11] *Liberty and Property,* no. 1, pp. 1, 3, and 5.

Man. The Association seems to have believed it wiser to combat reform with ignorance, and, as will be more evident later, with class hatred and insecurity, than with a consciously held conservative position.

The anti-intellectualism of the tracts can be justified by their assessment of the audience. The character of John Bull, revealed by his reply to his brother Thomas, demonstrates why reason was thought to be inappropriate:

I thank you for your kind letter. But you need not fear me . . . says I to myself; — *Who be ye? — What be ye? — Where d'ye come from; — What d'ye want?* — Says Reason directly, — *'Beware of wolves in sheeps' cloathing — Hypocrites — Robbers, Murderers, Fellows void of Principle. — Incendaries.* . . . Thy barn is well filled and they want to thresh thy corn. *John take heed!!' (2. 1-2)

Readers might be amused by John's simple pride, as when he describes himself as 'too apt to believe everybody like myself — sincere, just, and true' (2. 4), when he is obviously stupid. The tracts go further, however, than allowing more knowing readers the smug comfort of their superiority. The manifest possibility that John Bull could think anything at all, with great vehemence and intensity, makes him a frightening character. By portraying someone who relies heavily on the opinions of others, the *Liberty and Property* series presents the dreadful possibility of such a figure believing in the radicals as willingly as he believes Parson Orthodox or David Trusty. John Bull's exuberant stupidity makes his conservatism accidental and precarious. The exclamations, the dashes, and the underlinings define him as a loud-mouthed character. The education he had received at a charity school, the best his parents could afford (1. 1), does not redeem him from being a prime candidate for a riot.

Of several statements discussing how to contain the minds of the lower orders, none suggests convincing them by exchanging ideas. The statements assume that such minds are entirely passive and can be 'arranged' by various techniques. Lord Sheffield, organizer of the Association's branch at Sussex, advocated confusion followed by an admittedly delusive argument:

It appeared to me that nothing could be more advantageous than arranging the minds of the people under a good principle while they were in a ferment, and when once committed by their signature, it was likely they would be strenuous for measures which I endeavoured to make their own as much as possible.[12]

Sarah Trimmer wrote to the Association recommending that the poor be given a loaf of bread and a pamphlet a week to keep them happy for seven days. After several weeks 'their minds may be gradually impressed with the principles of loyalty, subordination, and every other virtue of humble life'. She maintains that such had been the effect of the programme in her own parish.[13] Edmund Burke advocated repression of the reading audience as well as of authors in the belief that the lower classes were incapable of understanding the complex argument that would justify their subordination: 'where a man is incapable of receiving Benefit through his reason, he must be made to receive it thro' his fears. Here the Magistrate must stand in the place of the Professor. They who cannot or will not be taught, must be coerced.' (*The Correspondence*, vi. 304.) Burke's letter hints at the difficulty; conservative pamphleteers could not address their readers as intelligent persons because to do so would deny the major justification for the subordination of the audience. Subordination could not be intellectually explained to a body of people who were excluded from political discussion on the grounds of their irrationality.

The tracts employ dialogues and allegories to portray rigid class division. Characters from the lowest order are invariably named John and those slightly higher on the social scale are named Thomas. Their betters have either individual names or are referred to by their social position, such as 'Parson Orthodox'. The dialogue form is well suited for the class specificity which the series hoped to encourage; the space on the printed page between the speakers graphically represents the social gulf between them. Different levels of intelligence, different political positions, and different classes are always aligned in the same way. The dialogues in themselves do not occur without explanation, as if members of different classes

---

[12] Cited from *Private Letters of Edward Gibbon*, ed. R. E. Prothero, 1896, by Mitchell, p. 61.
[13] BL Add. MS 16972, ff. 121-4.

never talked to each other without a discernible cause: a
tradesman talks to his worker because 'the Porter, being a
sober and industrious man, was usually treated with more
familiarity by his master than the rest of the servants, who
did not so well deserve it' (8. 1). The dialogues and stories
state the class for which they are intended and that of the
alleged writer. Those that appear to address an entire society,
such as 'people' or 'Britons' address the undistinguished part
of the population, as the language reveals: 'Do not leave the
plain wholesome ROAST BEEF of OLD ENGLAND for the meagre
unsubstantial diet of these political *French* Cooks' (5. 13).
Otherwise, a pamphlet written allegedly by a mechanic is
addressed only to mechanics, by a farmer only to farmers,
and by a small tradesman only to other tradesmen. This
fragmented portrayal of who talks to whom embodies several
beliefs which the writers hoped would order English society:
that the lower classes should not consider questions without
the guidance of a superior, that their only readers were their
peers, that their superiors did not disagree with each other,
and that no matter what one's status, there was always someone threatening in the rank below. Everyone has someone to
fear (4. 3). In a 'Ten Minute Caution from a Plain Man to
his Fellow Citizens', the speaker writes down his own
thoughts, a rare occurrence in the series. An inadvertent joke
lets readers know that the *Rights of Man* gave the author a
false confidence that enables him to write: 'I remember a
little of my Grammar as well as Mr. Paine' (1.9). Farmers,
masters, and self-sufficient tradesmen speak better English
than workers, sailors, or journeymen. None of them, however, are capable of speaking a language that extends beyond
their immediate experience; sailors talk about ships, farmers
about the English oak.

These dialogues and stories could have different effects,
depending on the social status of the readers. The tracts can
be read as instruction manuals to teach the upper classes how
to contain the minds and political inclinations of their
inferiors. By portraying gentlemen and masters successfully
telling their inferiors how to understand politics, the
pamphlets provide an imaginative experience of how to treat
one's own workmen should they become interested in the

reform movement. At the conclusion of 'A Dialogue between Mr. T— and his Porter John', the tradesman expresses his pleasure at the porter's decision not to return to the political club: 'for I should certainly dismiss you from my service if you were to go again, and that I should be very sorry to do, for I really esteem you' (8. 8). Such statements suggest various forms of flattery and intimidation. The tracts dismiss good behaviour, intellectual effort, financial sacrifices, curiosity, the efforts of parents, and even the unusual quality of the English as factors that make any substantial difference to the nature of the lower orders. None of the self-motivated activity of these classes alters their intractably ignorant and potentially violent nature. The lessons of how to treat social inferiors are accompanied by relentless assessments of their limitations.

Meanwhile, lower-class readers are continually reminded of their vulnerability to their own violence, illness, the birth of too many children, ignorance, and bankruptcy; and of the gratitude that they owe to English society and to the government for whatever security they have. Within such a world, charity becomes the major ground for defending the status quo, and radicalism becomes equated with augmenting the insecurity of the lower orders. By the act of writing these pamphlets, the authors diffused (and I do not mean weakened) their fears of political reform into vaguer fears which were appropriate for various social classes. If the pamphlets were at all effective, which they were, they taught the upper classes not to fear political reform so much as to fear the ignorant and violent character of their social inferiors and how to reassert control by intimidating conversations. They taught the middling and lower classes that gratitude and obedience were required to calm their fears concerning their precarious existences and their uncontrollable selves.

Throughout 1793, the Association's propaganda permeated the writings of radicals and reformers who either imitated its forms and methods, or attempted to refute its portrait of the reading audience by providing it with other fictional identities. On both counts, the propaganda was sufficiently powerful to interfere considerably with the development of an intellectual vernacular language and an adequate fictional characterization of the audience. Such pamphlets as *Liberty and Property* could more readily employ vulgar language because it was generally known to portray a character which was appropriate for the Association's purposes. Thus, the Association had only to bring a language to life, to provide specific speakers for a language which had already been delineated. To employ the vernacular language in a manner which disproved its alleged limitations, as Paine did, was a different type of task and a much more difficult one, because it required refuting the assessment of vulgarity with its own evidence. The difficulty might explain one reason why an intellectual vernacular language did not develop until after the wars. Although a few writers could write such a language in the 1790s, it was not available as a cultural resource until a generation later. The existence of *Rights of Man* makes its absence all the more glaring, for the book provided a model which might have been imitated. The unusual discrepancy between Paine's intellectual and literary influences, possibly unrivalled in English literary history, suggests that his style was not imitated because radicals were constrained by the hysteria which followed its publication and also by the status granted to the refined language. To a surprising extent, Paine's style vanishes.

The Soldier's Friend is an interesting and informative exception for the *Rights of Man*, Part One contributed to its political perspective and to its style. Its history, as well as its uniqueness, reveals the complexity behind the apparently simple act of learning from Paine's skilful prose. William Cobbett would not admit to writing the pamphlet either in 1792 or in 1805. My attribution of the anonymous pamphlet to him is stronger than M. C. Pearl's bibliography would warrant: 'Authorship dubious, probably written with Cobbett's assistance'.[14] As Pearl explains, Cobbett admitted to writing the pamphlet in two articles of the *Political Register* published in June 1832 and December 1833. The article of 1832 explains that a friend was responsible for the pamphlet's publication. Doubts concerning Cobbett's authorship are due to an article of 1805 where he states firmly and

[14] *William Cobbett: A Bibliographical Account of his Life and Times*, 1953, p. 19.

for the only time, that he neither authored nor published the pamphlet. He explains that he discussed a parliamentary speech with a friend 'to whom·I had communicated my information upon such subjects, [and who thought it] worthy of remark in print. Hence arose a little pamphlet, entitled the *"Soldiers' Friend"*. Of this pamphlet I was not the author; I had nothing to do either with the printing or the publication of it.' (*PR*, viii. 522.) Cobbett could well have been relying on the secondary meaning of 'author', in the sense of instigator or originator, to mislead his readers. He is discussing, after all, who first had the idea of writing it. Throughout the rest of the article and on no other occasion does Cobbett say that he did not write the pamphlet or that someone else wrote it. Moreover, he acknowledges writing it in several parenthetical comments that receive little attention in his otherwise emphatic prose: 'giving the authorship to me, and even the circulation if they will'; 'admitting, in their full extent, the assertions of these "Gentlemen", with regards to the authorship and circulation'; and 'having exerted my humble talents in that cause' (*PR*, viii. 523, 520). Throughout the remaining article, Cobbett discusses the pamphlet as if he had written it, as a subsequent citation will confirm. By mentioning the writing and the publishing of it together, Cobbett admits to writing it under the guise of making hypothetical statements which are justified by his lack of involvement in its publication.

The rebel Tory of 1805 had ample reason to disavow the writing of his more radical youth. Even in the headier days of 1791, the pamphlet was exceptionally audacious. In colloquial and persuasive language, Cobbett argues that the people have a greater allegiance to each other than they do to the king: 'I would have you consider the nature of your situation, I would have you know that you are not the servant of one man only: a British soldier never can be that. You are a servant of the whole nation of your countrymen, who pay you, and from whom you can have no separate interests.'[15] Cobbett's prose is easy to read, attentive to its readers, and paced with the energy and rhythm of spoken

---

[15] Unsigned, *The Soldiers' Friend . . . Written by a subaltern*, 1792.

language. No other radical writings are as close to Paine's either in style or in firmness of attack. (Even this early, however, Cobbett was writing as he would later, with one stylistic foot in the radical and the other in the conservative camp. Jonas Hanway's *The Soldier's Faithful Friend* (1776) apparently provided him with the title.) In the article of 1805, Cobbett explains that he could not have written the pamphlet except for certain unusual conditions: he had returned from living in Canada for eight years, he knew nothing about contemporary English society or politics, and he had just finished reading Paine's book. 'Let it be considered, that I had just arrived in England; that I was a perfect novice in politics, never having, to my recollection, read even a newspaper while abroad . . . and let it be considered, too, that I took up the book of Paine (just then published) with my mind full of indignation, at the abuses which I myself had witnessed.' (*PR*, viii. 523.) Cobbett explains that he was not inhibited by the pressures which restrained the writing of his English counterparts. As a result, the pamphlet stands out vividly among the generally more timid writing of the time.

Others took note of it. A letter mailed to the Association in 1792 mentions *The Soldier's Friend* with *Rights of Man* as the type of dangerous literature that frequently could be seen in poor people's houses.[16] In 1797, it was reissued and distributed before the mutiny of the Nore, and in 1805 a pamphlet was written that accused Cobbett of having written such a republican document, *A Review of the Reports made by the Naval Commission*. The pressure which Cobbett claims would have prevented him from writing *The Soldier's Friend* had he been living in England, increased in strength after the appearance of Part Two of the *Rights of Man*. Then, both parts were extensively distributed at an inexpensive price. The immediate and threatening response to its publication — the effigy burnings, Paine's trial, and the King's Proclamation — greatly lessened the likelihood of writers modelling their prose on Paine's style.

Burke's phrase, the 'swinish multitude' occurs more

---

[16] BL Add. MS 16919, fo. 1.

frequently than any trace of Paine's style, a phrase that could be used without dreading the repercussions. The journals, *Politics for the People or a Salmagundy for Swine,* and *Pig's Meat; Lessons for the Swinish Multitude*, reflect the phrase's popularity in their titles and also in pseudonyms of letters to the editors, in the content of various stories, and in several poems. Burke's phrase released one of the few strands of humour in radical literature during the 1790s, although the situation grew more comic around 1819. *Politics for the People* was especially obsessed with the phrase and begins with the ditty

> Thy magic Rod, audacious Burke
> Could metamorphize Man to Pork,
> And quench the Spark divine;
> But Eaton's Wonder-working Wand;
> By scattering Knowledge through the Land
> Is making Men of Swine. (*PP*, i. 1)

signed 'A Ci-devant Pig'. 'Gregory Grunter' (ii. 81), 'Porculus' (i. 10), 'Pigabus' (i. 13), 'Old Bristle-back' (ii. 128), 'Gruntum Snorum' (ii. 81), 'A Young Boar' (ii. 33), and 'Spare-rib' (ii. 78) are several of the pseudonyms of letters sent in by the readership. 'Your Brother Grunter', appears to be the editor of *Pig's Meat*, Thomas Spence, sending his new colleague, Daniel Isaac Eaton, some excerpts to include in his journal, or, as Spence prefers to call them, 'a few morsels from a store of Hog's Meat' (i. 2).

The charge of being swine was gleefully accepted, by many of those who included themselves among the swinish multitude. Compared to the social fragmentation conveyed in the Association's pamphlets, the phrase proclaimed a unity of thought and consciousness. Thus, Gilbert Wakefield, a classical scholar and influential Unitarian minister, aligns himself with the multitude in a pamphlet of 1798 for which he was prosecuted.[17] If the pseudonyms often genuinely represent the writings of people who did not previously participate in public debate, then Burke's phrase might have provided a catalyst that made people more apt to write. As

---

[17] Gilbert Wakefield, *A Reply to some parts of the Bishop of Landaff's Address*, 3rd edn., 1798, pp. 8-9.

mentioned in the second chapter, Thelwall praised Burke
for defining conservatism so clearly that many were made
radical by reading his book. The phrase 'learning will be cast
into the mire, and trodden down under the hoofs of a swinish
multitude' might have had an analogous effect (*Reflections*,
p. 173). By vividly defining a large part of the population
as brutish and inarticulate, Burke provoked them into speech.
The insult that embodied their social status as inadequate
thinkers became the chosen mode for disproving the
accusation by engaging in the act of writing. Any recognition
might be better than none, in such a case, for the concreteness of the image is what allows it to be refuted.

The phrase was also used as a basis for allegorical stories
which portrayed social subordination. Authors adopted the
personae of pigs to define the character of the audience and
to present radical thought as the opinion of humble swine.
The phrase formed a banner of identification, not only
among various classes in England, as in Wakefield's pamphlet,
but also with subordinate classes in Europe. A common
theme of the allegories is that of the pigs of England being
forced to fight the pigs of France. The basic image proves to
be flexible, and the pleasure in reading these stories lies in
anticipating what other activities will be contained within the
framework of the metaphor. In some respects, the image
clarifies forms of social behaviour by allowing readers to
imagine their social relations within an imaginative and
playful construct. The humour of the imagery alleviates the
bitterness that would have followed if these authors
described themselves or their audience more starkly as
subordinate human beings. The type of language used, the
personae, the characterization, and the themes of the stories
are sufficiently similar to maintain that the pig allegories
constituted a short-lived literary form that arose out of the
political tensions of the early 1790s.

The pig allegories contend with the confusing impact of
images which defined the audience as a revolutionary mob.
As well as the *Liberty and Property* series, denunciations in
Parliament and the King's Proclamation against Seditious
Writings are usually considered. James Parkinson, in his
unsigned *Address to the Honourable Edmund Burke from the*

Swinish Multitude (1792) describes the confusion which stemmed from these three occurrences in November:

Fearing we [the swinish multitude] were destined to furnish a meal for the host of *republicans* and *levellers* we suddenly plunged ourselves into the *stream of loyalty*, and suffered ourselves to be carried by the force of the current entirely out of our depth: not considering, that, in avoiding one evil we had rushed into a greater; nor was it until we had swam a considerable way down the stream, that we discovered we were all the time — *cutting our own throats.* (p. 21)

Such comments indicate that those who identified themselves as one of the multitude were frightened by the vivid depiction of their identity and that the confusion resulted in the inability to safeguard their own political interests. Other pig allegories allude to the Duke of Brunswick's manifesto of July 1792 which declared imperial and bloody war against the French Republic. These stories thus had a considerable array of imagery, threats, and hysteria to withstand. Parkinson's *Address* continues, claiming that the proclamation and Burke's speeches in Parliament had such an impact that the audience forgot that they were not the characters they were described as being; 'for a while we doubted, since you had asserted it, whether we might not have undergone an actual metamorphosis' (p. 6).

The difficulty which Parkinson discusses is evident in most of the pig allegories. Both the nature of political activity and the identity of the audience are sources of confusion within the stories themselves. The *Liberty and Property* series had only to delineate pre-existing social assumptions to present an horrific image of the lower classes. The radicals had no available means of refuting such characterizations in the hurry of the moment, except by relying on another manifestation of social hierarchy. The lesser of two evils — pigs are better than potential murderers — was developed into a narrative stance and a mode of address to counter the vulgar language and people portrayed by the Association. To refute the *Liberty and Property* series with Burke, however, is a confused and perhaps desperate gesture, for Burke's image likewise describes a violent lower class that is incapable of valuing civilization. Far from appropriating

Burke's phrase, radical adaptations of it sometimes betray a confused belief that such an image might be accurate.

Political expression and participation is denied by the construct of the basic metaphor; the lives of the pigs are the responsibility of the swineherds, and as long as the metaphor holds so will its advocacy of deference. 'The Remonstrance of the Swinish Multitude, to the Chief and Deputy Swineherds of Europe', published in Eaton's *Politics for the People*, is an eight-page article relentlessly controlled by Burke's metaphor. The article only momentarily suggests that people should take responsibility for their present situation. 'O swine! swine! when will ye be wise! when will ye consider these things? your future happiness and peace depends on your present conduct' (i. 59). The author's plea here is undermined by the article's content, its imagery, and its language. Passive verbs define the pigs' limitations; the pigs do not complain of their free will but are 'cruelly compelled to proclaim the grievances we labour under' (i. 54). Verbs which define emotional responses or subservience portray the activities which the pigs perform. The article becomes unclear as it discusses the political changes which the author recommends: 'We admire the good old way, let them repair its defects and we wish no innovation' (i. 55). By using Burkean language — 'we wish no innovation' — the writer evades mentioning precisely what reforms he favours. Otherwise, the article portrays the upper classes as responsible for the lower-class political needs ('let them repair its defects') and, ultimately, for the swines' behaviour. It asks the swineherds to behave in such a way as to prevent revolution, a request which means to save the multitude from acting against its own will: 'We shall, it is to be feared, recoil furiously on our drivers. . . . May the prudence of our swineherds prevent this extremity. . . . Let them act properly, and they will perceive that our tractability and docility are greater than they supposed.' (i. 60.) Docility is a promise granted in return for adequate care. The 'Remonstrance' responds to the fear of revolution by accepting the paternalist relation of quiet obedience.

The discontent which the story describes strives awkwardly against the restraints imposed by the imagery. Other pig allegories suffer from the same tension. 'An Address to the Numerous Herd of Tradesmen, Mechanics and Labourers, and Others, comprized under the Appellation of the Swinish Multitude', also in *Politics for the People*, parodies various techniques of the *Liberty and Property* series. Written as a letter to John, it mentions the Association, and the Duke of Brunswick's manifesto as well. Parodying the personae of *Liberty and Property* tracts, the narrator conveys someone else's thought and denies the validity of his own ideas: 'I beg leave to offer you some wholesome advice, which has been communicated to me by a great man, who has goodness enough to pity the hardships we endure' (i. 70). Later in the article he corrects himself for stating an opinion of his own: 'I forgot, however, that I have no right to form an opinion upon such subjects, because I am, like yourselves, *One of the Swinish Multitude*' (i. 72). The article vacillates between its recommendation to postpone political activity and its vivid portrait of the self-effacement required by both the threat of prosecution and social subordination. The article concludes by asking readers to accept the great man's advice by remaining quiet until the end of the war, after having parodied the Association's refusal to grant the lower orders any independence of mind. It performs the confusing gesture of advocating what it parodies.

Deferential pigism is a confused form partly because the authors do not have a sure sense of whom they are addressing. They rely on assessments of their audience by people whose perspective they know to be antagonistic to their own. Such an acceptance establishes limits which the allegories cannot transcend. They cannot recognize any political activity beyond uncontrolled rebellion motivated by extreme poverty: 'Our roots and mast, acorns and berries, are all we crave; if they would let us enjoy them in peace we should be happy' ('The Remonstrance', *PP*, i. 55). To varying degrees, these articles are unable to depict a politically conscious audience or to recommend a political strategy. The social gulf between pigs and swineherds leaves no alternatives other than outbreak or obedience. The abundant use of the 'swinish multitude' points out the need for and the dearth of other literary identities. The very newness of the audience, compounded by the hysteria which greeted its advent, seems to have precluded the ability to describe it accurately. The entity which these stories are addressing is not the readers primarily but rather contending images defined by the opposition.

Daniel Isaac Eaton's journal, *Politics for the People*, reveals the difficulties of addressing an audience that only gradually comes to be trusted. Initially the editor appears to be wary and uncertain of his audience. Material is carefully controlled and information is guarded; the audience is not represented and an appropriate language is admittedly absent. The early numbers are composed of extracts from former writers, Aesop's and more modern fables, and a serialized 'Sketch of the most memorable Events in the History of Old England', written by James Parkinson. The didacticism of Aesop's fables is inherent in their being basically a classical form and in their having been used by charity schools to teach students how to write. Also the morals, which are evident enough, are fully explained. Extracts from earlier writings discuss current problems in general, moral, or antiquated terms. An article about aristocracy discusses Romulus and Remus. Several discuss the horrors of war, but not the current war with France. Although the periodical alludes to contemporary issues, it does not discuss them directly.

The author of the 'Sketch' was aware that he was not addressing the audience as if it had an adequate language, a point which he makes ungraciously clear. As he discusses the differences between the language of a 'well meaning friend' and 'the poor', his own style veers from the simpler diction and syntax of the rest of the history:

The greater part of the poor know hardly any more of their native language than is just sufficient to express their wants; the advice of any well meaning friend must be carefully adapted to their small stock of language, or the unhappy object to whom it is addressed may undergo the imputation of hardiness and obstinacy, for not attending to the benevolent remonstrance, when the fault may only rest in his inability of comprehension. (*PP*, i. 34)

A 'language just sufficient to express their wants' is not

capable of much; even children have a more adequate language. Writers could not delineate characters who could express ideas, if they thought that the models of those characters did not have such a language themselves. Parkinson's evident desire to distinguish himself from his audience, his need to clear himself of the stigma of vulgarity, interfered with his democratic beliefs at that moment when thought turns into written language.

In Eaton's periodical and elsewhere, authors experimented with sentimental fiction in order to present a more respectable characterization of the audience than that presented by the Association's series. John Thelwall, a contributor to the periodical and leading member of the London Corresponding Society, chose to combine political content with sentimentality, believing that their relation was inherent: political abuses will perpetually distress 'the feeling observer' unless he suppresses 'every reflection that ought to awaken the tender sympathies of the soul'.[18] As sentimental fiction implies that a refined sensibility is of the utmost value and is nourished by an acquaintance with literature, the genre was in some respects unsuitable for describing either political conflict or the audience of Eaton's journal. The genre encourages readers to attend to private events, and worth is defined by the mind's silent workings. The 'Debtor's Tale', written by Thelwall and published in *Politics for the People*, clearly reveals the problem of employing a genre that concentrates on the emotions of the narrator and not on the story's ostensible subject-matter. An attorney tells the story of going to the debtor's house to collect money. His sensitive monologue dominates the story throughout: the debtor never appears, we never learn how he got into or out of debt, his house is not described, and the conversation of his family is not recorded. The clearest image of the debtor's family lies in the narrator's observation of 'the attractions of the little blooming maiden' (i. 118). The vagueness of the characterization and the absence of dialogue implies either that these are less important than the narrator's sensitivity or that the writer did not know enough about them to incorporate them

---

[18] John Thelwall, *The Peripatetic*, 1793, 3 vols., i. viii.

into the story. Despite the title, the main interest lies in the debtor's daughter, or more specifically, 'the unfolding rose of her simple loveliness' (i. 119).

When the story arrives at its political part, the fiction stops abruptly, and the simple, although adorned language becomes convoluted, multi-syllabic, and unclear. After mentioning that the debtor had obtained some money and was no longer threatened with imprisonment, Thelwall continues:

a circumstance agreeable enough to himself and family, who might otherwise have been irretrievably ruined; but not equally fortunate for his Grace the Duke of Grafton, the patriotic * * *, and some other exalted characters, equally honourable and equally useful to society, who lost thereby some of those fees and emoluments which the *Swinish Multitude*, who are *guilty of debt and poverty*, are justly doomed to pay for the support of their *benignant splendour*. (i. 119–20)

If the story had portrayed the debtor, readers would have known that the debtor was himself owed money that he could not obtain except through litigation which he could not afford. The information which explains the above paragraph does not appear for some time, while the relation between the story and the message remains confusing. The emotive heart and the political mind which Thelwall hoped to unite in his writings are kept apart by two styles of language, one for sentiment and another for thought. Other sentimental tales such as James Parkinson's *The Village Association* (1793?) and *A Sketch, Whilst the Honest Poor are wanting Bread* (1795?) also fail to portray politically knowledgeable characters speaking an adequate language, despite the author's depiction of a situation which calls for such a portrayal.

Eaton, Thelwall, and Parkinson were in the awkward position of being unable to align their political beliefs with their writings. *Politics for People* initially contains no traces of the authors' experiences as members of the London Corresponding Society, which they belonged to and where they presumably heard vulgar speakers discussing politics. The only stories that employ colloquial language with ease and inventiveness are the pig allegories, despite or perhaps because of their limitations. Writers apparently wrote more freely as pigs because their political identity and their audience were explained by the metaphor. Colloquial language was appropriate for pigs speaking to pigs; that is, for authors pretending to be as their political opponents imagined them. Without this mediating image, authors were less willing to speak in an identifiably vulgar style. The unity of thought portrayed by adapting 'the swinish multitude' could break down in the process of writing when authors were unwilling to claim the audience's language as their own. Like the humanitarian poems of the period, the sentimental tales might portray the poor as expressing their misery, but the need to assert the dignity of such characters requires their lack of understanding. They can be miserable and innocent but not respectable and knowing. Without the indirectness provided by the pig allegories, the poor are effectively silenced and, as linguistic conventions defined them, capable of expressing only their wants and needs.

Although Eaton's periodical does not begin to include narratives which portray the poor as politically competent, its other limitations gradually diminish. Step by step the periodical approaches the discussion of contemporary events in England. Former political trials, contemporary events in France and Poland, and finally the high treason trials in Scotland precede the periodical's declaration of a change in policy in the first issue of 1794. With Eaton's arrest and acquittal for three charges of seditious libel, the periodical directly discusses the present. Eaton's 'Address to the Public', written soon after his release, expresses his gratitude for the support he had received during his trial and announces his plan to include more original material sent in by his readers. From then on the periodical is almost entirely composed of contributions sent in by the readers. Parkinson's 'Sketch', the sentimental stories, and the fables no longer appear. Extracts from William Godwin, Erasmus Darwin, and Gilbert Wakefield replace those from Dryden and Smollett. Rather than speak primarily in moral terms and without reference to contemporary life, the periodical discusses such essential issues as suffrage, the King's hiring of foreign troops to be stationed in England, and the suspension of habeas corpus. Contemporary figures such as William Pitt and John Reeves are mentioned by name. Petitions and resolutions from several societies are published. The variety of tone and genre is striking, as is the quality of the entries. Dialogues, parodies, satires, and essays reveal the greater ease and flexibility of the periodical.

According to John Reeve's unpublished Report of Sedition, Eaton's acquittal led to greater freedom in other publications besides Eaton's own.[19] The unusual decision where the jury convicted Eaton of publishing the material but not of libel revealed that juries were willing to disregard the recommendations of the judge and to take full advantage of Fox's Libel Act of 1792. Until that date, juries could only decide upon the act of publication and not the verdict. Compared to the dread of the unknown, such a decision might well have emboldened radical writers. The greater freedom and creativity of *Politics for the People* stems also from Eaton's new willingness to trust and rely upon his audience: he thanks a 'generous Public for the liberal and uncommonly flattering support which he had experienced'. By composing the journal of pieces sent in by the readership, Eaton cannot fail to address his audience appropriately. Written by people who betray few traces of being hindered by literary values, the journal addresses its audiences directly and freely. Awkwardness with language is no longer apparent once Eaton hands the pen to his audience.

Eaton's journal, and Thelwall's and Parkinson's articles reveal various attempts, with varying degrees of success, to solve the problem of addressing an audience that was generally believed to have an inadequate language. Such experimentation was soon to be cut short by the passage of repressive legislation, in 1795 and 1798. While the experimentation lasted, however, it was of an extreme kind. Such writers were not attempting to alter the language slightly or to revise concepts of taste but to write in a language that was not acknowledged to exist according to either theories of language or social assumptions. Moreover, the experimentation existed under pressing conditions. At a time when there were few contemporary models of writing in an

---

[19] 'Report on Sedition', 29 April 1794, cited by A. Goodwin, p. 320.

intellectual vernacular prose, authors were trying to steer a political course between outbreaks of violence and accepting a corrupt and repressive regime: between bloodshed and silence. Experimentation at such a time demanded both nerve and creativity, with little chance for thought or emotion recollected in tranquillity. E. P. Thompson's depiction of John Thelwall — 'his lectures were thought out on his feet, to an audience which always included one of his Majesty's informers' (*The Making*, p. 179) — describes the predicament of any radical writer who was trying to find an adequate language for discussing political ideas.

Hannah More and Thomas Spence are something of a different case. They were the two most successfully innovative writers of popular political literature. Both were more experienced writers than Thelwall and Parkinson, who recognized that their audience already had a literature, the small, inexpensive books known as chap-books which had been printed and sold since the sixteenth century. Victor Neuburg credits chap-books with perpetuating literacy among readers who otherwise had very little to read until the sudden increase of printed material beginning in the 1790s.[20] Most chap-books were highly traditional stories, printed again and again, although some were abridged versions of what are now known as the popular classics, such as *Pilgrim's Progress* and *Robinson Crusoe*. Almanacs, jest-books, religious literature, and how-to books also appeared as chap-books. Hannah More studied the books in order to imitate the form and to alter the content. She wrote detailed descriptions of poor people's lives in order to advocate quiet obedience. Thomas Spence, whose work anticipates the more widely circulated and more skilful writings of William Hone, was too much a product of chap-book culture to need to study it. He extended the tradition, however, by adapting chap-books to convey political ideas. From opposing political camps, Spence and More do not have the difficulties of Eaton, Thelwall, and Parkinson. Their characters speak a credible language and express a range of emotions in stories which reveal no signs of groping for a language.

[20] *Popular Literature, A History and Guide*, 1977, p. 121.

Between 1795 and 1797 Hannah More wrote approximately fifty of the Cheap Repository Tracts, editing and publishing a total of one hundred.[21] She was well suited for such an enterprise. The Bishop of London, ever busy with propaganda, recognized that her founding of the Mendip Valley schools gave her an unusual knowledge of the lives and conversations of working people (*MLC*, ii. 343). From the start she was scornful of fashionable English and preferred the greater simplicity of earlier eighteenth-century writing. Her preference for the 'courtly ease of the style of Addison, the sinewy and clear precision of Swift' brought her own writing closer to the vernacular than that of many of her contemporaries (*MLC*, ii. 146). As a published poet and former friend of Lord Monboddo, Samuel Johnson, and Bishop Lowth, she did not need to prove her ability to succeed in a literary world nor did she particularly want to once she became more religious. Being female, she was by definition not a writer of the hegemonic language. During the Blagdon controversy, when the extremity of conservative rhetoric accused even her of being a radical, More was unwilling to defend herself in print and insisted that she did not initiate any activities without masculine encouragement. Believing in the 'defenseless state of our sex' as she then put it (*MLC*, iii. 123), she did not think of language as a means of asserting her value in a public sphere. She thought of writing for the poor as an act of humility appropriate to both her gender and her faith.

Hannah More's writing exemplifies the limited dignity that conservatives could convey to their audience, while it avoids some of the worst characteristics of conservative prose: she does not make jokes at the expense of her readers; she does not advocate hatred of radicals, distrust of one's peers, or scorn for social inferiors; and she does not imply that the efforts which her readers expend make no difference to their character. Unlike radical writers, she does not need to demonstrate the superiority of her language to that of the audience. Even when discussing the difference between the language of her social class and that of the audience, she

[21] G. H. Spinney, 'Cheap Repository Tracts: Hazard and Marshall Edition', *The Library*, 4th series, xx (1940), 295.

abstains from using refined language. Describing a well-educated man's inability to explain religion to his servant, she states, 'though his meaning was very good, his language was not always plain; and though the *things* he said were not hard to be understood, yet the words were, especially to such as were very ignorant'.[22] 'Compared to both radical and conservative writings, this is exceptional and a self-conscious *tour de force*. Moreover, the statement disagrees with familiar notions of language on several counts. Complexity is described as irrelevant to meaning, the inability to speak plainly is portrayed as a limitation of the refined speaker's, and the ignorance of the listeners does not imply their moral deprivation. Because Hannah More did not believe in widely current notions of vulgarity, she had exceptional freedom as a writer. Her Cheap Repository Tracts contrast sharply with both conservative and radical literature in the simplicity of the language, the portrayal of the poor as individuals, the use of credible dialogue, and the particularized portrayal of various situations, including different trades. Tracts describe apprenticeship, a family which breaks the game laws, being a servant, working in a coal-mine, an impoverished widow, getting drunk and attending an anti-Paine riot, and the process of weaving. The characters, the settings, and many of the events are realistic:

Jack, who, with all his faults, was a keen, smart boy, took to learn the trade quick enough, but the difficulty was to make him stick two hours together to his work. At every noise he heard in the street, down went the work — the last one way, the upper leather another; the sole dropped on the ground, and the thread he dragged after him, all the way up the street. If a blind fiddler, a ballad singer, a mountebank, a dancing bear, or a drunk were heard at a distance — out ran Jack — nothing could stop him. (*The Two Shoemakers*, p. 11)

This is Hannah More at her best, portraying ordinary work in detail, village life as potentially exciting, and a character who is both specific and familiar. The tracts can bring dignity to labour, unspectacular characters, and ordinary settings by the degree of attention which the author manifestly gives them.

---

[22] *The Shepherd of Salisbury Plain*, Part ii, p. 19. The tracts are not identified as a series nor are they dated. They will hereafter be noted in the text.

Realism breaks down, however, as More relentlessly demonstrates that the poor exist to be saved by the upper classes. In a *Lancashire Collier Girl*, an allegedly true story, a nine-year-old girl works in the mines. Her father dies, her mother becomes insane, and the girl's strength is ruined by her work. For years, she supports her mother and her siblings until a wealthy man learns about her history and employs her as a servant. The easy gesture of his charity is less impressive than the girl's ability to survive despite overwhelming odds and to continue caring for other people. *The Shepherd of Salisbury Plain* is based on a real shepherd named David Saunders. In the story, the shepherd's poverty is vividly described: his eight children, his rudimentary cottage, and his inability to procure sufficient food and medicine. A wealthy gentleman advises him to start a Sunday school, arranges it for him, and pays him a regular salary: 'I am not going to make you rich but useful' (Part Two, p. 28). The real David Saunders had sixteen children, he thought of starting a school on his own initiative, he was probably paid by his students, and he did not achieve the financial security of his fictional counterpart.[23] The capability of himself and of the collier girl before her rescue portrays a strength which More did not want her audience to have; that is, she wanted them to endure, but not to manage for themselves. She sometimes travels this fine line with astounding lack of tact, cheering on the poor for the suffering that enables the rich to be virtuous. The basic plot of a poor person saved by the chance arrival of a generous and wealthy man occurs over and over again. In the ballad, *The Riot, or Half a Loaf is Better than no Bread* (1795), written during a severe famine, labourers sing their willingness to starve:

> Besides I must share in the wants of the times
> Because I have had my full share in its crimes,
> And I'm apt to believe the distress which is sent
> Is to punish and cure us of all discontent.

.   .   .   .

[23] Mary Alden Hopkins, *Hannah More and her Circle*, New York, 1947, p. 217.

> So I'll work the whole day, and on Sunday's I'll seek
> At church how to bear all the wants of the week.
> The Gentlefolks too will afford us supplies;
> They'll subscribe — and they'll give up their
>   puddings and pies.

The unprecedented attention which More pays to her readers, thus comes with great cost — that of permitting her to quiet them by eventually betraying the recognition that she originally granted. The individuality of her characters dissolves as so many of them weep in gratitude. More attempts to take the discontent out of misery by this simple plot and also by the relentlessness of her tone and diction. The purity of her language, where every word means precisely what it says, implies that meaning on all levels is unquestionable. Word falls after word into its appointed place without question, stress, or ambiguity. The flow and certainty of the language is still soothing, in its lullaby way, and in a time of political disruption it would have been more so. Compared to the hysterical style and tone of the Association's tracts, Hannah More's are like oil upon the waters.

Having an unconfused concept of her readers, Hannah More knew how to address them. Whether discussing inexpensive radical writings or her own tracts, More describes them as 'alluring'. She considers the effectiveness of writings addressed to the audience to be of a particular kind — a matter of catching attention through the appetites of her readers. This leaves her in the odd position of describing her relation to her audience as one of righteously seducing people who have no control over their passions: 'Alas! I know with whom I have to deal, and I hope I may thus allure these thoughtless creatures on to higher things' (*MLC*, ii. 427). This potentially dangerous relation between a female author and her readers is secure only when the poor are pathetic and manipulable. Behind Hannah More's evident attention to the lives of her readers lies the quiet and usually unstated fear that they will disrupt the social system by becoming self-sufficient. Her diary entry of 2 November 1794 records her complex attitude towards her students, and will serve to describe her attitude towards her reading audience as well: 'Oh Lord, grant that this people may never' rise up in judgement against me, and that, with all the advantages of knowledge and education, I may not fall short of these poor ignorant creatures.'[24]

From the start, however, Hannah More's version of the vulgar life and language was regarded more highly by the upper than the lower classes, who went at them somewhat desperately. Two million tracts had been distributed by March 1796 but in January of that year Hannah More was worried that they were not reaching their intended readers. To remedy this, she decided to publish expensive editions in order to finance cheaper ones which would undersell the chap-books. In addition, she planned to distribute tracts to charity school children in London with the particular intention of reaching their parents: 'and we should thus get them introduced among a greater number of the lower class than we have yet been able to do' (*MLC*, ii. 461). The tracts were distributed through the army and navy, prisons, workhouses, factories, and parishes, as well as by private families. Despite this enthusiastic activity, little evidence exists of the tracts being bought for their own enjoyment or even of being ordered by the booksellers without solicitation. Albert Goodwin's claim that they 'outsold even Paine' disregards too many differences in the distribution of their work (p. 265). He is comparing the sales figures of a hundred entertaining tracts that were given away through large institutions to that of political essays that were sold inexpensively at great legal risk. One claim to their effectiveness is the story of rioters near Bath who disbanded after 'a gentleman of fortune' distributed her ballad, *The Riot, or Half a Loaf is Better than No Bread*', and induced the riotous colliers to sing it together (*MLC*, ii. 384). The Bishop of London wrote that a Quaker bookseller in York gave the tracts away to poor people who said they loved them (*MLC*, ii. 458), but such comments are noticeably rare. William Cobbett wrote More a letter in praise of them, but he was soon to change his mind: 'This flatterer, on coming to

[24] Martha More, *Mendip Annals,* 1859, p. 138.

England joined Mr Bere's party and became my mortal enemy'.[25]

Although very little praise from her intended audience was recorded, there were also few angry comments, such as those by William Hone and William Cobbett in 1817. Then, political turmoil again prompted Hannah More to write, but her writings had little effect. Her famous tract, *Village Politics*, which appeared in the *Liberty and Property* series, was rewritten as *Village Disputants*; she wrote some more tracts, and she contributed to the weekly, *Anti-Cobbett*, but these writings were powerless against the convincing radical publications of that time. The end of the eighteenth century appears to have been her moment. Her writings stand out for several reasons: because the radical press could not develop adequate fictional forms, because the alarmist portrayals of the Association required an antidote, and because the passage of the Two Acts dealt a heavy blow to the opposition. In the late 1790s, the several currents of alarmism, the awkward relation of radicalism to literature and conventions of language, and the passage of repressive legislation were all moving in her favour. Hannah More's ability to write simple, calming, and vividly detailed stories describing the lives of the poor might have comforted readers who had been publicly defined as immoral, vicious, and incapable of self-control by the *Liberty and Property* series. Without question, however, they comforted wealthier readers who grasped on to her tracts to allay fears which former conservative tracts had done their best to instill. Coming after the hysteria of the 1790s and before the even greater repression of 1800, her gentle propaganda was a harbinger of the encroaching silence.

Whereas Hannah More was freed from literary conventions, in part, by her religious faith in the distinction between social classes, Spence was freed by the depth of his commitment to social equality. He was impervious to the relation of language to class because he did not conceive of himself as someone who was inferior to those who spoke a more formal variant of English. As a writer, he was unhindered by the

---

[25] Cited from a letter to Zachary Macaulay by G. H. Spinney, p. 310.

disadvantages of having a better education or a higher social status than his audience. Eaton, the son of a fairly wealthy stationer, had a good education which included attending a French boarding-school. He was fully apprenticed and, unlike Spence, a freeman.[26] Spence was taught to read by his father who held various semi-skilled jobs and who was impoverished by raising fourteen children. Newcastle, the city where Spence grew up, was a centre for popular publishing and was presumably less ridden with social assumptions concerning language than the more literary world of London. Spence's writing manifests his lack of belief in any incompatibility between literature, his audience, and radical politics. He does not portray any speakers as having an essentially different language from his own, nor does he portray himself as different from his audience.

By his own account, his audience was small, but Spence had an impact both as an eccentric figure about London, and as the most vocal advocate of socialism. In his trial of 1801, he commented: 'I stand alone, unconnected with any party, and except by a thinking few am looked on as a lunatic'.[27] He tended, however, to be distinctly remembered. When Cobbett was an antiministerial Tory, he inadvertently attended Spence's trial. Fifteen years later, Cobbett expressed his admiration of Spence in the *Political Register*, and remembered him in surprising detail (*PR*, xxxi. 749). In the *Quarterly Review*, Robert Southey praised Spence in the midst of an essay denouncing all other radicals. Southey presumably found Spence's thought appealing because it was similar to that of Southey's youth. In 1816, Southey believed that Spence was especially dangerous because 'great and important truths, half understood and misapplied, are of all means of mischief the most formidable', and he consequently regretted that Spence had not been transported.[28] Spence was dead by the time of Southey's article but a small and influential group of followers, The Society of Spencean Philanthropists, continued to advocate Spence's land reform;

---

[26] Daniel McCue jun., 'The Pamphleteer Pitt's Government Couldn't Silence', *Eighteenth-Century Life*, v (1978), 38.

[27] *The Important Trial of Thomas Spence* [1801], p. 9.

[28] 'Parliamentary Reform', *Quarterly Review*, xvi (1816), 263.

one, Arthur Thistlewood, led the Cato Street Conspiracy of 1819.

Spence's politics, unlike those of other writers, were not drastically changed by the appearance of new publications or by the events of the 1790s: he was a socialist before the movement for a more democratic form of government began. In 1775, at the age of twenty-five, Spence delivered an essay to the Newcastle Philosophical Society which advocated parish ownership of land and the land's productions. The original essay is no longer extant, but Spence reprinted it in 1792 with the title *The Real Rights of Man* and again in 1796 in the third volume of his journal, *Pig's Meat*. There, he considers reforms in military organization, in taxation, in parish relief, in suffrage, and in the relation between parish and national government. Spence believed that land and fixed property, including houses, factories, and mines, were the means of life and should therefore be publicly owned: 'a right to deprive any thing of the means of living, supposes a right to deprive it of life; and this right ancestors are not supposed to have over their posterity'.[29] The essay concludes with the millennial cast to his thinking that is evident elsewhere in his writings, especially in his songs:

Now what makes this prospect yet more glorious is, that after this empire of right and reason is thus established, it will stand forever. Force and corruption attempting its down-fall shall quickly be baffled, and all other nations struck with wonder and admiration at its happiness and stability, shall follow the example; and thus the whole earth shall at last be happy, and live like brethren. (iii. 229)

Spence's thought could encourage such diverse movements as Robert Owen's and trade-unionism because it combined a political analysis based on the perspective of a labourer with a utopianism that relied on individual fulfilment rather than on centralized government as the primary means of achieving social order.[30]

[29] *Pig's Meat; A Lesson for the Swinish Multitude*, 1793-6, 3 vols., iii. 221. Later abbreviated as *PM*.

[30] Olive D. Rudkin, *Thomas Spence and his Connections*, New York, 1966, pp. 191–201; Iorweth Prothero, *Artisans and Politics in Early Nineteenth-Century London: John Gast and his Times*, Folkestone, 1979, pp. 88–91; T. M. Parssinen, 'Thomas Spence and the Origins of Land Nationalization', *Journal of the History of Ideas*, xxxiv (1973), 135-41.

As well as having formulated a political analysis before the 1790s, Spence had already considered the relation of language to class. Politics and language were the two consuming interests of his life, as he stated grandly during his trial: 'When I began to Study, I found ... every Art and Science a perfect Whole. Nothing was in Anarchy but Language and Politics: But both of these I reduced to order: the one by a New Alphabet, and the other by a New Constitution' (*Important Trial*, p. 59). The Introduction to Spence's *Grand Repository of the English Language* (1775) is composed almost entirely of a long excerpt from Thomas Sheridan's *A Dissertation on the causes of the difficulties which occur in learning the English tongue* (1761). The *Dissertation* in its original form was an unusual document, both critical of élitism and élitist in itself. Spence's omissions and additions, however, alter it significantly. According to Sheridan, grammarians had falsely increased the gap between written and spoken English because of their desire for spelling to retain traces of Greek and Latin etymologies. As a result, the 'true power and beauty' of English was not apparent in its written form and pronunciation had deviated from spelling to such an extent that the language was only the 'property of a few'.[31] Sheridan's apparent preference for spoken English and his critique of the written language were most unusual. But his solution to the gap between them was to formalize spoken English both by the teaching of oratory and by the standardization of pronunciation. Language spoken by 'the people of the best taste at court' was to provide a national standard (p. 35). Unlike most eighteenth-century theorists, Sheridan does not consider the level of language use as indicative of mentality. Hence, no reason exists for the language of different classes to vary as much as they do. That his theory was identified and appropriated by Spence is one measure of the scarcity of radical interpretations of language and of the subject's importance to a critique of class structure.

Spence extracted a considerable portion of Sheridan's preface but by shifting its emphasis from the language of

[31] EL no. 40, pp. 12 and 36.

the court to the literacy of the labouring classes, he alters Sheridan's remarks. Repeating Sheridan's intention as his own, Spence states that he wants 'to make the spoken language, as it ought to be, the archetype; of which the written language should be considered only as the type'.[32] But here the spoken language is not eventually defined by that of the court. Whereas Sheridan advocated the formalization of pronunciation and the teaching of elocution, Spence advocates altering the alphabet to make it accord phonetically with spoken English. Relying on the accent of a minister and apparently unconcerned with the prospect of having to learn a new pronunciation himself, Spence devised a new phonetic alphabet. His *Grand Repository of the English Language* transposes vocabulary into Spence's variant of English. In one of his few additions to Sheridan's Preface, Spence concludes: 'I cannot but think it possible such a method of spelling may take place, especially among the laborious part of the people, who generally cannot afford much time or expence in the education of their children, and yet they would like to have them taught the necessary and useful arts of reading and writing.' Spence thus directs Sheridan's comments to a different target, the needs of the 'laborious part of the population'.

Compared with the other spelling reformers of his time, such as Benjamin Franklin and James Elphinstone, Spence's work has been evaluated as 'consistent, following a definite convention, and apparently fairly reliable'.[33] Shields argues that both Spence and Sheridan rely on Anne Fisher's *A New Grammar*, briefly mentioned in the first chapter. Anne Fisher taught and published in Newcastle, where Spence grew up, and her grammar forms the basis for the ten-page grammar which appears in Spence's *Repository*. Spence continued to be interested in alphabet reform, despite the political intensity of the 1790s. William Hone wrote in an unpublished memoir of Spence that he saw him working on a dictionary in 1797,[34] and in 1803 Spence published

[32] Thomas Spence, *The Grand Repository*, 1775, EL no. 155, unpaginated Preface.

[33] Anthea Shields, 'Thomas Spence and the English Language', *Transactions of the Philological Society*, Oxford, 1974, p. 61.

[34] BL Add. MS 27808, fo. 314.

an account of his trial in his new language. Copies of *Dh'e imp'ortánt Triál ŏv Tóm'is Sp'ens For a Pól'it'ik'al Pámfl'et entitld 'Dhĕ Rĕstorr ŏv Sosiĕte tw ĭts năteŭral Stat'* were given to the two people who came to his aid. Spence's earlier story, 'The Rise and Progress of Learning in Lilliput' (1782) imaginatively conveys his expectations of introducing an alphabet that would simplify the process of learning English. Altering the distribution of language, like wealth, would put an end to corruption and encourage the fulfilment of individual citizens: 'the very poorest soon acquired such Notions of Justice, and Equity, and of the Rights of Mankind, as rendered unsupportable, every Species of Oppression'.[35]

'The Rise and Progress of Learning in Lilliput' was one of Spence's stories based on chap-book literature, which appeared as a chap-book itself. From the start, Spence's work was referential, pointing to the existence of a literary tradition that was known by both the readers and the writer. A *Description of Spensonia* (1793), the only chap-book which he wrote after the 1780s, loosely derives its plot from *A Tale of a Tub, Robinson Crusoe*, and recent American history. A father bequeaths a constitution to his three sons who sail towards America. When a storm sends them off course, they are stranded on an island where they must decide how to form their government. Such stories raise the possibility that popular literature was not simply a form of expression which Spence employed as a propagandist but that it contributed to his understanding of politics by enabling him to imagine a different type of future, another world.

One type of chap-book especially appears to have encouraged Spence's radicalism. Spence claims that legends about giants, a common chap-book plot, portray the antagonistic relation between landowners and their tenants: 'I can compare them and their Castles to nothing but the Giants, and their Castles in Romances, who were said to be a Terror and Destruction to all the People around; and must certainly

---

[35] *Supplement to the History of Robinson Crusoe*, new edition, Newcastle, 1782, p. 42.

have been invented for a Satire against Landlords.'[36] In the case of Thomas Hickathrift, one of the oldest and most well-known chap-books, Spence's comment proves to be correct. According to G. L. Gomme, the legend is an extremely old story about a physical dispute between the inhabitants of Ely and a landlord over the boundary of a manor.[37] Tom Hickathrift, the lazy son of a day labourer, lounges about, unwilling to help his mother after his father's death. He becomes happy when he discovers his strength (Paine would have appreciated this). After a forester tells Tom's mother that she can have any amount of wood they can carry, Tom takes an entire tree. Tom later meets the giant who addresses him with a speech that combines several forms of intimidation: 'How dare you assume to do this? . . . Do you not care what you do? I'll make thee an example of all rogues under the sun; does thou not see how many heads hang upon yonder tree that have offended my law!' And Tom replies in language that is vulgar in every eighteenth-century sense — crude, monosyllabic, and, in context, radical: 'A turd in your teeth for your news' (pp. 8-9). After killing the giant, Hickathrift gives the land to the poor for a common, keeping some of it for himself and his mother: 'Many more good deeds he did' (p. 12). In a second part, added to the story in 1780, the ungrateful poor rebel: 'Many dissatisfied persons, to the number of ten thousand and upwards drew themselves up in a body, presuming to contend for their pretended Rights and Liberties' (p. 17). Hickathrift fights and defeats 'the headstrong giddy-brained multitude' and is rewarded with a pension by his grateful king. This alteration of the story indicates that the antagonistic relation between the propertied and unpropertied classes expressed in the chap-book were evident to others besides Spence. As we shall see, *Pilgrim's Progress* was similarly depoliticized. Margaret Spufford argues in a recent book that chap-books were without political content of any kind and demonstrates

---

[36] 'The History of Crusonia; Or, Robinson Crusoe's Island' in *A Supplement*, p. 12.
[37] *The History of Thomas Hickathrift*, ed. G. L. Gomme, 1885, unpaginated Introduction.

her argument by discussing Thomas Hickathrift.[38] Spence, however, was sufficiently sure of this component of the tradition that he titled his last journal, only two issues of which were published in 1814, *The Giant-Killer*.

Moving from Newcastle to London in the 1790s, coincided with Spence's beginning to write again after a nine-year hiatus. He no longer wrote only chap-books but relied on all of the political genre of the period: he wrote dialogues, essays, and songs. He even stamped commemorative coins and wrote political graffitti on the walls about London. Unlike less practised radical writers, Spence was undaunted by the intensity of the conservative backlash. The *Liberty and Property* series, Burke's phrase 'the swinish multitude', fear that popular political activity was uncontrollable, and the government's repressive measures — Spence had a quick and courageous reply to all of these. Rather than refute the character of John Bull, Spence taunted his audience for being confused and rendered more passive by the tracts:

> For poor Johnny Bull
> Who is now so dull
> A few plain answers
> To suit his thick skull.[39]

Instead of writing a story in the persona of a pig and thereby remaining bound by the metaphor, Spence discusses the phrase in a dialogue called 'The Rights of Man by Question and Answer'. Ostensibly about Burke's phrase, the dialogue concentrates on the quietude espoused by the pig allegories. Spence points out that pigs differ from people in that they will 'scream most seditiously' when imposed upon (*PM*, i. 263). Such dialogues portray labourers speaking a confident and politically conscious language. In the *Rights of Infants* (1797), Spence writes a pamphlet in which an angry woman defies an aristocrat, a rare moment in the pamphlet war when vulgarity gets the better of refinement. The

---

[38] *Small Books and Pleasant Histories: Popular Fiction and its Readership in Seventeenth-Century England*, 1981, pp. 247–9.

[39] 'A Letter from Ralph Hodge to his Cousin Thomas Bull' (1795?) reprinted in *Essays in Honour of William Gallacher*, no editor, Berlin, 1966, p. 326. This book reprints several of Spence's pamphlets and includes an interesting essay about Spence by P. M. Kemp-Ashraf.

defiance of a 'Woman' leads her to accept the opprobious terms that had been used to denounce Mary Wollstonecraft and that would be used against Hannah More: 'Ask the she-bears and every she-monster, and they will tell you what the rights of every species of young are. — They will tell you in resolute language and actions too, that their rights extend to a full participation of the fruits of the earth.' (p. 5.) To encourage women's political activity would have been unusual, but to speak as a politically conscious, articulate, and defiant woman measures Spence's extreme political stance and his exceptional ability to write without ideological restrictions. Other radicals advised him to quieten down, and instead he wrote a bitter and sardonic *Recantation of the End of Oppression* (1795), in which he agrees with other radicals who were limiting their political aspirations to suffrage. Spence aimed higher, for social equality; and it is not coincidental that a socialist was the only radical writer to address the audience with this degree of creative freedom.

By the end of the 1790s, Spence had become increasingly critical of radicals who were contrasting themselves with the undeserving poor and advocated the causes of the semi-literate whom he believed were otherwise ignored. During his trial in 1800, he describes himself as the defender of 'all those who have no Helpers' and exclaims, what kind of land reform is it 'that Admits the very Babes, and their Mothers, the Blind and the Lame, the Dumb and the Eloquent, to an equal Participation of the Rights of Nature? — I say, will such a levelling Constitution as this, do for proud Men of Abilities and conceited Excellence' (*The Important Trial*, p. 48). Critical at an early stage of what would later become known as 'meritocracy', Spence addresses an audience that was barely literate, without condescension or sentimentality. His political commitment informs his writing, an act which might sound simple enough but which becomes self-contradictory when one is committed to people excluded from the privileges of literature.

Spence solves this contradiction in the third volume of *Pig's Meat*, where he serializes a seventeenth-century account of a rebellion of the labouring classes, a story which focuses on the political capability of the vulgar. In case anyone might miss the point, Spence follows the first excerpt with a passage from Joel Barlow's *Advice to the Priviledged Orders*, a book of great notoriety in the early 1790s: the possibility of revolution 'depends not on me, or on Mr. Burke, or any other writer. . . . It depends on a much more important class of men, the class that cannot write; and, in a great measure on those who cannot read' (*PM*, iii. 56). Originally translated by the royal historiographer of Charles II, James Howell, from a first-hand Italian account, the history's appearance in *Pig's Meat* is most unusual.[40] The story, which from Spence's perspective serves as a model for autonomous political activity, was used throughout Europe as a warning to the upper classes of the potential violence of their social inferiors. According to Peter Burke, it was not published elsewhere by radicals for the purpose of describing a radical movement.[41]

With remarkable objectivity, 'The Rise and Fall of Masaniello' portrays political conflict in detail, describing how people react to unfamiliar ideas, how they can be deluded by the administration, how they can direct political strategies, and how those strategies can become confused. Several details and events of the history were probably exceptionally vivid to Spence's readers whose political situation paralleled that of the citizens of Naples. Descriptions of bread riots in Italy described those in England, where rioters also carried bread on spikes decorated with black ribbon:

They boldly advanced towards the palace of the viceroy, many of them carrying loaves of bread on the tops of their pikes, to signify the dearness of bread. . . . The posse of boys, consisting of about 2000, marched in the van, with *Masaniello* at the head of them, and to make the procession the more affecting, every one tied to the top of his cane, a sort of flag of black cloth; and walking solemnly and dolefully along, they cried out in a most lamentable tone. (iii. 38-9)

The passage describes and confirms political traditions which

[40] *An Exact History of the late Revolution in Naples*, trans. James Howell, 1650.
[41] Peter Burke, 'Religion and Crisis in Seventeenth-Century Naples', unpublished paper read at the University of Birmingham, 28 Jan. 1980. See Burke's 'The Virgin of the Carmine and the Revolt of Masaniello', *Past and Present*, no. 99 (May 1983), 3-21.

were rarely noticed in print. Spence's followers buried him in 1814 with a similar display of iconography. At the head of forty Spenceans, one carried 'the scales, as the emblems of justice, immediately after the corpse, containing an equal quantity of earth in each scale, the balance being decorated with white ribbons to denote the innocence of his life and example'.[42]

As the story comes to a close, the analogy between contemporary events in England and the Italian rebellion comes sharply into focus. The withdrawal of the charter of rights in the history parallels the suspension of habeas corpus and the passage of legislation which curtailed basic freedoms. The Two Acts, passed in December of 1795, had recently extended the definition of high treason to include acts of speech or writing. The danger of an internal war becoming engulfed by a war between European powers was evident in the recent history of France and was greatly feared in England. Spence's conclusion, added to an otherwise faithful rendering of Howell's original, extends these similarities. In Howell's translation, the final passage points to the moral: Masaniello's history exemplifies the fickleness of fortune, a lesson one might think Charles II knew well enough from the fate of his father. Spence's version omits Howell's conclusion and ends with a statement blaming government ministers for the rebellion and declaring the people's ability to act on their own behalf:

The authors of it, unimproved by so recent an example of what an injured and exasperated people can do in their own defence, and the defence of their liberty, soon saw themselves and their country involved in all the calamaties and horrors that attend intestine feuds and dissentions: And some of them, by meeting with a more hasty and exemplary punishment, have left behind them, an everlasting monument of the wrath of Heaven, against perjured and avaricious ministers. (iii. 212-13)

The phrase 'perjured and avaricious ministers' could describe an administration that was asking the public to finance a war against republicanism while claiming it was being fought to

---

[42] Allen Davenport, *The Life, Writings, and Principles of Thomas Spence* [1836], p. 5.

preserve liberty. The phrase might also refer more specifically to William Pitt, who had verged on perjury during Horne Tooke's trial for high treason. He made a poor showing of himself by claiming to have forgotten his earlier activity in favour of extending suffrage and reforming Parliament.[43] Spence's final paragraph brings together various analogies and parallel situations into a culminating statement that is both a promise and a threat. Spence, under the guise of a moral and backed by the wrath of God, tells his readers that they have considerable political power which they can apply if the government remains unresponsive. By retelling a seventeenth-century account of Italian history, Spence published the only narrative which considers events rising from political tensions and admits the possibility of an autonomous movement of the labouring classes.

Primarily on account of his millennialism, Spence has been described as an anachronistic thinker, a 'mutation of the past, testimony to the latent and diverse radicalism of England's traditions and institutions'.[44] Such an argument can be made. It can be said as well that Spence, unlike Eaton, Parkinson, and Thelwall, was not writing in a cultural vacuum; but that his millennialism, his chap-books, his songs, his Swiftian, Defoeish, and biblical imagery were literary manifestations of a culture which enabled him to know and to trust his audience. Spence had developed an informal and flexible use of language that existed independently of both conservative concepts of literature and of conservative images of his audience. He could use conservative imagery and rhetoric as he used radical imagery, as a stylistic resource. He could portray his characters speaking in a vivid and informal language because he did .not perceive that language as demonstrating their intellectual and moral limitations. For the 1790s, this was a rare achievement, one which would not be matched until after 1815 when William Cobbett, William Hone, and others similarly provoked their audience by extending its own literary traditions. For the 1790s, one could even call it avant-garde.

[43] Simon Maccoby, *English Radicalism: 1786–1832*, 1955, p. 86.
[44] Thomas R. Knox, 'Thomas Spence: the Trumpet of Jubilee', *Past and Present*, no. 76 (Aug. 1977), 98.

When the Two Acts were passed in December 1795, Spence, Eaton, and Thelwall, with considerable courage, continued to lecture and to write until they were worn down by conviction, intimidation from local communities, poverty, and isolation. *Politics for the People* was not published after the first issue of 1795. Convicted in 1796 of seditious libel for publishing Pigot's *Political Dictionary* and *The Duties of Citizenship*, Eaton went into hiding until he fled to the United States in 1797 after publishing Paine's *Age of Reason*. James Parkinson stopped writing in 1796 after he wrote *A Vindication of the London Corresponding Society*. John Thelwall continued proudly to give political lectures under the guise of classical history, although part of the Public Meetings Act mentioned him by name. He describes his intention of evading the acts in his pamphlet, *Prospectus of a Course of Lectures . . . in strict conformity with the Restrictions of Mr. Pitt's Convention Act* (1796). Though Thelwall managed to evade the law, local magistrates and loyalists wore him down by intimidation, even in a rural Welsh community.[45] Thomas Spence also continued to write. Arrested immediately after the suspension of habeas corpus in 1794, he was in gaol for six months waiting to be charged while the trials of Tooke, Hardy, and Thelwall were in progress. During this time, he continued to publish *Pig's Meat* without weakening its content. Released in December 1794, Spence wrote a letter complaining to the *Morning Chronicle* that it had previously refused to advertise his journal and that he was in financial difficulty as a result of his imprisonment. Presumably, Spence stopped publishing *Pig's Meat* because he could no longer afford it. Spence's most radical work was published between 1796 and 1800.

The passage of more repressive legislation in 1798 and 1799 placed even greater restrictions on written works, and by 1800 very little radical material was being written. After the publication of his trial in 1801, Spence's publications ceased altogether until 1814, with the exception of a broadsheet in 1805 and a collection of songs. William Hone

---

[45] John Thelwall, *An Appeal to Popular Opinion against . . . the late atrocious Proceedings at Yarmouth*, 1796 and *Poems written chiefly in Retirement with Memoirs of the Life of the Author*, 2nd edn., 1801.

described Spence in 1809 as very poor, and selling pamphlets from a barrow.[46] Eaton was also silenced by poverty and imprisonment. Reappearing in London in 1803, Eaton was immediately arrested for two outstanding convictions. He was sentenced to fifteen months' solitary confinement and his stock of books — that is his means of livelihood — was publicly burned. After receiving a Royal Pardon in 1805, Eaton stated that he would not publish any more political material. In 1812 and 1813 he was convicted for publishing radical religious works. After serving a sentence for publishing the misleadingly titled *Age of Reason* Part Three, he was convicted for publishing *Ecco Homo*. The judge excused him from his last sentence due to his extreme old age and ill health. Both Eaton and Spence died in 1814, a year before political turmoil and the audience began to revive. During this grim interlude from 1800 to the end of the war, language and literature were being debated before a more traditional audience. Horne Tooke published a book on language which radically challenged orthodox theories, and Wordsworth and Colderidge wrote the Preface to *Lyrical Ballads* at a time when conservative rhetoric was reaching a pitch of confused ecstasy.

---

[46] BL Add. MS 27808 fo. 315.

Chapter IV

Winged Words: Language and Liberty in John Horne Tooke's *Diversions of Purley*

The task of developing an informal and intellectual language for the new audience was left largely to the self-educated, to such writers as Thomas Spence, Thomas Paine, William Hone, and William Cobbett. They achieved it both by the innovative practice of their writings and by considering conventions of language use. Comments ranging from Thomas Paine's, which associate different styles of language with different forms of government, to Spence's advocacy of a new alphabet, to Hone's defence of vernacular English during his trial, and to William Cobbett's discussion of class and language in the columns of the *Political Register*, were contributing to an awareness among the audience that ideas about language were an integral part of a social system which they desired to change. Such comments, however, had a limited effectiveness, for although they enabled more of the audience to contribute to public debates, they did not discredit ideas about language which justified class division nor alter the assessment of language by the literati. The self-educated writers who were most aware that eighteenth-century assumptions concerning language hindered the articulacy of the audience, were least apt to be able to challenge the grammar books, the dictionaries, and the theories of language on which those assumptions were based. A comment by William Wordsworth, which discusses the difficulty of re-educating literary critics, also serves to describe the more general difficulty of learning new ideas about language: 'For to be mistaught is worse than to be untaught; and no perverseness equals that which is supported by system, no errors are so difficult to root out as those which the understanding has pledged its credit to uphold.'[1]

---

[1] 'Essay Supplementary to the Preface', *Prose Works of William Wordsworth*, ed. W. J. B. Owen and J. W. Smyser, Oxford, 1974, 3 vols., i. 66.

The conservative linguistic 'system' of the last half of the eighteenth century was sufficiently pervasive to discourage extensive criticism. Dictionaries, grammars, theories of language, and the attitudes towards language disseminated by the reviewers presented a remarkably uniform code of values that was an integral part of all levels of literary trainïng. Moreover, this code of values was immensely flattering to those who considered themselves to be literary, and scornful of those who were not. 'Credit', in this instance, was pledged by the distinction which the system itself granted. John Horne Tooke, as notorious as a radical as he was renowned as a linguist, was one of the few who had the political acumen and the knowledge of languages to refute prevalent conservative theories.

Horne Tooke believed himself to have been severely hindered both intellectually and politically, by language theory and particularly by the obscurity of definitions. His experiences validate the charge, frequently expressed by his contemporaries, that intellectual confusion and political oppression were efficiently interwoven. While a student, Tooke found that the study of philosophy had been rendered difficult by the attempts to define the parts of speech according to philosophic categories. By attempting to align the parts of speech with either the types of things or the different operations of the mind, philosophic systems claimed validation by the very nature of language. Language, by becoming incorporated into philosophy, was no longer an independent means of analysis. Moreover, language itself became confused until it was no longer an effective tool of thought.[2] Tooke first studied language in an attempt to sort out this confusion: 'I long since formed to myself a kind of system, which seemed to me of singular use in ... my younger studies to keep my mind from confusion and the imposition of words' (i. 12-13). Almost thirty years later, he pulled out his 'loose papers in my closet' (i. 74), when his trial of 1777 convinced him of the public significance of his previous research. To a remarkable extent, his encounters with the law pertained to questions of language, when, as

[2] ΕΠΕΑ ΠΤΕΡΟΕΝΤΑ *or the Diversions of Purley*, 1798-1805, EL no. 127, 2 vols., i. 21-4.

Hazlitt expressed it, he examined, 'with jealous watchfulness, the meaning of words to prevent being entrapped by them'.[3] The defence and appeal of his first trial depended on the discrepancy between what words appear to mean and what they actually say, and on the part of speech of the word 'that'.

In 1777 Horne Tooke was arrested for publishing an advertisement for a subscription to raise money for the widows and orphans of the soldiers who had died in the Battle of Lexington. The charge against Tooke was aimed specifically at a statement which claimed that the King's troops had committed murder. Once the jury proclaimed his guilt, Tooke attempted to arrest the judgement with the startling remark, 'your lordship will instantly perceive, by looking at the record that I am not therein charged with any crime'.[4] Horne Tooke argued that the necessary averments (statements of fact) were not a part of the written information on which he was charged. He was not charged with a specific act but simply with accusing the troops of murder, which was in itself not necessarily criminal. 'If any one [situation] can be imagined, in which it would not be criminal to say, the king's troops have committed murder, then your lordships cannot, upon this information, proceed to judgement.' (Stephens, i. 471-2.) As the King's troops had been tried for murder nine years earlier, Tooke's objection was all the more tenable. The information did not include the mention of a specific illegal action, and the trial had been based on an unwarranted assumption of meaning. The court adjourned after the judge, Lord Mansfield, asked the Attorney-General to return the next day with precedents establishing that others had been sentenced for crimes without the averments being specified in the charge. The next day, Lord Mansfield supplied them himself, and, as they were stated by the judge and not the barrister, Tooke did not have the legal right to challenge them. Horne Tooke, with resentful grace, bowed out of the argument. Later, he appealed with a writ of error to the House of Lords; John Dunning was his counsellor.

---

[3] 'The Late Mr. Horne Tooke', The Spirit of the Age or Contemporary Portraits, *Complete Works of William Hazlitt*, 1930-4, 21 vols., xi. 55.
[4] Alexander Stephens, *Memoirs of John Horne Tooke*, 1813, 2 vols., i. 470.

A Letter to J. Dunning (1778) was written from the King's Bench Prison, after the failure of Tooke's appeal. In this pamphlet, Tooke discusses the disagreement between himself and the judge in terms of language theory. His trial is the starting point of his refutation of contemporary notions of language. One of the precedents brought against him was a sentence which was interpreted by the House of Lords as providing an example of a person's being convicted although statements of fact had been omitted: '"She knowing that Crooke had been indicted for forgery, did so and so"'. Horne Tooke argued that the sentence literally read '"Crooke had been indicted for forgery," (there is an averment literally made) — "She, knowing that, did so and so".' The court claimed '"It was not positively averred that Crooke was indicted; it was only laid that she sciens that Crooke had been indicted"'.[5]

The confusion here was facilitated by contemporary language theory which argued that the particles (conjunctions, prepositions, articles, and certain adverbs) had no meaning but represented acts of the mind. 'That' was not one word, but rather various words according to the part of speech it represented, a pronoun, an article, or a conjunction, each part of speech representing a distinct act of the mind: 'Though they have the same sound, it is universally imagined that there is not any the smallest correspondence or similarity of signification' ('Letter', p. 686). From the belief that the particles indicated a mind perceiving and expressing relations, Harris and Monboddo developed a theory that an abundant use of particles indicated a highly developed language and intellect. A language such as English which was deficient in particles, indicated an essentially different type of mind which was incapable of the abstract and rational thought which allegedly constituted a human being's most valuable attribute. The theoretical formulations of Harris and Monboddo established language as a means of class division while, at the same time, these theories perpetuated the obscurity of language. The status of the particles as the

[5] 'A Letter to John Dunning, Esq.', ΕΠΕΑ ΠΤΕΡΟΕΝΤΑ *or the Diversions of Purley to which is annexed his Letter to John Dunning*, ed. Richard Taylor, 1860, p. 685.

distinguishing characteristic of the refined language, depended upon their complete and utter lack of meaning. The debate over the nature of the particles and the parts of speech generally, had vast implications, and 'that' in this context becomes a very important word. According to Tooke, the word 'that' was always one word with one unchanging meaning which had evolved to serve various but basically similar functions in different sentences. Its use as a conjunction was the same as its use as a pronoun and article, in such a sentence as 'I wish you to believe THAT I would not wilfully hurt a fly, I wish you to believe THAT' ('Letter', pp. 686-7). Tooke thus proved that the various parts of speech or types of words did not represent different types of relation or different acts of the mind but rather merely the syntax of a word in a particular sentence.

While being tried for high treason in 1794, Tooke waged his last semantic battle with the court. Overly zealous ministers interpreted the following note he had received as a call to arms: '"Dear Citizen, This morning, at six o'clock, citizen Hardy was taken away, by order from the secretary of state's office: they siezed every thing they could lay hands on. – Query, is it possible to get ready by Thursday?"' (Cited by Stephens, ii. 119.) The question concerned a publication date and not a revolution. Tooke has been described as encouraging his arrest by telling false tales to a man he suspected of being a spy and, in an unsubstantiated charge, of anticipating the government's reaction to the letter.[6] Whatever happened, the government's misreading points to the problem here; that some people could say very little without their words being misconstrued. Such semantic hysteria is not unusual at moments of political conflict, but Tooke believed that it was compounded by mistaken philosophies of language and by the inadequacy of definitions. The *Diversions of Purley* discusses a similar distortion of meaning. Canning's exclamation '"Whenever I hear of the word RIGHTS, I have learned to consider it as preparatory to some desolating doctrine. It seems to me, to be productive

---

[6] *Dictionary of National Biography;* Minnie Yarborough, *John Horne Tooke,* New York, 1926, p. 157. Yarborough claims that Tooke actually posted the letter to himself.

of some wide spreading ruin, of some wasting desolation."'
(ii. 2.) Tooke argues that the word 'rights' evolved from the
past participle of a Latin verb, *regere*, meaning 'ordered'
or 'directed', and that all the modern meanings of the
word initially evolved from this original definition. Thus,
'nothing can more evidently shew the natural disposition of
mankind to rational obedience, than their invariable use of
this word RIGHT, and their perpetual application of it to all
which they desire, and to every thing which they deem
excellent.' (ii. 3.) The political bias of Tooke's etymology is
evident enough, but it needs to be recognized as a reply to
such specific events as Canning's extravagant and threatening
rhetoric and to the more fundamental problem of what
Tooke calls the 'imposture' which ambiguous terms allow.
His intention of granting words a more discernible meaning
amid such intense verbal confusion was intended to be a
political act.

From the 1790s to the present, however, the political
content of the *Diversions* has rarely been taken seriously.
Recent American studies have ignored Tooke's claim that
his theory has political significance and have criticized the
Diversions severely. Hans Aarsleff (whose book is seminal),
Stephen K. Land, and Jonathan Culler concur in their
evaluation of Tooke as a theorist who interfered with the
development of English language theory. Patrice Bergheaud
evaluates Tooke's work more highly from the same perspective as most of Tooke's recent commentators.[7] Here, Tooke
will be studied according to the claims that he makes in the
Diversions — that he had political reasons for wanting to
disprove previous theories, and that language, as it was
generally understood, was a source of distortion which
interfered with political life. Tooke's theory was an
exceptionally retaliatory one, which was aimed at previous
theories and at ideas about language both philosophically and

---

[7] Hans Aarsleff, *The Study of Language in England 1780-1860*, Princeton,
1967; Stephen K. Land, *From Signs to Propositions: the Concept of Form in
Eighteenth-Century Semantic Theory*, Longman Linguistic Library, 1974;
Jonathan Culler, *Ferdinand de Saussure*, Modern Masters series, New York,
1976; Patrice Bergheaud, "De James Harris a John Horne Tooke; Mutations de
l'analyse du langage en Angleterre dans la deuxième moitié du XVIIIe siècle,
Historiographia Linguistica, vi (1979), 15-45.

as they impinged upon social life. Without concentrating upon both these targets of Tooke's argument, his ideas are not situated as he intended them to be. The *Diversions* loses fullness and range, when its political component is not taken into account.

Commenting upon the charge made since his own day, that his political comments were inappropriate and bitter, Tooke replies, 'my politics will never be changed, nor kept back on any occasion: and whilst I have my life, it will neither be embittered by any regret for the past, nor fear for the future' (footnote, i. 230). Tooke's political commitment was deep and his admittedly bitter remarks vary from attacks upon political adversaries to protests against the withdrawal of civil liberties such as the suspension of habeas corpus. Tooke makes some sharp comments, especially by eighteenth-century standards, but perhaps he can be granted legitimate cause: he had been tried for sedition in 1777 for a statement published in 1775; he had been refused admission to the bar in 1779, 1782, and 1794 despite his obvious skills as a lawyer; in 1794 he was imprisoned for seven months without being charged; he was indicted for high treason with little justification, and in 1801 he was denied a seat in Parliament because of a ruling passed after his election. At a time when very few people were protesting, Tooke's continuous protest against the withdrawal of civil liberties might be considered as admirable. His most bitter comments appear in the second volume of 1805. Many of them were prompted by the trial and death of Gilbert Wakefield, a good friend of Tooke and a fellow scholar who had died from general ill health after serving a two-year sentence for sedition. In such a life, personal bitterness and warranted political criticism are not always distinct. The *Diversions* contains several kinds of political comments: some personal, some critical of recent legislation, and others concerned with the nature of language.

Certain problems present difficulties in interpreting Tooke's work. To start with, he wrote the *Diversions* over an unusually long time, approximately thirty years. His first published comments on language appeared in the short pamphlet of 1778, *A Letter to J. Dunning*. The letter was later incorporated into the first volume of the *Diversions of*

Purley published in 1786. A second edition appeared in 1798, which is now the most frequently studied edition, and a second volume in 1805. Between 1798 and several years after 1805, Tooke's work was especially prominent, frequently debated, and either extravagantly praised or damned. A third volume was written but not published. Tooke burned the manuscript and the rest of his papers before he died in 1812. In that volume, Tooke intended to explain his own ideas more fully, while the former volumes were designed to refute 'the false philosophy received concerning language and the human understanding' (i. 148). Such chronological sprawl without definite end raises difficulties in discussing 'the work' as if it were a single and compact entity. In some respects the volumes differ from each other, as one might expect of ideas formulated over a period of thirty years. Moreover, by concentrating on disproving others' theories, Tooke fails to produce a coherent theory of his own. The discrepancies and omissions are not brought under control in a definitive statement of his own theory of language.

Tooke was apparently uninterested in straightforward exposition for he chose to write his book in the form of a dialogue between various characters. In the first volume, the characters are H, T, and B: John Horne Tooke, who later changed his name from John Horne at the request of his friend; William Tooke, his friend and owner of the estate of Purley; and Dr Beadon, then master of Jesus College, Cambridge. The second volume is dedicated to his jury during the trial of 1794, and the dialogue is between H and F, John Horne Tooke and Sir Francis Burdett, a protégé of Tooke and a famous radical member of Parliament who will be mentioned again. The content of the characters' fictive conversations varies between concise dialogues and long lists of etymologies, neither of which fully elaborate on Tooke's basic ideas. The dialogue form enables Tooke to evade prosaic explanations and to answer any objections that his companions might raise. He can make surprising and grand statements, as he clearly enjoys doing, and turn etymology, as much as it ever could be, into repartee. We might enjoy the pleasure Tooke takes in being a slippery opponent, but the approach does not encourage the fuller explanations that are sometimes needed. Because Tooke burned all his papers, other records such as letters and note-books cannot help to clarify his ideas. Even the minor fact that he changed his name interferes with study of his work. Some time passes before one realizes that he might appear in indexes and catalogues as 'Horne', 'Tooke', or 'Horne Tooke'.

Without these difficulties, the *Diversions* would defy ready categorization. The work can be discussed in ways that traverse the century and as simultaneously old-fashioned, contemporary, and advanced. Tooke's preoccupation with Locke seems misplaced by the end of the century, although Priestley also revived Locke's centrality. He can be described as a 1770s primitivist of an extreme kind, or as a 1790s radical who more sharply than anyone theoretically defended the capability of the general population. He can be considered as a theorist who formed a point of transition from eighteenth-century theories of language to major, philosophical statements of the nineteenth, such as the Preface to *Lyrical Ballads* and the *Analysis of Phenomena of the Human Mind*. As did other radical thinkers, Tooke found political and intellectual resources from the early part of the century to formulate a challenging and forward-looking argument.

Despite this apparent waywardness, Tooke held clearly to his original intention of refuting theories which he under-stood to be intellectually and politically misguided. He undertook to write *A Letter*, as he explains in the first volume, because his trial made clear to him that the mean-ings of words were important 'to the rights and happiness of mankind in their dearest concerns — the decisions of Courts of Justice' (i. 79). Tooke's political intention went deeper however. As we shall see, he hoped that by clarifying signification with etymology, he would discredit what he called 'metaphysics', which he claimed was 'founded on the grossest ignorance of words and the nature of speech' (i. 399). Tooke's argument against metaphysics is not only one against a particular philosophic tradition but also against its political manifestations. His refutation of conservative philosophers discredits the distinction between vulgar and refined English, challenges the ambiguity and status of complex terms, and counters theories of language that withdrew attention from temporal and human concerns.

The fundamental premise of Tooke's *Diversions* is that the parts of speech represent neither types of things nor acts of the mind. Only two parts of speech can be said to be ultimately distinct and to be necessary for the act of communication: the noun and the verb. All other parts of speech evolve from these two. Nouns are the only parts of speech which represent an act of mind, that of receiving impressions.

> The business of the mind, as far as it concerns Language, appears to me to be very simple. It extends no farther than to receive Impressions, that is, to have Sensations or Feelings. What are called its operations, are merely the operations of Language. A consideration of *Ideas*, or of the *Mind*, or of *Things* (relative to the Parts of Speech) will lead us no farther than to *Nouns*: i.e. the signs of those impressions, or names of ideas. (i. 51)

Most words 'are the signs of other words' which have evolved from nouns and verbs which alter their appearance as they occupy new syntactical functions. Adjectives, adverbs, prepositions, conjunctions, and participles evolved because the dynamic of language developed new forms which made, and will continue to make, language more capable of concise expression. All parts of speech except nouns and verbs are called 'abbreviations', signs of nouns or verbs that indicate their new function by their altered forms and syntax. Technically speaking, these words are corrupt in that they are words worn down and altered by frequent use, the remnants and ruins of other words. Tooke's calling the abbreviated forms corruptions does not imply, however, that he yearned for a pure language. Far from it. Tooke praises the abbreviations highly for making as much difference to language as the wheel did to transportation; he calls them 'the *wheels* of language, the *wings* of Mercury' (i. 25).

Tooke wanted not only to contribute ideas to the study of language, but to alter the way that language was understood. He argues that language had been studied in relation to other disciplines but not in relation to its own history and capabilities. Language, according to Tooke, continually evolves because the people speaking and writing it incessantly attempt to have it 'keep pace in some measure with their minds' (i. 29). The means which language has of increasing the speed of meaning, that of abbreviation, affect every aspect of language, although Tooke will only investigate one, the division of vocabulary into 'sorts of words'. If all aspects of language were studied with the same method, then it would be studied according to the principles of anatomy, as a self-contained subject whose composition and characteristics could explain itself (i. 14). Because language had been studied in conjunction with the study of the mind and of ideas, philosophy and language itself had become confused. The *Diversions* would consider language without the burden of other concerns. The history of language would explain its properties. The meaning of individual words and the dynamic of language, its ability to create new forms, would then be clarified.

Tooke, with great frequency, presents his own ideas in relation to those of other grammarians, especially James Harris and Lord Monboddo, the 'metaphysical' philosophers whom he most wants to discredit. Language, according to Tooke, is not the manifestation of the quality of the soul or of civilization, but merely an evolutionary development in which most words evolve from previously existing nouns and verbs. Prepositions and conjunctions – the particles – are not words without meaning that indicate the mind's ability to perceive relations that have no reference to the material world. Tooke fully explains Harris's interpretation of prepositions and conjunctions in order to explain the confused and unsatisfactory explanations of former theorists. Harris believed that conjunctions expressed various relations of union and diversity and that prepositions expressed various relations of place. Neither had any meaning whatsoever. In a passage which Tooke discusses (and cites) at length, Harris defines a preposition as a *'Part of Speech, devoid itself of Signification; but so formed as to unite two Words that are significant, and refuse to coalesce or unite of themselves'* (i. 290). Because prepositions have no meaning, one preposition can represent different relations, even contradictory ones. A preposition could transfuse meaning even though it had none, and different meanings in different sentences. The use of the word 'from' exemplified for Harris how one preposition could represent contradictory relations.

'FROM, he says, denotes the detached relation of Body; as when we say — *These Figs came* FROM *Turkey*. — So as to *Motion* and *Rest*, only with this difference, that *here* the preposition *varies its character with the Verb*. Thus if we say — *That lamp hangs* FROM *the ceiling* — the preposition FROM assumes a character of *quiescence*. But if we say — *That lamp is falling* FROM *the ceiling*, the preposition in such case assumes a character of *Motion* . . .' (cited by Tooke, i. 341)

Tooke refers to the habit of defining prepositions and conjunctions by listing various categories as an example of detrimental scholasticism — a means of perpetuating mystery which disguises ignorance by making fine but useless distinctions (i. 111). He also criticizes Johnson's *Dictionary* on these grounds, for it does not explain the word 'from' according to its meaning but solely according to twenty different categories of relation, which Tooke also cites: 'Privation, Reception, Descent or Birth, Transmission, Abstraction, Succession, Emission, Progress from premises to inference, Place or Person from whom a message is brought, Extraction, Reason or Motive, Ground or Cause, Distance, Separation or Recession, Exemption or Deliverance, Absence, Derivation, Distance from the past, Contrary to, Removal' (i. 345-6, paraphrased). Tooke believed that listing categories was an inadequate means of defining the particles and that etymology could more adequately serve the purpose.

According to Tooke, 'from' has one essential meaning which derives from its initial form as an Anglo-Saxon and Gothic noun meaning '*Beginning, Origin, Source, fountain, author*' (i. 342). The preposition is the sign of another word which was once a noun but which develops a new 'manner of signification'. Harris and Johnson had confused the alleged various relations of the word with the meaning of the verb which accompanied it: 'The "*characters of quiescence and of motion*," attributed by Mr Harris to the word FROM, belong indeed to the words *Hang* and *Fall*, used in the different sentences. And by the same manner of trans-

ferring to the *preposition* the meaning of some other word in
the sentence, have all Johnson's and Greenwood's supposed
different meanings arisen.' (i. 347.) An evolutionary and
strictly linguistic progression had been mistaken for evidence
of universal relations and the mental acts of perceiving them.
All of the particles, according to Tooke, originate in
definable words which represent ordinary objects (i. 318).
The particles appear to be meaningless because their transformation from one grammatical function to another alters
their appearance. Prepositions, as well as other particles,
are not the sign of '*a pure idea of intellect*, which *never can
be apprehended by sense*', as Monboddo had claimed and
whom Tooke quotes (i. 397–8). Their existence does not
demonstrate that the mind is capable of acting without
reference to the material world because all vocabulary, even
the most apparently meaningless words, derives from common objects. Instead of particles representing acts of mind at
which the Greeks had particular skill, they are the invention
of 'artless men' who applied the same terms 'as they
employed upon other occasions to mention the same *real
objects*. For *Prepositions* also are the names of *real objects*'
(i. 318). If particles are still to be considered 'the glory of the
grammatical art', then Anglo-Saxon and common perception
deserve some credit for being the basis of those parts of
speech which are allegedly the signs of an act of pure
intellect.

   Thus, what had previously been accounted for as act of
the mind or universal ideas, Tooke accounts for by the
impulse of language to evolve new forms for the sake of
brevity and cohesiveness. Adjectives do not represent the
mind's ability to distinguish a quality from its substance nor
do they represent the natural concord between qualities and
substances, as Monboddo and Harris had argued. The
difference between the parts of speech is merely an evolutionary and syntactical one. That an adjective must be
joined to a noun does not demonstrate that an adjective
represents a particular act of mind, type of idea, or thing.
It merely represents an evolved form of a noun constructed
so as to indicate its special function: it is 'the *name of a thing*
which is directed to be joined to some other *name of a*

thing' (ii. 431). Its construction and its place in the sentence distinguish it from other parts of speech and manifest its 'manner of signification'.

Aspects of language which are complex such as terminations of the verb and which appear to have been deliberately created are products of language's evolution. 'However *artificial* they may now appear to us, they were not originally the effect of premeditated and deliberate *art*, but separate words by length of time corrupted and coalescing with words of which they are now considered as the *Terminations,'* (i. 352.) Such a statement refutes Monboddo's and de Brosses's concept of the 'artificial language', a language that was consciously invented by philosophers and artists seeking to express abstract ideas and relations. 'Language, it is true, is an Art, and a glorious one. . . . But an art springing from necessity, and originally invented by artless men; who did not sit down like philosophers to invent *"de petits mots pour etre mis avant les noms".'* (i. 317.)

At this point, Horne Tooke's work has vast repercussions. His etymologies ignore many of the fundamental points of conservative theorists: the distinction between refined and vulgar language, the alleged limitations of primitive language, and the vernacular's lack of intellectual potential. Horne Tooke's tracing of all parts of speech to nouns and verbs disregards the prevalent assumption that two distinct vocabularies exist for the learned and the vulgar, one which was pure and the other corrupt or barbaric. His method does away with the concept of a refined language by demonstrating that all words originate in the material, transitory world. Because particles, like all other terms, are the abbreviated forms of words with clear meanings, they no longer demonstrate the existence of a pure act of mind, and therefore can not be said to distinguish a refined quality of mind or level of civilization from that of the vulgar. In effect, Tooke invalidated the eighteenth-century dichotomies of civilization and barbarism, abstract and experiential modes of thought, and learning and vulgarity. Tooke's work begins and ends on remarkable assumptions: that language is unified, that it pertains only to human interchange, and that it alters, not according to the quality of civilization or the speaker's soul, but because it forms abbreviations of vocabulary and syntax according to its own laws and in the process of time.

Primitive, vulgar, and unlearned languages are equal to more cultivated ones. Primitive languages were frequently described as having a small number of terms because primitives had few ideas. Certain mental operations, the perception of relation and abstract thinking, could not be performed by savages. According to Tooke, uncultivated languages can express ideas and relations as well as cultivated ones can. The only characteristic difference between barbaric and civilized language lies in the number of abbreviated terms. Primitive languages cannot express ideas with the same degree of 'dispatch' as cultivated languages, but they can express the same ideas:

> Savage languages are upon an equal footing with the languages (as they are called) of *art*, except that the former are less corrupted: and that savages have not only as *separate and distinct ideas* of those relations as we have, but that they have this advantage over us (an advantage of intelligibility, though it is a disadvantage in point of brevity) that they also *express* them separately and distinctly. (i. 399)

The speakers of primitive languages employ fewer abbreviated terms, but they perform the same mental operations as the speakers of civilized languages.

Such an understanding of language forms the background of Tooke's re-evaluation of Anglo-Saxon and 'mere native English'. He insists that early authors and Anglo-Saxon are the proper foundations for understanding English: English is a continuation of Anglo-Saxon 'with a little variation of the written character' (i. 503). Thus, Tooke includes the Anglo-Saxon and Gothic alphabets in the first volume because they were not readily available elsewhere and were rarely studied. English had become confused, according to Tooke, because of the priority granted to the study of Latin and Greek. Harris's and Lowth's writings had had the effect of altering the language by prohibiting certain English expressions which did not accord with the classical languages (i. 325, ii. 475). Tooke claims to be less concerned with these alterations than with the 'false philosophy' which motivated them and the accompanying disregard of early English writings and of 'common speech' (i. 325–7). Appropriately, Tooke bases his analysis of the evolution of the parts of speech on unusual writers and works: Chaucer, Douglas, Gower, Boethius, *Astrolabye,* Sir T. Eliot, Chillingworth, Percy's *Reliques*, statements by Queen Elizabeth, sixteenth-century records of the Privy Council, a thirteenth-century translation of the Bible, *Piers Plowman*, and the *Fabian Chronicles* make an exceptional appearance in an eighteenth-century study of universal grammar. Tooke's reference to words as they appear in 'common speech' or 'common vulgar pronunciation' or in particular dialects elevates the status of spoken English (i. 326, ii. 453, i. 460). By employing early English and the spoken language as evidence for his argument, Tooke presupposes that the language merits the scientific attention that had previously been granted to the classical languages and that language as it is spoken is not a less genuine form of the language than written English.

Instead of there being distinct languages for the vulgar and the refined, Tooke discusses language as a single entity and implicitly criticizes the concept of vulgarity. Tooke claims to have been unable to discover any word that substantiated Johnson's notion of 'cant', which he paraphrases as words 'belonging only to the vulgar; and which have therefore no certain origin nor precise meaning' (i. 526). As Johnson had described a 'great measure' of lower and middle-class diction as of this type, Tooke's remark was a major reinterpretation of the characteristics of vulgar speech. Tooke protests against words being cautiously 'shunned and ridiculed' in common conversation, as 'a vulgarity' (i. 474) or castigated as appropriate only in '"low language"' (i. 516, quoting Johnson). Other commentators considered native English to be inadequate because of the composite nature of its vocabulary. James Buchanan, for instance, had maintained that English derived from all the European languages and that 'the far greatest as well as the most excellent part of it is chiefly derived from Latin and Greek'.[8] Lord Monboddo described English as exceptionally corrupt because its vocabulary did not have a single point of origin. Its terms derived from Gothic, Teutonic, the modern European

[8] *Linguae Britannicea Vera Pronunciatio*, 1757, EL no. 39, unpaginated Preface.

languages, and Ancient Greek and Latin: 'we have the roots of our language scattered through different languages' (ii. 185). According to Tooke, Anglo-Saxon is one foundation of English which has improved by adapting terms from other languages. Instead of being a sign of its degeneration, the adaptation of terms indicates the culture's extensive contact with other countries (i. 147).

Like all primitive languages, Anglo-Saxon does not suffer from an inadequate supply of abstract terms. Such terms

compose the bulk of every language. In English those which are borrowed from the Latin, French, and Italian, are easily recognized; because those languages are sufficiently familiar to us, and not so familiar as our own: those from the Greek are more striking; because more unusual: but those which are original in our own language have been almost wholly overlooked, and are quite unexpected. (ii. 17–18)

The quantity of abstract words derived from Anglo-Saxon demonstrates that the language is not as limited as had been supposed, and that the classical languages are not uniquely adapted to express abstract thought. Responding to a pamphlet written after the publication of the first edition of the first volume, Tooke replies, 'It is not true that any people are now, or ever were in the condition he represents the Anglo-Saxons; viz. of having "hardly a conveyance for one idea in a thousand"' (i. 160-1). Abstract terms do not indicate the existence of an act of mind which speakers of primitive languages are incapable of performing but are a syntactical development of every language. They are nouns merely because of their syntactical function in a sentence and because the evolution of language has formed them into nouns. They are derived from participles and adjectives used without accompanying nouns and are 'therefore, in *construction*, considered as Substantives' (ii. 17). 'Truth', then, is not an archetypical idea (as Harris would have maintained) but a derivative of an Anglo-Saxon verb meaning 'To think, to believe firmly, to be thoroughly persuaded of, *To Trow*' (ii. 402). By listing interminable etymologies, mostly derived from Anglo-Saxon, Tooke intends, not only to argue that the speakers of supposedly primitive languages are capable of abstract thought, but to prove that abstraction is not an act of mind: 'But, I trust, these are sufficient to discard that imagined *operation of the mind*, which has been termed *Abstraction*: and to prove, that what we call by that name, is merely one of the contrivances of language, for the purpose of more speedy communication.' (ii. 396.) As with the discussion of the particles, Tooke's consideration of abstraction refutes its status as the special achievement of civilized or refined languages. Tooke, once again, disproves the evidence which distinguished a rational language from one incapable of rationality.

In the last two chapters of the second volume, Tooke discusses the limitations of English and Anglo-Saxon by examining the two types of words which he believed were inadequately represented, the participle and the adjective. At this point, Tooke's assessment of the capacities of English becomes more complex. Several statements continue to advocate the capacities of ordinary English, while others undercut this predominant tendency of the *Diversions*. Tooke argues that the major benefit we derive from foreign languages is not an increased number of complex terms but new types of words which bring to the language a new 'manner of *signification*' (ii. 512). Types of words were borrowed directly from the Greek and Latin in order to form a new type of abbreviation. Words such as those ending in 'ible', 'able', 'il', and 'ile' derived from the Latin potential passive participle. These abbreviations and others entered the language when translators could discover no type of word in English which would match the original. Although these types of words were originally foreign or classical, 'the frequent repetition of these words has at length naturalized them in our language' (ii. 479). Even 'the most illiterate of our countrymen' understand suffixes which derive from the Latin (ii. 491). Works written by 'our ancient writers' contain the same abbreviations as modern English. By discussing such early authors as Chaucer and fourteenth-century translators of the Bible, Tooke indicates how thoroughly and for how long English had benefited by the importing of types of words from the classical languages. Yet again, the alleged distinction between primitive and civilized language has become less clear.

The Bible occupies a unique and somewhat awkward place in language theories because its language was clearly not refined, although it was sacred. The book was valued and disparaged by the same theorists. Monboddo, for instance, describes the Bible's language as the most perfect English — 'the standard of our language as well as of our faith' (i. 479-80). He maintains, however, that writers should imitate classical authors whose language does not suffer from the weaknesses of English. If a writer does not know the classical languages, he should imitate writers who wrote a classically-based English (iii. 402). Monboddo's criticisms of modern English also describe biblical language: the sentences are short, the diction concrete, the words often monosyllabic, and the particles are strikingly absent (ii. 422). Bishop Lowth, as mentioned, argued that the language of the Bible is inappropriate to express the advanced reasoning of contemporary life. Tooke, however, points to the intellectual adequacy of biblical language as he discusses the new capacities brought to the language by the process of the Bible's translation. Tooke highly praises its translators, as well as those of other early works, for altering the language in a manner which enabled people to think more precisely: 'A short, close, and compact method of speech, answers the purpose of a map upon a reduced scale: it assists greatly the comprehension of our understanding: and, in general reasoning, frequently enables us, at once glance, to take in very numerous and distant important relations and conclusions, which would otherwise totally escape us.' (ii. 513-14.) Types of words which have existed in the language for centuries and which are extensively distributed by the Bible's publication facilitate rational thought. As Tooke's own language demonstrates, short and ordinary words, concrete terms, and metaphor are compatible with an intellectual language.

It is difficult to discern precisely how much of the population Tooke intended to credit with a competent language. By concentrating on various passages of the *Diversions*, one could justify various arguments about the minds of the vulgar population. His discussion of the particles, by disproving the existence of an act of mind which characterized civilized speakers, could be applied to defend the minds of even the non-literate. Similarly Tooke's analysis of abstract terms defines abstraction as a linguistic operation performed by speakers of allegedly primitive and vulgar languages. His discussion of the Bible's language, however, could be applied to defend those who could benefit from reading it. The difference is analogous to that between the language of 'rustics' advocated in the Preface to *Lyrical Ballads* and that of the man of 'common sense' in Coleridge's *Biographia* whose language was informed by an extensive knowledge of the Bible. There, Coleridge makes the difference between the two as great as they could possibly be to argue against the Preface.[9] Neither type, however, was acknowledged as having an adequate language by conventional late eighteenth-century theories, and the language of either figure would have been dismissed on the basis of what it revealed about the speaker's mind. Nowhere in the *Diversions* does Tooke maintain that language demonstrates the value of the mind or that it reveals intellectual capabilities that are not available to all speakers. At the end of the second volume, published in 1805, he none the less withdraws slightly from the radicalism of the rest of the book by discussing English as a deficient language. Whereas he had described language as in a constant state of improvement, he describes the languages of Europe as in a 'corrupt and deficient state' (ii. 513). In contrast to another comment in the same chapter that the abbreviations had been 'naturalized', Tooke now states that an 'unlearned native can never understand the meaning of one quarter of that which is called his native tongue' (ii. 452). Despite this tendency to become more critical of vernacular English, Tooke maintains his former position that allegedly primitive language could express abstract ideas and intellectual relations and that the deficiencies of language are merely linguistic ones (ii. 512).

One might regret Tooke's failure to examine the capacities of vernacular English fully and directly. If he had discussed the notion of vulgarity as its own topic, he would have exerted more control over the impact of his book and

---

[9] Ed. J. Shawcross, Oxford, 1907, 2 vols., ii. 38-9.

clarified both political and linguistic debates by making the
relation of language to class more generally known. Commentators would then not have been puzzled by, and finally
dismissive of, the political component of his work. It appears
that Tooke was uncertain and possibly disillusioned about
the potential of the lower classes. He bases the dialogue
which composes the *Diversions* on H's defence of the
capacities of a 'plain man of sense without what is commonly
called Learning' (pp. 3-4) but also states that he no longer
has the faith in the 'understanding of the generality' that he
once had (i. 13). Although Tooke disproves ideas which
demonstrated the incapacities of the vulgar, he does not
present another coherent assessment of the mentality of the
lower classes. One is left with separate pieces of evidence that
do not always fit together. The disproof in itself, however,
achieves a great deal. By disrupting the ideological construct
of language's relation to the mind and 'civilization', Tooke
refuted the major philosophical justification of class division
in the last half of the century, and the myriad ideas which
depended on it. Tooke's new theory of language, as we shall
see, challenged people not only to write new considerations
of language but also new grammar books, new theories of the
mind, and a new theory of poetry. By refuting concepts that
claimed to define both society and the individual, Tooke's
work had a grand scope of its own.

Tooke had yet other ambitions for his book. He intended
not only to dispute the grammarians' assessment of vulgarity
but also what he called their 'system' or their 'metaphysics'.
Tooke's ultimate protest against the theories of Harris and
Monboddo was for their espousal of a particular type of
consciousness. What he wanted especially to refute was the
very type of thinking which he believed to be encouraged by
the 'false philosophy'. The conservative identification of the
parts of speech had implications which even its proponents
were not fully aware of:

But his lordship [Monboddo] and his fautors will do well to contend
stoutly and obstinately for their doctrine of language, for they are
menaced with a greater danger than *they* will at first apprehend:
for if they give up their doctrine of language, they will not be able to
make even a battle for their Metaphysics; the very term *Metaphysic*

being nonsense; and all the systems of it, and controversies concerning it, that are or have been in the world, being founded on the grossest ignorance of words and of the nature of speech. (i. 398-9)

James Mackintosh, considering the above passage, claims that Tooke objected to the term because it literally meant 'what is above or beyond nature';[10] and this literal meaning includes the full range of ideas that Tooke was opposing.

Previous theories had castigated an interest in the present, the particular, and the worldly in order to advocate a language which was allegedly 'pure' of time and matter. According to James Harris, language was designed to represent 'COMPREHENSIVE and PERMANENT IDEAS, THE GENUINE PERCEPTIONS OF PURE MIND, that WORDS of all Languages, however different, are the SYMBOLS' (p. 372). Such a definition places attention on an isolated and disembodied mind's relation to abstract ideas. In contrast, Tooke's discussion of language concentrates attention on human life and public exchanges. The value of words depends on their temporal evolution to facilitate a necessarily and strictly human exchange. While Tooke discusses the definition of 'truth', he reveals the shift in consciousness which he wanted the *Diversions* to encourage. 'TRUTH supposes mankind: *for whom* and *by whom* alone the word is formed, and *to whom* only it is applicable; if no man, no TRUTH. There is therefore no such thing as eternal, immutable, everlasting TRUTH.' (ii. 404.) Words are formed by the process of their being spoken; they are neither atemporal, nor mysterious, nor the representations of ideas which are superior to human life.

A specific example, the noun 'law', might serve to explain how politics, language, and philosophy could become entangled, and how Tooke tries to disengage them. Harris had argued that nouns were a genus with three different species; natural objects, artificial objects, and abstractions. The three were considered to represent different types of things, and their division to imitate the logic of the universe, 'the nature and division of things' (Harris, p. 40). Harris did

[10] *Memoirs of the Life of the Right Honourable Sir James Mackintosh,* ed. Robert James Mackintosh, 1835, 2 vols., ii. 231.

not consider the problem of one noun being used both abstractly and concretely: species by definition were supposed to be distinct. Also, the species existed in a hierarchical order. Any words pertaining to a specific time or place were of less value than those which represented universal ideas, which language was designed to describe. 'Law' then was not worth considering in the particular, and if it were considered abstractly, it already had a limited nature; that is, it was not man-made, it was a universal idea, and it was significant precisely because it was a philosophical idea and not a political actuality. Abstract words were thus immediately self-validating. Certain questions would not need asking because an abstraction was, from the start, valuable, mysterious, almost magical. Monboddo similarly believed that the object of the 'arbitrary' language was to express ideas which were entirely disconnected from time, place, and matter. In contrast, Tooke derives 'law' from the past participle of an Anglo-Saxon verb meaning '*Laid down*' or '*Ordered*' (ii. 8). Far from being a 'PERMANENT and ALL COMPREHENSIBLE IDEA', law is a human activity susceptible to discussion and change. Tooke's derivation of such words from verbs implies that abstract words are general terms which describe a plurality of single actions once performed at particular times and places. By depriving them of the authority which previous grammarians had granted them, Tooke intends to make abstract terms more distinctly defined, and what they represent more open to question. If 'law' is a verb, then actions can alter it.

The dynamic of the argument, where a radical political perspective merges with an emphasis on history and human experience to argue against what is portrayed as idealism, vague vocabulary, and conservative theories of government, is familiar from the arguments of John Locke. In *A Letter to J. Dunning*, Tooke states his belief that conservative theories of language were based on the urge to refute Locke, and that he considers himself and Locke as allies sharing a common enemy. If his reader

should think that I have treated them [Monboddo and Harris] with too much asperity, to him I owe some justification. Let him recollect, then, the manner in which these gentlemen and the *Common Sense Doctors* [Beattie and Reid] have treated the *'vulgar, unlearned* and *atheistical'* Mr Locke (for such are the imputations they cast upon that benefactor to his country); and let him condemn me if he can. ('Letter', p. 723)

The second chapter of the *Diversions* is entitled 'On Locke's Essay'. There, and with a fell swoop, Tooke appropriates the *Essay* by stating that Locke's analysis of ideas makes more sense if it is applied to terms. Locke's study of 'composition, abstraction, generalization, relations etc. of Ideas, does indeed merely concern *Language*' (i. 39); that is, various types of words, and not the mind, compose, abstract, generalize, and relate. With his history of language, Tooke demonstrates that language performs intellectual operations that had been mistaken, even by Locke, for operations of the mind. According to him, complex ideas (moral, intellectual, and general terms) are essentially different from simple ideas because the mind actively forms them, transcending the passivity of experiencing sensations. According to Tooke, complex terms are the products of the evolution of language devising a new type of term: they do not prove the existence of certain acts of the mind nor the existence of certain types of ideas. If Locke had understood the relation of terms to the mind

he would not have talked of the *composition of ideas;* but would have seen that it was merely a contrivance of Language: and that the only composition was in the *terms*; and consequently that it was as improper to speak of a *complex idea*, as it would be to call a constellation a complex star: And that they are not ideas, but merely *terms*, which are *general* and *abstract*. (i. 36-7)

(The French philosopher Condillac similarly appropriates Locke's *Essay* by redefining it as a theory of language.[11]) Apparently on the verge of proving the existence of another theory of the mind, Tooke states that Locke's theory of ideas could be disproved by 'Locke's own principles and a physical consideration of the Senses and the Mind' (i. 38-9).

Other comments suggest that Tooke is primarily concerned with providing a theory of language that could explain the

[11] *An Essay on the Origin of Human Knowledge, being a Supplement to Mr. Locke's Essay on the Human Understanding,* trans. Mr Nugent, 1756, p. 10.

mind, especially his discussion of the verb and the etymology of 'thinking'. Although Tooke does not fully define the verb, he describes it as a noun with *'something more'* (ii. 514). All words are therefore ultimately nouns and ultimately represent the act of receiving impressions. Tooke's definition of the word 'thinking' confirms this interpretation of the mind, if it can be called that. Tooke derives 'think' from 'thing', an etymology which seems slightly less bizarre when one knows that 'thing' is now derived from the Old-English term meaning 'discussion' (Culler, p. 30): *'Res* a thing, give us *Reor*, i.e. I am *Thing-ed*. . . . Remember, where we now say, *I Think*, the ancient expression was — *Me thinketh*, i.e. *Me Thingeth, It Thingeth me'* (ii. 405–6). Such a derivation describes apparently active mental processes as passive and thinking as the act of receiving the impressions from concrete objects. Despite these strong indications that the *Diversion* would elaborate a theory of the mind, Tooke stops himself from doing so. After stating that Locke's theory of the composition of ideas could be disproved by a theory of the mind, Tooke twists the argument yet another turn by claiming that he will not perform the proof, because it would be a digression: 'it is not necessary to the foundation for what I have undertaken' (i. 38).

Such an argument, followed by such a dismissal, makes sense if we consider Tooke as subordinating his interest in language's relation to the mind to his interest in language as a public form of expression which could be abused. The concentration of former theories on the expression of the soul or the quality of the individual or of civilization is entirely absent. Tooke refers to a theory of the mind and expected his theory of language to accord with it, but he none the less asserts strongly that language should be studied without including other concerns and that his primary concern is with language as a public form. Rather than discuss the composition of ideas in relation to an isolated mind in a temporal vacuum, Tooke discusses language with reference to public institutions. Tooke's trial led him to publish his ideas about language because it 'afforded a very striking instance of the importance of the meaning of words; not only (as has been too lightly supposed) to Metaphysicians and Schoolmen, but to the rights and happiness of mankind in their dearest concerns – the decisions of Courts of Justice' (i. 79). The political necessity for greater clarity is one aspect of his attack on conservative theories. While alluding to Locke's *Essay*, Tooke expresses both of his political intentions concerning his study of etymology: he expects it to

Lead us to the clear understanding of the words we use in discourse. For, as far as we 'know not our own meaning;' as far as 'our purposes are not endowed with words to make them known;' so far we 'gabble like things most brutish.' But the importance rises higher, when we reflect upon the application of words to Metaphysics. And when I say Metaphysics; you will be pleased to remember, that all general reasoning, all Politics, Law, Morality, and Divinity, are merely Metaphysic. (ii. 121)

Tooke thus vehemently protests against the presence of the concept of universal ideas in disciplines and institutions which had a crucial social presence. Furthermore, he criticizes ideas about language for their contribution to forms of public behaviour, to a 'metaphysical jargon and false morality, which can only be dissipated by etymology' (ii. 18). Tooke opposes ideas about language which he believed infused English society at intellectual, institutional, and personal levels.

Others, as well as Tooke believed that current ideas about language emphasized metaphysical, abstract, or general ideas to a degree which falsified perception and increased the distance between social classes. Thomas Paine, James Gilchrist, Samuel Coleridge, William Wordsworth, and William Blake made similar observations. Thomas Paine's style depends heavily on deflating the mystery of abstractions which served to protect the state. James Gilchrist, author of a *Philosophic Etymology* (1816) believed that the vagueness and authority of abstract terms created a perplexity that he likens to slavery (p. 15). And Coleridge, writing about the Napoleonic War argued that the abstract and technical terms disguised the complexity of experience and that their ability to do so enabled the body politic to justify its actions:

The poor wretch, who has learnt his only prayers
From curses, who knows scarcely words enough
To ask a blessing from his Heavenly Father,
Becomes a fluent phraseman, absolute
And technical in victories and defeats,
And all our dainty terms for fratricide;
Terms which we trundle smoothly o'er our tongues
Like mere abstractions, empty sounds to which
We join no feeling and attach no form!
As if the soldier died without a wound;
As if the fibres of this godlike frame
Were gored without a pang; As if the wretch,
Who fell in battle, doing bloody deeds,
Passed off to Heaven translated and not killed;
As though he had no wife to pine for him,
No God to judge him! Therefore, evil days
Are coming on us, O my countrymen!
And what if all-avenging Providence,
Strong and retributive, should make us know
The meaning of our words, face us to feel
The desolation and the agony
Of our fierce doings?

('Fears in Solitude', 11. 108–28)

Like Coleridge, Wordsworth protested that 'mere abstraction', what he calls 'general notions', ignored the actuality of
human experience. In the following passage from Book
Twelve of the 1805 *Prelude*, he describes such terms as
perpetuating class fragmentation:

Yes, in those wanderings deeply did I feel
How we mislead each other, above all
How Books mislead us, looking for their fame
To judgments of the wealthy Few, who see
By artificial lights, how they debase
The Many for the pleasure of those Few
Effeminately level down the truth
To certain general notions for the sake
Of being understood at once, or else
Through want of better knowledge in the men
Who frame them, flattering thus our self-conceit

With pictures that ambitiously set forth
The differences, the outward marks by which
Society has parted man from man,
Neglectful of the universal heart. (11. 208-19)

An extensive critique of abstract, general, or metaphysical ideas occupied the attention of many radical writers. The *Diversions* justified this prevalent discontent by discrediting theories of language which asserted an extreme dichotomy between experiential and abstract modes of thought.

According to Tooke even Locke, whom he admired greatly, had been misled by metaphysics. His thought was confused by the status and authority which he granted to abstract terms. The following comment, recorded by Samuel Rogers, refers to the chapter of Locke's *Two Treatises of Government* which is titled 'Of Political Power':

When I first read the first book of Locke, I was enchanted. It seemed to be a new world — when I proceeded I stept into darkness. . . . He puzzled about Power, &c. as some strange things which he could not define, thinking these words an authority for the existence of these things. If he had gone into their derivations, the difficulty would have vanished.[12]

Locke's political thought had been thwarted by his concept of ideas, a concept of ideas which Tooke set out to disprove by writing the *Diversions*. There, Tooke analyses vocabulary according to its history in order to study language as it existed in public life, as a form of interaction. The use of the dialogue form, which is often cumbersome, appropriately directs attention to language as a means of communication. Far from being the expression of the soul or the measure of refinement, the language of the *Diversions* always exists as an interaction between two speakers. Tooke's method of study and the dialogue form are aligned with his ultimate intention, to direct attention towards public nature of language and its possible abuse.

In the last volume, Tooke applies his concept of metaphysics to that of 'imposture'. After referring to the term occasionally in the course of the two volumes, Tooke grants

---

[12] *Recollections*, ed. W. Sharpe, 2nd edn., 1859, p. 134.

it a sudden importance when he states that 'Metaphysical (i.e. verbal) Imposture' will be the major subject of the third volume (ii. 516). Tooke does not define what he means by the term, nor does he directly discuss why he gives it such sudden importance, but the word appears whenever he describes the political and intellectual abuse that allows one group or institution to dominate others. Thus 'mankind in general are not sufficiently aware that words without meaning, or of equivocal meaning, are the everlasting engines of fraud and injustice: and that the *grimgribber* of Westminster Hall is a more fertile, and a much more formidable, source of imposture than the *abracadabra* of magicians' (i. 75). To associate the term with 'metaphysics' stresses Tooke's concern with metaphysics as a philosophy which impinges on political life by providing institutions with a means of domination. Tooke wanted both to clarify political thinking and to clarify words as they were used by political bodies because he believed that institutions would thereby be deprived of an unsound basis of power. One and perhaps the ultimate aim of Tooke's book is to lessen the obscurity which perpetuated both ignorance and subordination. By reforming ideas about language, Tooke intended to clarify the meaning of discrete words and to contribute to the reformation of social relations.

The illogicality of former theories, the 'false philosophy', has its most significant consequence in the defence and abuse of power. Such crucial words as 'innocence', 'truth', or 'spirit' derive from verbs and adjectives and have no significance other than as the actions which they represent. Referring to them as if they otherwise existed is not a consequence of the nature of reality but merely of the way that people speak: 'JUST, RIGHT and WRONG, are all merely Participles poetically embodied, and substantiated by those who use them' (ii. 19). Johnson's definitions of the word 'rights' exemplify how obscurity enhances power: Johnson did not 'acknowledge any RIGHTS of the people; but he was very clear concerning Ghosts and Witches, all the mysteries of divinity, and the sacred, indefeasible, inherent, hereditary RIGHTS of Monarchy' (ii. 5). Tooke attempts to provide a theory of language which will lessen the hold of what William

Blake called 'the mind-forg'd manacles' and what Paine described as being 'immured in the Bastille of a word' — the force of words which prompted submission to oppressive forms of government.

Through somewhat meandering logic, even Tooke's attack on the withdrawal of civil liberties has a bearing on his theory of language. The war against France and the passage of repressive legislation evoked much of the 'false morality and metaphysical jargon' which Tooke describes as justifying political abuse. The text of the *Diversions* bears the scars of the 'imposture' which Tooke claims is substantiated by mistaken theories of language. In the 1805 volume, Tooke describes England as in a 'state of siege'. The comment was omitted and a blank left in its stead due to the printer's fear of prosecution.[13] The frequent blanks in the second volume add urgency to the discussion by demonstrating a specific instance of 'imposture'. Canning's response to the word 'rights', which Tooke discusses at the beginning of the volume, is a significant detail in his advocacy of repressive legislation. The legislative power and political effect of such uncontrolled vocabulary as Canning's is manifest in the blank spaces. 'Imposture' and 'false philosophy' perpetuate each other because subordination depends upon distorted meaning. According to Tooke, the laws of God, nature, and government are essentially the same: 'I revere the Constitution and constitutional LAWS of England; because they are in conformity with the LAWS of God and nature: and upon these are founded the rational RIGHTS of Englishmen.' (ii. 14.) Although his language is now archaic, the concept that truth, freedom, and good government are interdependent, still continues to be persuasive. In such a scheme, legitimate government and correct reasoning either co-exist or do not exist at all. The accurate understanding of language would lessen the likelihood of imposture both by clarifying meaning and by minimizing the semantic confusion which encourages an unconscious submission to authoritative terms.

Far from being irrelevant, the political impetus and content of the *Diversions* grants it cohesiveness and direction.

---

[13] Richard Taylor's edition of the *Diversions of Purley* prints the omitted phrases of the 1805 volume in square brackets. Taylor, p. 404.

Tooke states that his etymologies are important for what they disprove and it is here that the *Diversions* has significance and scope. As Tooke understood it, his theory of language would be politically contentious if it were fully elaborated. He states as much while discussing his plans for the third volume: 'We may still perhaps find time enough for a further conversation on this subject [the verb]. And finally (if the times will bear it) to apply this system of Language to all the different systems of Metaphysical (i.e. verbal) Imposture.' (ii. 516.) Although the third volume was not printed, the first and second contain many ideas with radical implications. The possibility of thinking without reference to the material world, the credit that was granted to the classical languages for being pure and exceptionally capable of abstract thought, the concept of 'cant' vocabulary — the first two volumes disprove every linguistic notion that defined the vulgar as a group whose mentality was inferior to those who were allegedly civilized. After a long period in which the study of language was dominated by that of the mind and civilization, in a particularly obnoxious combination, Tooke began to make language an autonomous study which would be analysed by its own properties and history. By clarifying meaning, he reduces what was often considered to be the awesome power of words, their tendency to grant a necessary existence to whatever they represented. His concept of 'imposture' is insufficiently developed but it none the less initiates a new way of considering ideas about language, as an unsound means of political dominance. Even though Tooke does not explain his ideas adequately and does not fully answer several questions that his argument raises, he opens a subject that had appeared to be firmly closed. A social critique of language practice had a basis from which to develop. And the relation of language to the mind and to class could be extensively reconsidered.

The *Diversions'* argument did not enter a neutral field, where it could have simple effects. Publishing it in the tumultuous year of 1798 and the grimly quiet year of 1805, Tooke would have been naïve if he thought it would be entirely accepted. Most reviewers dealt with the book's political content in the simplest of all possible ways: they repeatedly dismissed it. Review after review extravagantly praises the knowledge and the clarity of Tooke's work, while condescendingly rebuking him for his politics, 'if we smile at the patriot, we must applaud the scholar'.[14] Literariness and political radicalism were considered antithetical, and if one was literary, one's political criticism was a meaningless aberration, an unfortunate tic of the eye. Samuel Johnson, commenting upon Tooke's first trial and *A Letter to J. Dunning*, vividly presents the assumption that literary characters are contradictory and superior to political ones: 'I hope they do not put the dog in the pillory for his libel; he has too much literature for that'.[15] The effect of this assumption on the *Diversions* was to justify overlooking the political content because Tooke understood language too well. An article in the *Monthly Review* performs this characteristic manoeuvre. After disagreeing with Tooke's discussion of the word 'rights', the article continues,

If he stumbles in the vestibule, let us only follow him into the interior of the temple, and we shall discover the strength, symmetry, and beauty which characterize the fabrics of truth; though we observe, placed here and there, utensils and ornaments which are very little in character with the nature and design of the edifice.[16]

Even those who agreed, at least somewhat, with Horne Tooke's politics failed to recognize any reasons for associating them with language. James Mill's article in the *Literary Journal* gives little thought to the subject, no more than the following remark:

Even with regard to his criticisms on politics and politicians, which seem the least connected with the subject, they are in general naturally introduced, and have always in them a keen point, and not infrequently real justice. They are often however in such bitter language, as, if mild and respectful words ought always to be used respecting the great, must be condemned as indecorous.[17]

[14] *Monthly Review*, lxxvi (1787), 2 (a review of the first edition).
[15] James Boswell, *Life of Johnson*, ed. R. W. Chapman, 3rd edn., 1970, p. 996.
[16] *Monthly Review*, 2nd series, li (1806), 391.
[17] *Literary Journal*, i (1806), 1.

Mill's sense of decorum here interferes with his question of what politics have to do with language. Instead of fully considering the question, Mill evaluates Tooke's manners.

Clearly, Mill did not understand the social and political implications of Tooke's work. He was, however, acutely conscious of the *Diversions'* tendency towards materialist epistemology. Despite Tooke's statement of what he plans for the third volume, Mill confidently states that Tooke will explain the nature of the mind and describes how he will do so. Aarsleff has pointed out that what Mill fearfully describes here, he will do later himself by relying upon the *Diversions* to write his *Analysis of the Phenomena of the Human Mind* (p. 94).

Circumstances in the book appear, we say, to us, to point out a system of materialism, which it is his intention to raise upon a new foundation, the analysis of language; a system which, whether cast in the mould of Helvetius or Hartley, appears to us equally abhorrent from reason, and mischievous in tendency; but a system which he will not find to stand with much security upon the *names of sensible objects*. (*Literary Journal*, p. 14)

Mill was unexceptional in considering the *Diversions* as primarily a book about the mind. If one considered Tooke's political comments seriously, and not many did, it would require a new way of thinking about language. To recognize and develop the work's tendency towards a theory of the mind would be much simpler, because that would not require altering the perspective from which language was understood. Furthermore, a theory of language that could establish a theory of the mind was anticipated because of the formulations of previous theories. By in part satisfying this demand, Tooke distracts attention from his main concern, 'Metaphysical (i.e. verbal) Imposture'. The momentum of the debate, the pre-existing need to reply to the full range of conservative theories, had its own power, as Tooke recognized. In describing his intention to separate the study of language from that of the mind, Tooke depicts his intellectual isolation: 'the full stream and current sets the other way' (i. 126). The most forward-looking ideas of Tooke's theory — his attempt to distinguish the study of language from that of the mind and to formulate a political analysis of language — were the most challenging and the least developed. The self-same conventions that Tooke was challenging impinged on some of his own ideas, and distorted the readings of his work.

It is an odd state of affairs when Mill, an eventual advocate of the book, cannot understand one of its major concerns and when the book's severest critic appreciates it more astutely. Unlike Mill or other reviewers, the Scottish philosopher Dugald Stewart does not divest the book of its attributes but discusses it in its own terms. Thoroughly opposed to Tooke's political stance, Stewart discusses the political implications of the *Diversions* more fully and explicitly than anyone. His essay, 'On the Tendency of some late Philological Speculations', attempts to recover the essential conservatism of previous theories from the persuasive challenge of the *Diversions*. At its conclusion, Stewart arrives at an impasse by asking that the study of language proceed in two contrary directions, that it limit its concerns and also that it maintain class distinctions.

According to Stewart, the study of language relies on two errors: 'the error of confounding the historical progress of an art with its theoretical principles when advanced to maturity; and, secondly, that of considering language as a much more exact and complete picture of thought, than it is in any state of society, whether barbarous or refined'.[18] Here, Stewart criticizes Tooke for ideas which Tooke himself had argued. Tooke had stated that the study of the mind needed to be distinct from the study of language and that language did not prove any difference between the minds of primitive and civilized people. Although other theorists had enthusiastically studied language in relation to the mind and civilization, Stewart concentrates on Tooke because of his dread of the book's consequences. Stewart understood the political implications of the *Diversions* and argued against it accordingly. He advocates obscurity for those reasons which Tooke had described — to maintain distinctions between the vulgar and the refined, to concentrate attention on abstract rather than experiential modes of thought, and even to restrain the expectations of the multitude.

[18] *The Collected Works*, v. 166.

On several counts, Stewart describes etymology as a dangerous science and gives reasons why its study should be restricted. Words have very little meaning and can be understood only according to their relation to other words in a sentence: 'Words, when examined separately, are often as completely insignificant as the letters of which they are composed; deriving their meaning solely from the connection, or relation, in which they stand to others' (pp. 154-5). Vocabulary can not be understood by hearing words or by formal definition. Meaning must be inferred by the frequent experience of reading. Such an extreme sense of vocabulary's lack of inherent meaning requires the silence of all but the literati. Only those with leisure, taste, and wealth are entitled to write according to Stewart's philosophy.

Tooke had emphasized the origins of vocabulary because he intended to situate abstract terms within a temporal rather than an idealistic context. Such an orientation would open up the possibility of asking certain questions and allow for greater possibilities of change. Stewart's discussion of intellectual terms favours permanence, and he recognizes a benefit in the 'obscurity of their history' which he desires to maintain: 'Such words have in their favour the sanction of immemorial use; and the obscurity of their history prevents them from misleading the imagination, by recalling to it the sensible objects and phenomena to which they owed their origin' (p. 174). Words become more delicate, fanciful, and suitable for philosophy as they become more obscure and increasingly distanced from their material origins. In a footnote, Stewart's rhetoric is less restrained, and the political context of his remark becomes clearer. There, he advocates what Tooke criticized as 'Metaphysics' by agreeing that intellectual vocabulary leads the imagination away from the material world. In speaking of the word 'harbinger' from a line in *Paradise Lost*, Stewart states: 'The power of *this* (which depends wholly on association) is often increased by the mystery which hangs over the origin of its consecrated terms; as the nobility of a family gains an accession of lustre, when its history is lost in the obscurity of the fabulous ages.' (p. 182.) Radicals also believed that the mystery of terms and the authority of the aristocracy depended upon obscurity and ignorance. Thomas Paine had said as much himself.

Stewart's reply to Tooke marks another stage in the Burke and Paine debate. Such terms as 'mystery', 'consecrated', 'obscurity', and 'fabulous ages' had gained unusual prominence with the publication of Burke's *Reflections on the Late Revolution in France*. Moreover, Stewart relies on the political rhetoric of the 1790s as he explains that one essential purpose of the study of the mind is to confirm the superiority of his own social class. Whereas Paine had performed a stylistic *coup* by reducing Burke's theatre image to a puppet show, Stewart, in turn, extends and appropriates the meaning of Paine's image:

When I study the intellectual powers of Man, in the writings of Hartley, of Priestley, of Darwin, or of Tooke, I feel as if I were examining the sorry mechanism that gives motion to a puppet. If, for a moment, I am carried along by their theories of human knowledge, and of human life, I seem to myself to be admitted behind the curtain of what I had once conceived to be a magnificent theatre; and, while I survey the tinsel frippery of the wardrobe, and the paltry decorations of the scenery, am mortifed to discover the trick which had cheated my eye at a distance. This surely is not the characteristic of truth or of nature; the beauties of which invite our closest inspection, — deriving new lustre from those microscopical researches which deform the most finished productions of art. If, in our physical inquiries concerning the Material World, every step that has been hitherto gained has at once exalted our conceptions of its immensity, and of its order, can we reasonably suppose, that the genuine philosophy of the Mind is to disclose to us a spectacle less pleasing, or less elevating, than fancy or vanity had disposed us to anticipate? (pp. 175–6)

Stewart states his agreement with Cicero that a philosophy deserved to be discounted if it '"savoured of nothing grand or generous"'. Stewart's main objection to such an unflattering philosophy is not the disillusionment of the 'we' and 'us' of his essay but rather its encouragement of aspiration among subordinate classes. It fails to restrict the expectations of the 'multitude': 'Nor was [Cicero's] objection so trifling as it may at first appear; for how is it possible to believe, that the conceptions of the multitude, concerning the duties of life, are elevated, by ignorance or prejudice, to a pitch, which it is the business of Reason and Philosophy to adjust to a humbler aim?' (p. 175.)

Stewart's initial request that the study of language be clarified becomes ambiguous as his essay progresses. His belief that language study should not be treated as a means of studying the mind or the growth of civilization is undermined by what he asks of 'Reason and Philosophy'. Previous conservative theories effectively satisfied the requirement that theories of language maintain social distinctions by simultaneously considering the nature of the mind and of civilization. To sever the study of language from that of the mind might be a means of discrediting the potential application of Tooke's argument, but it would also discredit the basis for aligning concepts of language with those of class. Stewart did not want to do this.

At this point, the two opposing camps are in remarkable agreement, and language has become a diminished component of a much larger argument. Stewart fulfils the charge brought by Tooke and others that vague vocabulary served the purpose of class division and that an ignorance of language, and of history as well, protects the state. Tooke fulfils Stewart's fears of the diminishment of the grandeur of the literati and of the dangers of materialism and radical politics. In political awareness, they match each other down the line. When two sides are this thoroughly aware of the implications of the study of language, new information will not alter either of the perspectives which formulate their ideas. An intellectual debate cannot proceed after such a deadlock. Either Tooke's theory would have to be extracted from its motive and its context or leading theorists would have to accept a radical critique of language.

Amidst these complications, Tooke's book was received with overwhelming enthusiasm. Several reviewers, even the staid *Annual Review* and the *British Critic*, called it the best book which had ever been written about language: 'There is no work in the English language or indeed any language with which we are acquainted, that stands higher in our estimation.'[19] As Mill initially feared, materialist philosophy received a tremendous boost from Tooke's work, both

---

[19] *British Critic,* xxix (1807), 647; *Annual Review,* iii (1805), 679.

through his own later work and that of Jeremy Bentham. Aarsleff describes the eagerness with which various materialist thinkers responded to Tooke's theory of language: as well as Bentham and Mill, William Hazlitt, Erasmus Darwin, James Mackintosh, and Henry Brougham were 'too dazzled by the flash of light to examine its source' (p. 73). Hazlitt and Mackintosh should not be included in this list for they criticized the *Diversions* for its potential to prove a materialist theory of the mind. Hazlitt evaluated the *Diversions* with a careful and critical eye in his grammar of 1809, in his essay on Tooke in the *Spirit of the Age*, and in his *Lectures on English Philosophers, 'On Tooke's Diversions'*. Comments by these and other writers explain various other reasons for the *Diversions'* popularity besides its materialism. It was praised for its contribution to grammar, education, semantics, and, by a few radicals, the contemporary political debate. Hazlitt, Mackintosh, Hunt, and Darwin all state that the sudden clarity brought to language revealed how inadequately it had been understood. Leigh Hunt, for instance, defines himself as 'one of the very many who, at first sight of it, bade adieu to the leaden *Hermes* of Mr Harris'.[20] Many comments express enthusiasm for Horne Tooke's clarification of the particles, as if the understanding of language had been bound and tied by the misunderstanding of myriad little words. Sir James Mackintosh's comment is not unusually extreme: 'Horne Tooke's is certainly a wonderful work; but the great merit was the original thought. The light which shines through such impenetrable words as articles and pronouns, is admirable — "the" and "it." No single book, perhaps, ever so much illustrated the language.' (*Memoirs*, ii. 230-1.) Maria and Richard Edgeworth state that because of Tooke, and Wilkins as well, students will no longer be puzzled as they were when learning the language: 'Fortunately for rising generations all the words under the denominations of adverbs, prepositions, and conjunctions, which are absolute nonsense to us, may be happily explained to them and the commencement of instruction need no longer lay the foundation of implicit acquiescence in nonsense.'[21] The sense of jubilee, of being liberated by clarity, characterizes many comments.

Noah Webster and William Hazlitt claim in their grammars that the *Diversions* offered the first possibility of writing an accurate grammar of the language.[22] Grammars written to accord with the *Diversions of Purley* — Hazlitt's, Webster's, John Fell's (to a lesser extent), and possibly William Cobbett's — have several distinctive characteristics in common.[23] Each respects the spoken language as equally genuine and pure as the written language, as does the full title of Hazlitt's *A New and Improved Grammar of the English Tongue in which the Genius of our Speech is especially attended to and the discoveries of Mr. Horne Tooke and other modern writers on the formation of Language, are for the first time incorporated.* Hazlitt, Cobbett, and Webster do not present language as a gentlemanly attribute or as a moral virtue, although Webster became more moralistic later in his career. Colloquial expressions frequently provide these writers with examples, and eliptical phrases are given an unusual degree of attention. The parts of speech are not distinguished by definition but by their syntax: their 'difference does not, however, arise from any intrinsical difference in the ideas to which those words relate or from the nature of the things spoken of, but from our manner of speaking them' (Hazlitt, ii. 20).

These grammarians and other writers recognized the political implications of the *Diversions*. In their grammars, Cobbett and Fell present a radical variant of the English language and discuss the contemporary practice of language as socially and politically divisive. Tooke's influence on Cobbett will be discussed in chapter six. Fell's grammar was written before the *Diversions* was published but he praises *A Letter to J. Dunning* highly, which was incorporated into volume one. Noah Webster, in his theoretical work

---

[21] *Practical Education*, 2nd edn., 1801, 3 vols., ii. 209.

[22] Hazlitt, 'A New and Improved Grammar of the English Tongue', *Complete Works*, ii. 5; Webster, *A Philosophical and Practical Grammar*, New Haven, 1807, p. 3.

[23] [John Fell], *An Essay Towards an English Grammar*, 1784; William Cobbett, *A Grammar of the English Language in a Series of Letters*, New York, 1818. London edition 1819.

Dissertations on the English Language (1789), develops the political implications of Tooke's work. Webster states his debt to Tooke in the Preface and in the subheading to one of his chapters, 'Horne Tooke's theory of the Particles'. Tooke's redefinition of language enables Webster to construct an alternative to contemporary language practice. Webster maintains that contemporary English was socially divisive and that for Americans to imitate it would encourage prejudices that were inimical to democracy (p. 174). He criticizes the attempt of English grammarians to differentiate written from spoken English and states firmly that a fundamental purpose of language is thwarted when grammarians make people of different social classes less willing to listen to each other, and even less intelligible (p. 205). Although these grammars did not achieve the authority or popularity of Lindley Murray's, they taught a more colloquial language that provided an alternative to hegemonic texts.

Others appreciated Tooke's theory for its demystification of vocabulary. Henry Tuckerman, an American, discusses the *Diversions* as a theory which distinguishes words from ideas in a manner which benefited literature, philosophy, and politics: 'He certainly opened many new vistas in the dense and tangled forest of words. . . . He proved how often ideas had been mistaken for terms, words identified with things, and the inevitable confusion that results; that science, politics, and literature had essentially suffered from this cause.'[24] And William Hazlitt, although critical of the book in some respects, praises it for divesting words of their accumulated meanings:

There is a web of old associations wound round language, that is a kind of veil over its natural features; and custom puts on the mask of ignorance. But this veil, this mask the author of *The Diversions of Purley* threw aside and penetrated to the naked truth of things, by the literal, matter-of-fact, unimaginative nature of his understanding, and because he was not subject to prejudices or illusions of any kind. (xi. 54)

[24] *Characteristics of Literature illustrated by the Genius of Distinguished Writers*, 2nd series, Philadelphia, 1851, p. 116.

The training which the book provides in distinguishing vocabulary from its associations might well have been in special demand at the turn of the century. Radicals and other thinkers had to protect themselves and their ideas from an aggressive rhetoric employed to persuade people to accept repressive legislation, to stabilize political disruption, and to meet the demands of the Napoleonic Wars. Prejudice and illusion abounded in the form of propaganda and in the new acrimony of theoretical debates. The *Diversions* warns readers thoroughly against the powers of vague vocabulary and the dangers of political confrontations being lost due to the false authority granted to certain terms. To demystify rhetoric and to assist people to penetrate 'to the naked truth of things' is a considerable achievement even in the quietest of times. More vaguely and more grandiosely, Coleridge described the *Diversions* as politically effective because it clarified vocabulary as it refuted theories which promulgated superstition. Coleridge regarded it as an enlightenment text, one which simultaneously encouraged political and intellectual liberty. His poem in praise of Tooke was written after Tooke's defeat in the Westminster election of 1796:

> Patriot & Sage! whose breeze-like Spirit first
> The lazy mists of Pedantry dispers'd
> (Mists in which Superstition's *pigmy* band
> Seem'd Giant Forms, the Genii of the Land!),
> Thy struggles soon shall wakn'ing Britain bless,
> And Truth & Freedom hail thy wish'd success.
> ('Verses addressed to J. Horne Tooke', 11.13-19)

As Coleridge explains in a letter to Estlin, the phrase 'breeze-like Spirit' refers to the Greek title of the *Diversions,* ΕΠΕΑ ΠΤΕΡΟΕΝΤΑ, meaning 'winged words'.[25]

And finally, by refuting the categories of civilized and primitive modes of thought, as well as speech, Horne Tooke wrote a theory of language which granted experience and 'vulgar' discourse new status in literary works. 'Refined' and 'vulgar', 'primitive' and 'civilized' might continue to describe types of language but they could no longer scientifi-

[25] *Collected Letters of Samuel Taylor Coleridge*, ed. Earl Leslie Griggs, Oxford, 1959-71, 6 vols., i. 225.

cally explain the mind according to the intellectual and moral capabilities of two social classes. The rudimentary theory of knowledge contained in the *Diversions* allowed perception and feeling to regain a position in theories of knowledge without being dismissed as the characteristics of the vulgar: 'The business of the mind, as far as it concerns Language, appears to me to be very simple. It extends no farther than to receive Impressions, that is, to have Sensations or Feelings'. As will be discussed, the *Diversions* challenged Coleridge to reconsider ideas about language in the late 1790s, while contributing to the Preface to *Lyrical Ballads*. The *Diversions*' influence was thus pervasive and diverse. By addressing the central problematic of the study of language, the *Diversions* touched upon a range of issues: grammar, poetics, class differentiation, and the study of the mind. For the literati, it was without question a tremendously challenging and significant book.

It is more difficult to evaluate how Horne Tooke's theory might have affected any but its well-educated audience. We do not have the means of assessing how a work which profoundly influences the literati extends its range until it eventually alters a wider public's sense of things. It is clear from the records of trials and from comments in reviews that Tooke did not so weaken the hegemonic theory of language that it was incapacitated. Vulgar language continued to be considered as the sign of a poorly developed and uncivilized mind, and unrefined English was still characterized as 'barbaric'. Major eighteenth-century texts which encouraged such assumptions might have been philosophically disproved by the *Diversions*, but they continued to meet increasing demands for a language that was immediately distinguishable from vulgarity. Blair's and Campbell's works on rhetoric, Johnson's *Dictionary* with its Preface, and Lindley Murray's grammar sold more copies during the nineteenth than the eighteenth century. In terms of how prevalent assumptions about language maintained class boundaries or were applied during political conflicts, no single book could have a sudden and immediate power.

The *Diversions* none the less weakened a hegemony of language which had previously been complete and intact.

Those who disagreed with contemporary language theory and linguistic practice, Hazlitt, Coleridge, Webster, and Cobbett, had a means of operating, of bringing previously undeveloped ideas into coherent focus. When considering the greater availability of a certain type of language, the notion of 'influence' is inadequate. A vernacular discourse emerged after the wars for other reasons than the writing of the *Diversions*. But the book appears everywhere, whenever the vernacular is strengthened, making it difficult to conceive of the book's absence. The two most effective writers after 1815, William Cobbett and William Hone, relied upon it at important moments. Cobbett's grammar was one means by which the *Diversions* extended its range. For the first time, educated writers had a grammar book that was designed for them to be able to participate in public discussion. Perhaps less randomly than one might expect, the self-educated writer William Hone refers to the *Diversions* during his self-defence for blasphemous libel. Discussing the piracy of the book, Hone parenthetically describes it as 'a work which every man who knew the English language read and admired'.[26] Having to withstand a judge who relentlessly denounced his language as vulgar and indecent, Hone's ideas might well have been confirmed by his reading of a theoretical work that vindicated his own 'mere native English'. Hone, as we shall see, found his three trials to be excruciating, and confidence in his 'vulgar' language could not have been more severely strained. Under such circumstances, any contribution is a significant one. Like many radical writers, Hone knew of Tooke both as a political leader and as a theorist of the English language. Presumably, Tooke's comments about 'imposture' were especially vivid to those like William Hone who remembered the treason trials, who wrote a vernacular English, and who were threatened with prosecution themselves. The *Diversions'* contribution to a trial that uncovered bias in the selection of special jurors and which defended the freedom of the press, suggests that Tooke's work might have intervened at the level that he most hoped it would, that of safe-guarding political liberties. Although the *Diversions*

---

[26] *The Three Trials of William Hone*, ed. William Tegg, 1876, 3rd trial, p. 181.

did not singly overwhelm and defeat the previously existing relation of language to class, it appears at crucial moments when that relation is challenged.

Chapter V

The Power of the Press and the Trials of William Hone

On the title-page to one of William Hone's parodies, an encircled printing press sheds rays like the sun blasting and blinding the two lawyers who wrote the repressive legislation of 1819.[1] The illustration reveals the strength that Hone and other writers felt themselves to have despite their poverty and lack of formal education. It illustrates a new sense of mightiness that makes the writers after the Napoleonic Wars seem vastly different from those before. Cobbett, Hone, Wooler, and Carlile are unimaginable in the earlier period because they did not sense the constraints which are evident in the writings of Thelwall, Parkinson, Eaton, and less so of Spence. They trusted their audience, they could portray it convincingly, and they achieved a bold vernacular language. None was hampered by the concepts of vulgarity and refinement, although the presence of these concepts was otherwise felt. The weakening of the hegemony of the concept of vulgarity was one of numerous changes occurring between 1780 and 1815 which encouraged the greater creativity and strength of writers after the war. John Horne Tooke's book, with its critique of a dominant philosophical tradition, was part of this fundamental change. Also literacy had increased, the laws of copyright had become less restrictive, national newspapers became more informative and independent, and the technology of printing advanced significantly. Insufficient work has been done on these economic, technological, and legal changes in the practice of reading, despite Marjorie Plant's excellent book, and only a brief account based on others' work will be given here. Although a considerable array of developments can be listed, the differences between the non-literati press in 1790 and 1820 cannot be entirely

---

[1] 'A Political Christmas Carol', with *The Man in the Moon,* 16th edn., 1820, unpaginated.

accounted for. More mysteriously, some mental barrier had broken. Thomas Paine's hope and Dugald Stewart's fear that the loss of mystery would diminish the supremacy of the upper classes were in part fulfilled. The radical press scrutinized the government's behaviour and attacked traditional practices by which the government protected itself. Cabinet ministers, especially Sidmouth, Canning, and Castlereagh, were exposed and reviled, as was the Prince Regent. The 'mind forg'd manacles' frequently mentioned in the 1790s, no longer called for comment. For several years, from 1819–22, writers and readers released themselves from previous constraints. They were incessantly aggressive and wilfully, hilariously rude. The manacles had broken and the people laughed and laughed.

Custom as well as theory had differentiated refined from vulgar literature. Before 1780, reading material addressed to the audience was in short supply and of a specific kind. Copyright laws, distribution, and the technology of printing helped to confine popular literature to that of chap-books, almanacs, jest-books, religious works, and broadsheets. Hand-bills and pamphlets were also read during times of political excitement. Books were prohibitively expensive and their price continued to rise between 1780 and 1830. Because perpetual copyright was enforced until 1774, inexpensive editions of books had to be published clandestinely or imported from Scotland and Ireland. Charles Knight referred to the book market, even after it had expanded somewhat, as an 'unnatural, bigoted and unprofitable system'.[2] Book-sellers controlled the price of their products by selling as few books at as high a price as possible. Remainders were burnt or sold as wrapping. Old second-hand copies were the only cheap copies available. Remarkably few books (excluding pamphlets) were even published: less than one hundred titles a year between 1714 and 1774; an average of 372 between 1792 and 1802; and 580 a year between 1802 and 1827.[3] As with the literacy rate and advances in printing technology,

---

[2] *The Old Printer and the Modern Press*, 1854, p. 239.
[3] Marjorie Plant, *The English Book Trade, An Economic History of the Making and Sale of Books*, 2nd edn., 1969, pp. 92, 414.

the rate of book production stagnated during most of the century, gained momentum at its end, and then significantly increased in the early stages of the nineteenth century.

Not surprisingly, autobiographies of self-educated writers discuss the scarcity of reading material. James Lackington, a London bookseller, and Thomas Holcroft, a novelist and radical charged with high treason in 1794, both forgot how to read.[4] After receiving a minimal education in dame schools, they did not see enough printed material to maintain their skills. Holcroft stated that after reading the Bible and two chap-books, he read nothing for six years. Moreover, he did not see any printed material except ballads and broadsheets hung in taverns.[5] William Lovett, born a generation later in 1800 and a leader of the Chartist movement, did not see any printed material other than chap-books and religious books until he moved from an isolated village in Cornwall to London at the age of twenty-one.[6] Among such a scarcity, luck could count a great deal. Holcroft rediscovered his ability to read when he roomed with a fellow apprentice who owned a few books. Supplies were better in London than the provinces, and, in several autobiographies, the move towards London is also one towards greater literacy.

The gulf between refined and vulgar literature was narrowed by the breaking of the practice of copyright. Until 1774, perpetual copyright guarded the market, enabling a publisher to maintain sole rights to a book no matter when the firm negotiated with the author. Declared illegal in 1709, it was upheld by the practice of booksellers (they called it 'curtesy.') and even by later decisions of the court.[7] In 1774, the Scottish bookseller, Alexander Donaldson appealed against a former decision which had prohibited him from publishing an inexpensive edition of Thomson's *Seasons*. The House of Lords upheld the 1709 law, admitting new

[4] James Lackington, *Memoirs of the First Forty-Five Years of the Life of James Lackington*, 2nd edn., 1792, p. 99.

[5] *Memoirs of the Late Thomas Holcroft written by himself*, ed. William Hazlitt, 3 vols., 1816, pp. 134–5.

[6] William Lovett, *The Life and Struggles of William Lovett*, 1876, p. 17.

[7] Richard Altick, *The English Common Reader: A Social History of the Mass Reading Public, 1800–1900*, Chicago, 1957, pp. 53–4. I am indebted to Altick generally and for several references.

works into the public domain after the passing of twenty-eight years and already existing titles after twenty-one. Meaning to criticize, Samuel Johnson compared Donaldson to Robin Hood because he stole from the rich.[8] From 1774 onwards, refined literature was published in cheap editions. Excepting contemporary literature, copyright law no longer helped to maintain a sharp distinction between vulgar and refined literature, between vulgar and refined· readers. Between 1777 and 1783, John Bell published 104 volumes of poetry at an unusually low price, *The Poets of Great Britain complete from Chaucer to Churchill.* A fine edition sold for one shilling and six pence, and a cheaper edition sold in six penny weekly numbers. A group of forty London booksellers attempted to forestall the success of Bell's project by publishing a fancier collection of British poets, for which Samuel Johnson was employed to write his famous prefaces, *The Lives of the English Poets.*[9] Bell also published *Bell's British Theatre* and *Bell's Editions of Shakespeare's Plays.* John Cooke and James Harris also produced inexpensive serial editions of refined literature. Cooke's editions, which were illustrated, were remembered with special fondness by Hone as well as others.

Innovative booksellers devised other new ways of expanding their commerce. William Lane founded the Minerva Press and Library in the 1770s. Before the 1790s, he sold traditional popular literature — jest-books, almanacs, travel books, and pamphlets. From the 1790s to the 1820s, he sold and published novels which were often written specifically to be distributed in circulating libraries. William Lane would post instructions and books to anyone in the provinces hoping to start a circulating library. Because only shelves and a few books were required to begin, a library could readily be added to an already existing shop. According to Dorothy Blakely, Lane was instrumental in the extension of the circulating· libraries to the provinces, even though such libraries had existed since much earlier in the century.[10]

    [8] *Boswell's London Journal,* ed. Frederick A. Pottle, New York, 1950, pp. 312-13.
    [9] Stanley Morison, *John Bell, 1745-1831,* Cambridge, 1930, p. 6.
    [10] *The Minerva Press, 1790-1820,* 1939, p. 119.

James Lackington began his extremely successful bookshop by selling books as a shoemaker. Lackington's business expanded because of his disregard for the customs of the trade. He bought books in as large a number, and sold them as cheaply as possible. Whereas a batch of remainders would normally be mostly destroyed and those left sold at full or nearly full price, Lackington kept all remainders and sold them at a quarter or half price. Booksellers counter-attacked as they had against Bell (Lackington, p. 374). Lackington was prohibited from attending trade auctions and became the object of a slander campaign. His London shop, magnificently titled the Temple of the Muses, did not suffer greatly from the consequences. Claiming to sell one hundred thousand books a year in the 1790s, he took pride in enabling more people to read and to purchase books (p. 453).

More so than books, however, newspapers, pamphlets, and serial publications provided the steady supply of reading material which brought the audience into the public sphere. While book production remained largely the same, the distribution and contents of newspapers altered considerably. The political debate of the 1790s, the Luddite Riots, the Napoleonic War, and the political turmoil after 1815 engaged the public interest over an exceptionally long period. During the last quarter of the century, newspapers changed rapidly: whereas mid-eighteenth-century papers were designed primarily as advertisers, later ones were both critical and informative. Although editors established the privilege of reporting parliamentary speeches in 1771, it took considerably longer for editors to become unhindered by government interference. During and after the wars, newspapers gained sufficient circulation to be able to operate without government assistance or protection by the opposition. Direct support, franking privileges, access to official information, printed contracts, and income from advertising were various means by which the government interfered with the press.[11] Direct assistance from the Treasury or the Home Office was common before the war, the government spending approximately £5,000 a year on subsidy during the early 1790s.

[11] Arthur Aspinall, *Politics and the Press, c.1780–1850*, 1949, p. 9.

The Times travelled the course from direct subsidy of £300 a year, to indirect subsidy, and finally to financial independence between the years 1790 and 1805. Losing the subsidy in 1799, *The Times* received priority of information and a valuable printing contract. The contract was lost in 1805, when the paper continued to support Addington despite Pitt's return to office. The second editor, John Walter jun., then strove to keep it independent and concentrated on increasing circulation. As such a history and others recorded by Aspinall reveal, government assistance could be precarious. After the war, extensive circulation proved to be more advantageous than government support, and, by 1815, the government-supported press was frowned upon. Although the *Courier* was quite successful, many sponsored papers had a short life. They did not compare well to the more independent and usually impoverished radical press.

An increase and steadiness in the demand for news also prompted advances in printing technology. The period between the 1790s and 1815 again reveals a great deal of activity after a long period of stagnation. Although various improvements had been added, the same basic wooden press had been used since the invention of printing. Between the 1790s and 1810, several new presses were invented: the Stanhope, the Columbian, and the Albion among them. Although these eased the process of printing, they did not substantially increase the rate of production. The wooden press produced 200 sheets an hour and the Stanhope 250. Substantial advances in technology were frustrated by the primitive technology of paper-making. Until 1812, all paper was commercially produced by hand in separate sheets. In 1799, the Frenchman Nicholas-Louis Robert invented a paper-machine which was improved in England by Henry and Sealy Fourdrinier. Paper could then be made in a continuous sheet, up to six miles long. From five weeks, the time required to make paper was reduced to five days (Plant, 329–31). Major changes in printing technology were then possible. The German inventor of a cylinder steam press was brought to England by *The Times* in 1806. Within a few years, Koenig had invented several presses designed for various purposes. In November 1814, *The Times* was the first paper to be printed on a steam press. Compared to the Stanhope's 250 sheets, it printed 1,100 an hour. Soon machinery would print 5,000 sheets an hour on both sides (Plant, 275-6).

Circulation was restrained by the stamp duty which increased the price of every paper sold by 3½d. in 1797 and 4d. in 1815. Advertisements and paper were also taxed. In 1792, circulation was approximately 15,000,000. In 1811 it reached 24,420,000, a figure that would increase by only 400,000 until the stamp duty was repealed in 1835 (Aspinall, p. 23).

Considering that the illegal, unstamped press is not included in these figures and that one paper served twenty to thirty readers, information was readily available compared to the period before the war. The audience skirted the restraints imposed by the stamp duty by reading papers in whatever way they could. Newspapers could be rented by the hour, children were hired to read while others worked, people purchased papers collectively or read them in taverns and coffee-houses. Radical publishers also evaded the effects of the stamp duty by publishing weekly political pamphlets. As these were essays containing information rather than direct presentations of the news, they were not newspapers by legal definition. William Hone, T. J. Wooler, Richard Carlile, and John Wade printed weekly periodicals at an inexpensive price. Also, in November 1816, Cobbett began to publish the leading article of the *Political Register* separately, thereby reducing its price from over a shilling to a mere two pence. The unstamped press, as it came to be called, and Cobbett's *Weekly Political Pamphlet* had a sizeable following that was not recorded in the number of stamps sold. Cobbett's pamphlet sold forty to sixty thousand copies a week, a circulation 'several times larger than that of any other newspaper' (Pearl, p. 95). Cobbett stopped publishing it in April 1817 after repressive legislation altered the definition of a newspaper to include inexpensive and regularly issued periodicals. Others continued to publish. T. J. Wooler's *Black Dwarf* had a circulation of 12,000 which was probably larger after Peterloo (E. P. Thompson, *The Making* p. 718). Despite the impact of the stamp duty, the practice of reading newspapers had drastically changed since the 1790s, and even since 1815 when inexpensive papers did not exist. The notion of gentlemen reading in their closets, a phrase used by attorney-generals to describe trustworthy readers, makes little sense in newspaper culture. Information and ideas were no longer private.

People were too literate, too interested. Despite the difficulties of measuring literacy, historians agree on a long national period of stasis in literacy levels between 1675 and 1775. The impetus given to literacy and education by the supremacy of Puritanism was followed by a long and severe backlash that lasted more than a century. Lawrence Stone calculates the literacy of the urban and rural middle classes as remaining the same for a hundred years and then rising from 75 per cent to 95 per cent between 1780 and 1840.[12] Literacy of the lower classes, according to Stone, did not rise until 1800 when it reached a level of 35 per cent to 40 per cent. In the early nineteenth century, it rose more dramatically to 60 per cent. Richard Altick argues for a temporary rise in lower-class literacy during the 1790s, followed by another stasis until after the Napoleonic War (p. 22). The questions of active or inactive literacy and variations in the quality of literacy further complicate the figures. Stone suggests five levels of literacy ranging from that of reading with difficulty to the advanced reading and writing skills of the literati. Moreover the non-literate, especially in London, were not as excluded from political debate as one might assume. Political cartoons and other pictorial prints were designed to be 'read' by the non-literate.

The problem which worried contemporaries of the 1790s and the post-Napoleonic War period, was not so much that the lower and middle classes were reading but that they were reading unconventional material. A significant difference exists between reading chap-books, ballads, and almanacs and reading pamphlets and newspapers that challenge one's social status or criticize the government. Although some chap-books and ballads expressed class conflicts, they were restricted forms of expression. Material such as the Luddite

[12] 'Literacy and Education in England, 1640–1900', *Past and Present*, no. 42 (1969), 109–12.

ballads expressed the discontent of a region and a class, but
it did not constitute a part of a public dialogue. While the
audience read chap-books and ballads, no one appears to have
noticed that they read. Reading the news, however, puts
readers into a relationship with both the state and other
readers, without making distinctions according to class.
Although newspapers were usually aimed at skilled readers,
they did not specify the class of their audience either by
distribution or by presentation. The basic classlessness of the
newspaper press developed new problems. In 1798, Parliament discussed the problem of newspapers reporting speeches
in the House that would be seditious if spoken outside it.
It was again a question of audience. Speeches addressed to
the gentleman concerning the 'unjust and unnecessary war'
differed in character from those comments addressed to the
paper's relatively unspecified audience (*PD*, xxiv. 140-65).
The availability of papers in taverns, where even their price
did not restrict the readership, was also of concern. Unlike
handbills, the daily and weekly appearance of newspapers
implies that a large body of readers is continuously interested
in public affairs. Newspapers both depend on and propagate
the notion that readers participate in public life along with
many other citizens, and that the workings of government
can be scrutinized by anyone capable of reading, or even of
listening to someone else read.

The war also shifted the relation of the lower and middling
classes to the state. After having been disciplined and self-
sacrificing during the war, these classes could no longer be
convincingly portrayed as a body of the population that had
no relation to public life. Whereas the French Revolution
had justified conservative propaganda by demonstrating the
potential violence of radicalism, the war against the French
required the propagandists to alter their descriptions of the
lower classes. The government could not ask a despised
population to defend that government's existence. To
persuade the lower classes to fight, propaganda was produced
in quantities that greatly surpassed that of the 1790s.[13]
Broadsheets and handbills depicted their readers as guaran-

[13] Clive Emsley, *British Society and the French Wars, 1793–1815*, 1979,
p. 115.

tors of the freedom of the press and the Magna Carta against a tyrannical and arbitrary government. From the stupid, loud-mouthed, hysterical character of the 1790s, John Bull became an heroic and intelligent defender of political liberty. Even his vulgar language became a virtue in 1803. In *Plain Answers to Plain Questions in a Dialogue between John Bull and Bonaparte,* Napoleon criticizes John Bull for the 'unmannerly Way you Englishmen have of calling every Thing by its vulgar Name'. John Bull asks informed questions concerning Napoleon's conduct during the war, and, in turn, criticizes Napoleon for employing a refined language that disguises the reality of oppression. Although much of the conservative propaganda of 1803 is repulsive, it often claims that 'John Bull' has a relation to the state and is responsible for safeguarding political liberties.

These depictions were remembered bitterly after the war when repressive legislation was passed and habeas corpus suspended. During his self-defence for seditious libel, T. J. Wooler states that ministers

declared over and over again that we were fighting the cause of social order, good government, and legitimate monarchy; that all our hopes of Heaven and all our blessings on earth depended upon a vigorous resistance to the dreadful principles of the French revolution ... neither [the Attorney-General] nor any man will be able to challenge from the page of History, the unhappy — the delusive result of all those promises and pledges.[14]

The sense of betrayal and the certainty that the audience had made an unrewarded contribution to the country alleviated the awkwardness, the hesitancy, and the fear of the audience that characterized much of the writing of the 1790s. Combined with developments in the press and advances in literacy, this confident knowledge of the audience prompted a new power and freedom among radical writers. Whereas in the 1790s, conservative propagandists had had the most effective style, the most dreadfully convincing portrayal of the audience, and a greater flexibility with language, they lost these advantages. After 1815, radical writers achieved an

---

[14] *A Verbatim Report of the Two Trials of Mr T. J. W., Editor of the Black Dwarf,* 1817, p. 33.

indigenous and persuasive literature which conservatives tried to contain by imitation and more stridently by repression.

During the decade following the war, the government energetically opposed radical writers and editors. Other measures besides the suspension of habeas corpus in 1817 were evoked in the attempt to restrain the effectiveness of radical writings. Lord Sidmouth, secretary of the Home Office, issued a notorious and legally dubious circular letter authorizing local magistrates to arrest anyone selling apparently seditious material and to charge bail without a hearing. Publishers, printers, booksellers, and hawkers were all legally responsible for the contents of whatever material they made public. Proceeding by ex-officio information also ·eliminated steps which normally protected citizens. Initially intended to prevent treason by allowing suspects to be apprehended immediately, ex-officio information allowed the Attorney-General to seize a suspect and charge bail. Those suspects who could not afford bail were imprisoned for an unspecified time. Up to seven years could pass between the indictment and the trial. Often the trial was never called, while the threat of it remained. T. J. Wooler and William Hone were two of the sixteen people who were prosecuted by ex-officio information in 1817. Their trials are famous among historians for preserving freedom of expression and uncovering the process of illegal selection of special jurors. Both successfully defended themselves in a total of five trials. Wooler was indicted twice and Hone three times. Having suffered these major defeats, the government indicted no one for libel during 1818.

The quiet was broken by the massacre at St. Peter's Fields, 16 August 1819, when Manchester cavalry attacked an outdoor mass meeting for reform, killing eleven and wounding hundreds. The ensuing outrage provoked numerous arrests and the passage of repressive legislation, familiarly known as the 'Gagging Acts'. The punishment for blasphemous and seditious libel was extended to include banishment for a second offence. Richard Carlile, who had been on the platform at Peterloo, began a determined attack on the government's restriction of civil liberties. Indicted twice for publishing Thomas Paine's *Age of Reason* and Palmer's

Principles of Nature, Carlile was found guilty of both. Twenty-five other ex-officio indictments were issued against those who sold weekly newspapers edited by Carlile, the *Republican* and *Sherwin's Register*, which contained articles about the massacre.[15] Sentenced for three years, Carlile was released after six because he could not afford sureties for his behaviour. Meanwhile Carlile's wife, his sister, and recruits from London and the provinces continued to publish and to sell seditious material, particularly the writings of Thomas Paine. All told, one hundred and fifty volunteers served a total of two hundred years in gaol (E. P. Thompson, *The Making*, p. 725). Although convicted, they proved their point.

Hone was in the midst of this push and pull, the simultaneous expansion and repression of the press. The relation between the state and his audience was not only the main subject of his writings but also a central fact of his life. *The Political House that Jack Built*, for instance, emerges from this conflict. After his three trials for blasphemous libel, Hone placed advertisements in every London paper, promising not to publish any more scriptural parodies and suggesting that others do likewise. He did not write any parodies until the Peterloo Massacre prompted him to do so in the autumn of 1819. The event of a cavalry attacking a peaceful reform meeting manifested the antagonism which, Hone had argued, characterized the state's attitude towards the disenfranchized population. With the writing of *The Political House*, Hone reached his mature style and developed the genre for which he was most famous, a mock innocence which is reminiscent of Blake and which was frequently imitated during the next several years. The parody sold one hundred thousand copies, becoming a definitive interpretation of what happened at Peterloo. Although it was more incisive than the parodies which Hone published in 1817, it was an unprosecutable form. Having made fools of themselves already, the

[15] William Wickwar, *Struggle for the Freedom of the Press, 1819–1832*, 1928, p. 97.

government ministers could well imagine the outcome of prosecuting a satirist for writing a seditious nursery rhyme.

Having promised to write no more scriptural parodies, Hone was perhaps forced to seek an unconventional vehicle for his satire. By satirizing a nursery rhyme, Hone maintains some of the advantages of satirizing well-known religious works. Both were very familiar to his audience, even to those who could not read. Hone, however, takes special advantage of the original rhyme. For one, it had had a special history. In 1794, Lord Erskine referred to it during Thomas Hardy's trial for high treason in order to describe the prosecution's reliance on circumstantial evidence: 'Gentlemen, if the cause were not too serious, I would liken it to the play with which we amuse our children. "This is the cow with the crumpledy horn, which gored the dog, that worried the cat, that ate the rat etc ending with the house that Jack built."'[16] More explicitly, Hone refers to his own trial in a manner that also defines the form as a riposte to the Attorney-General's tendency to distort information. He dedicates the parody to his audience, as the Attorney-General understood it to be to

THE NURSERY OF CHILDREN
SIX FEET HIGH
HIS READERS
for the delight and instruction of
their uninformed minds;
THIS JUVENILE PUBLICATION
is affectionately inscribed.[17]

The childish rhyme contains a bleak and damning portrayal of the government and its relation to the audience. The simplicity with which Hone manages to convey his analysis implies that the predicament is so obvious, so glaring that a child could understand it and be repelled. Its motive, its content, its childish language, and its form — throughout — *The Political House* expresses the antagonism which culminated with the massacre.

Looming illustrations by George Cruikshank co-operate with the archly simplistic text. The original chain of caus-

---

[16] Cited from *State Trials*, xxiv. 596 by A. Goodwin, p. 349.
[17] *The Political House that Jack Built*, 13th edn., 1819, unpaginated.

ation becomes a chain of oppression: the Constitution protects civil liberties, which are attacked by local authorities, who are denounced by the press, which is attacked by the Attorney-General, who is supported by the military, who are thanked by the Prince Regent, for attacking the people, who are persecuted by the Cabinet, that attempts to block reform. The parody gradually builds up, one segment at a time, each segment contributing a new element which redefines the extent of the conflict and the temporary victor. At its conclusion, an entire complex relationship is conveyed in one long, winding sentence, a syntax of oppression and resistance. The succession of the illustrations and the passages, the knitting together of the entire chain, is an aspect of the satire that cannot be conveyed except by reading it in its entirety. Each segment, however, has its own power. An illustration of the Regent, with bulging stomach, decorated with feathers, insignia, and a corkscrew, accompanies the rhyme

> This is THE MAN — all shaven and shorn,
> All cover'd with Orders — and all forlorn;
> THE DANDY OF SIXTY,
>   who bows with a grace,
> And has *taste* in wigs, collars,
>   cuirasses and lace:
> Who, to tricksters, and fools,
>   leaves the State and its treasure,
> And, when Britain's in tears,
>   sails about at his pleasure.

The treasure is the Magna Carta and the Bill of Rights; the tricksters and fools are Sidmouth, Castlereagh, and Canning; and the Prince Regent had truly gone sailing.[18] Thus factual details confirm the structure of oppression which Hone portrays. The ease with which Hone arranges information, his scathing lightness of touch, are immediately persuasive. The more one knows, the truer the parody becomes. The simplicity and quickness with which Hone mentions overwhelming difficulties ('when Britain's in tears') grants each

---

[18] Edgell Rickword's *Radical Squibs and Loyal Ripostes: Satirical Pamphlets of the Regency Period, 1819–1821*, Bath, 1971, annotates *The Political House*.

phrase a tremendous amount of strength even if it could otherwise be trite.

Similar to early eighteenth-century satire, *The Political House that Jack Built* could be called a modern, political *Dunciad*. Its extreme allusiveness proclaims the existence of an informed and critical public, sharing particular values, activities, and ideas. The allusions point out that the audience both shares a body of information and composes it within a similar analytical framework. Unlike *The Dunciad*, however, the parody does not make a virtue of excluding those without adequate knowledge to understand it fully. Although readers might not know that the Regent went sailing, their lack of information would not interfere with their reading of the poem. The simplicity of the language, the method of illustration, the parody's length, and its inexpensive price are reminiscent of the chap-book. Call it a chap-book *Dunciad* then, simultaneously esoteric and available to anyone. The language is basic and the sequence of illustration is significant in itself. Anyone who had heard of the massacre or who knew the original rhyme would find it meaningful.

This extreme demotic form is coupled with a vehemency of attack that is inconceivable in the 1790s. Hone was clearly unhindered by deference, or any trace of the concept of vulgarity. He does not fear that his audience will be provoked into uncontrolled behaviour by his writings, and he does not hesitate to portray the audience as it was at the massacre. The people are described with stark simplicity. After the illustration of the Prince Regent, the reader sees that of a dispirited and impoverished small group of people, whose fellow reformers are being attacked in the background:

> these are
> THE PEOPLE
> all tatter'd and torn,
> Who curse the day
> wherein they were born,
> On account of Taxation
> too great to be borne,
> And pray for relief,
> from night to morn;

Who, in vain, Petition
             in every form,
Who, peaceably Meeting
             to ask for Reform,
Were sabred by Yeomanry Cavalry,
             who,
Were thanked by THE MAN,
             all shaven and shorn,
All cover'd with Orders —
             and all forlorn;
The DANDY OF SIXTY
             who bows with a grace . . .

The formal capacities of the nursery rhyme are stretched to
the full as they align simplicity with artifice, innocence with
knowledge. The childish language, stripped of any refinement
or propriety, seems strangely naked, devoid of any vocabulary that might identify the speaker as a member of a
particular social group or class. Hone takes full advantage of
the disembodied voice of the original rhyme — the brief lines,
the unusually long single statement, the inevitability of its
rhythm, and the relentlessness of the syntax. In the 'House
that Jack Built', the chain of events leads to a marriage
between a tattered and torn man and a forlorn woman.
In the parody, the massacre occurs where the marriage ought
to have been.

The Political House is a creative analysis of information
made public by a national press which had only recently
come into being. Hone's creativity flourished in this interim
moment, between a restricted and a relatively free press,
between limited and advanced technology, and between
eighteenth- and nineteenth-century literary markets. Because
advances in technology were recent, Hone could produce *The
Political House* under conditions of two forms of production.
The growth of newspapers and the development of the
cylinder press allowed for a new allusiveness in radical
writings. Readers could be depended upon to know the
information that would enable them to recognize the
significance of particular phrases. Whereas in the 1790s,
radical writing was severely limited by the unavailability of

knowledge, this limitation no longer existed after 1815. *The Political House* was printed, however, on a wooden press and contained illustrations printed with a type of wood-block that had long been out of use and that had previously appeared only in chap-books and broadsheets. Hone adapted the old form of illustration to provide contemporary inexpensive prints that were first used in *The Political House*. Hone controlled and to some extent designed the illustrations, he wrote the text, he printed, published, and sold it. Wooden presses and even the more advanced Stanhope press were inexpensive to purchase and to operate, allowing relatively poor authors complete authorial control. Nor had advances in technology established new forms of constraint, such as the necessity of large investment, the division of labour, and the need for large sales. Hone was in the exceptional position of presenting a product which he entirely controlled to an informed public of various social classes.

In other respects, Hone occupies an interim moment. He demonstrates an unusual degree of flexibility by being able to take full advantage of both vulgar and refined cultures. He has Spence's freedom from the concept of vulgarity with the advantages of wider reading. He has Thelwall's wider reading without his dread of vulgarity. Hone writes as if the distinction between vulgarity and refinement had not imposed upon his capacity as a writer but rather contributed to it. He is impervious to linguistic hegemony in part because of the exceptional cultural conditions in which he grew up. Both popular and refined literature were available to him as a young reader as they were not to Thomas Spence or to the older William Cobbett. Hone writes with the advantages of eighteenth-century popular culture with its relatively distinct tradition of chap-books, ballads, broadsheets, and a few novels, such as *Pilgrim's Progress*, and without the major limitation of that culture, its confinement to a limited range of styles, genres, and themes. Traditional ideas about language had been challenged by changes in the market, by such writing styles as Thomas Paine's, and by a radical theory of language. Hone grew up in the midst of this radical and evolving culture, before the audience existed in such numbers that a new mass culture was created for it. Growing up with newspapers and with refined, political, and popular literature not only available but largely thriving, Hone co-ordinates them as if they were self-evidently parts of a unified, organic whole.

In his unfinished autobiography, Hone describes a much richer and more varied culture than other self-educated writers who similarly describe their initial encounters with books.[19] Born during the Gordon Riots (3 June 1780), he grew up in London during the 1790s. The contrast between the few books owned by his parents and the variety of books Hone owned himself is telling. The Bible, a cookery book, a book of farriery, some religious pamphlets, and a 'mutilated' copy of *Paradise Lost* were owned by Hone's family. For four years, Hone studied reading and writing from the Bible. The first book he owned himself was *Pilgrim's Progress*, a book which astounded Hone as it did many others. During the French Revolution, Hone's family began to take a daily paper which Hone read aloud to his mother and her sister. His family bought the Association's pamphlets, and Hone's first published writing was distributed by the Association. Written when he was twelve, the broadsheet included a poem which is indistinguishable from those written by adults for the Association. The child had a peculiar ability to be precociously crude:

> Come Britons unite, and in one Common Cause
> Stand up in defence of King, Liberty, Laws;
> And rejoice that we've got such a good Constitution
> And down with the barbarous French Revolution!
>
> (cited by Hackwood, p. 45)

Other early reading included gruesome Protestant works, detailing the joys of persecution and death. Foxe's *Book of Martyrs*, and James Janeway's *A Token for Children* had a strong effect on him. The latter was distributed without cost by the Society for the Promotion of Christian Knowledge among the Poor. Little stories describe the children weeping for their sins and then dying gladly. The introduction entices

[19] Reprinted in Frederick W. Hackwood's *William Hone His Life and Times*, 1912, pp. 13–60.

young readers to confess their 'miserable state of nature' to sympathetic adults: 'Come, tell me truly, my dear child; for I would fain do what I can possibly to keep thee from falling into ever lasting fire'.[20] No wonder that Thomson's *Seasons* and Goldsmith's poems struck him as delightful. At thirteen, Hone began to read poetry in John Cooke's editions. His generation was the first to have refined poetry more readily available. The new radical literature was also an unprecedented cultural resource. His father's gift of Bishop Watson's *Apology for the Bible* introduced Hone to the possibility of scepticism and led him to read Paine's *Age of Reason*. Soon, Hone became a convert to the New Philosophy, that contemporary sin without a name, more bluntly referred to as Godwinism. Inspired by reading the *Tryal of John Lilburn*, Hone decided to become a lawyer in order to defend 'Constitutional Law', an ambition which he would eventually fulfil but not as he first intended.

Nor was Hone's early culture confined to reading. At the age of six, Hone met John Wesley under bizarre circumstances. Visiting his ill teacher, Hone watched the famous Methodist prepare her for death. Hone attended church with his father for many years and heard the sermons of the Revd William Huntingdon, a famous preacher and voluminous writer. Hone began buying second-hand books and poking around bookstalls at a young age. From his account, various people were receptive towards him and responsive to his curiosity. One neighbour, a cobbler, had a collection of fragments of old books printed in the heavy Gothic type known as black-letter. Another neighbour, a copperplate engraver, let Hone watch him work and examine his prints which Hone did for three years. Illustration and the black-letter press were interests which Hone developed later in his career. At fourteen he became a member of the London Corresponding Society and attended various debating clubs until his father, a lawyer's clerk, insisted upon his leaving the dangerous influences of the city. Growing up in the midst of radical London familiarized Hone with ideas which were once new and disturbing but now more confidently and

[20] 1797, p. vii.

surely held. Hone, for one, had the advantage of coming after Thomas Spence. He kept a wary and interested eye on the extremist and in 1830, sent Francis Place an account of his knowledge and opinion of him. In 1800 Hone watched Spence being arrested by Bow Street Runners.[21] Hone must have been twenty years old at the time — a young adult of the second generation watching the first and little knowing that his future lay precisely there.

Arrested on 3 May 1817, on three ex-officio informations, Hone appeared to be charged before Lord Ellenborough on three counts of blasphemous libel. Hone had printed three parodies based on the church service: *The Late John Wilkes's Catechism, The Political Litany,* and *The Sinecurists' Creed.* Only· the *Sinecurists' Creed* was written by Hone, a fact which had no bearing on the trials. Because Hone could not afford the extravagant bail of £1,000, he was imprisoned for five months. Released in September, he was not informed when or if his trials would take place. Despite the overhanging threat, he continued to publish satires which strongly criticized the government but soon stopped publishing his two-penny paper, the *Reformist Register* (1 Feb. to 17 Oct. 1817). Held on 17, 18, and 19 December Hone's trials were a resounding success for Hone and for his audience. Hone, however, was not invigorated by his victory, and published no more satires for a year. From 1819 to 1823, he published and wrote numerous pamphlets attacking the government and supporting reform: *The Queen's Matrimonial Ladder, a National Toy; Hone's Political Showman — At Home!; A Political Christmas Carol; Non Mi Recordo; A Slap at Slop and the Bridge St. Gang;* and *The Bank Restriction Barometer* among them.

Soon he was permanently silenced by vicious articles in the *Quarterly Review.* In his *Apocryphal New Testament* (1820), Hone published Apocryphal stories of the Bible and introduced them with a discussion of how and when the Apocrypha were excluded from the texts which achieved sacred status. Such knowledge was previously available to scholars, and the *Quarterly Review* denounced Hone, among

---

[21] BL Add. MS 27808, fo. 314.

other things, for casting doubt on the sacredness of Scripture in a book that did not have a limited audience.[22] Initially deciding not to reply, Hone responded in 1824 with *Aspersions Answered*. The *Quarterly Review* retaliated by reviewing it (lxi (1824), 472-81), and William Hone replied with *Another Article for the Quarterly Review* (1824). In *Aspersions Answered*, Hone states that hè will write only one more book, presumably his history of parody and popular literature which was to be his final vindication from the charge of blasphemy. After spending a great deal of time and money on the project, Hone was forced to sell his collected material when he went bankrupt in 1826. For two years, he lived within the rules of King's Bench. Although he wrote no more books, he compiled and edited several. Too scarred to be willingly contentious, he announces in his *Every-Day Book* that his ambition is to 'communicate in an agreeable Manner, the greatest possible variety of important and diverting facts without a single sentence to arouse an uneasy sensation, or an embarassing enquiry.'[23] *The Every-Day Book* (1825-6), *The Table Book* (1827), and *The Year Book* (1832) are anthologies that portray a full and varied cultural life of popular legends, customs, and traditions.

In 1832, Hone became increasingly religious and was accepted formally into the church two years later. A poem describing his new faith describes also his new belief that his political opponents had correctly identified him as God's enemy. There, Hone surrenders his will and his pen to God:

> The proudest heart that ever beat
> Hath been subdued in me;
> The wildest will that ever rose
> To scorn Thy cause and aid Thy foes
> Is quelled, my God, by Thee.
>
> Thy will, and not my will be done;
> My heart be ever Thine —
> Confessing thee, the mighty Word,

---

[22] xxv (1820), 348-65.
[23] *The Every Day Book and Table Book; or the Everlasting Calender of Popular Amusements,* 1837, 2 vols., p. viii.

> I hail Thee, Christ, my God, my Lord,
> And make Thy name my sign.
>
> (cited by Hackwood, p. 343)

His is a life of painful victories and welcomed defeats, his last poem a sad judgement of what he once thought of as his moral integrity. The burst of creativity from 1819-23 was accompanied by and succeeded with a profound discomfort concerning his notoriety, not as a radical but as a blasphemer and aetheist. As was Coleridge, Hone was extremely sensitive to the charge of irreligion.

Nor did he have the hardness of head that protected other radical writers such as Richard Carlile and William Cobbett. Many others beside Hone suffered from the slanders and the persecutions of the state, but because Hone participated in literary culture, he was vulnerable in perhaps different ways and gained enemies of yet another kind. An exceptional literary radical, Hone was angered by the active opposition of the literati to the reform movement. Southey, Coleridge, Wordsworth, John Murray, Sir Walter Scott, and the *Quarterly Review* appear in his satires along with government ministers. (William Hazlitt, John Hunt, and Charles Lamb were his friends.) Whereas Cobbett's books were greeted with complete, stony silence by the major reviewers, the *Quarterly Review* attacked Hone's with the insults which were already familiar to him from the newspaper press and personal encounters. The reviewer describes him as 'a poor illiterate creature, far too ignorant to have any share in the composition either of this, or of his seditious pamphlets. He only supplies the evil will and the audacity'.[24] If Hone had been less 'literary', critics might have been more capable of believing in his existence as an author. He might have had Cobbett's slightly better luck of being entirely ignored rather than given this virulent attention. Cobbett could be more readily ignored in part because his practice as a writer did not disrupt the relation of language to class. Cobbett usually specified the social status of his audience and addressed it accordingly. Hone's satires were more obviously literary and written for any and everyone. His imaginative use of

[24] xxv (1824), 362.

vernacular language, his ability to make mundane forms significant such as nursery rhymes, toys, and banknotes, and his ability to learn from the literati without sacrificing his attention to his audience were extraordinary skills that denied the restrictive basis of concepts of language and literature.

Hone thus wrote in the midst of major cultural disruptions concerning the conditions of production, the distribution of literary texts, governmental interference with the press, and the relation of language to class. It was neither a comfortable nor a lasting position to occupy. Not only did Hone eventually deny his own worth as a writer but few people appear to have learned from him after numerous imitators of the early 1820s. It could be argued that he contributed to the resources of innovative novelists such as Thackeray and Dickens, and that his adaptation of wood-block printing continued to provide an inexpensive form of illustration, but as a political writer he left few traces. Perhaps his position was too anomalous, too contradictory for either himself or others to sustain.

Hone's three trials articulate the political and social pressures which such writers encountered. Hegemony of language gains an unusually discernible form as the Attorney-General and the Judge attempt to prove that Hone's language is sufficiently indecent and improper to be criminal. Although the vocabulary to describe vulgar language tended to shift from 'barbaric' and 'vulgar' to 'indecent' and 'improper' between the 1790s and 1817, the concept remained largely the same and served the same purpose of defining the inadequacy of various classes according to their language. Had Hone lost his trials, such vague concepts would have gained legal currency, becoming evidence of criminality in themselves. The prosecution expected an easy victory but Hone had unforeseen resources. To defend himself, Hone applied the literature of his own culture and based his standards of language on the literature of his class. His familiarity with popular literature enabled him to withstand the arguments of the prosecution by providing him with a vernacular language that he knew was not vulgar and with conventions of an appropriate genre, that of trial literature. *The Three Trials of William Hone*, the edited and published account of the trials, is of interest because it enacts a conflict of ideas about language and because it is a work of literature in itself, dependent on previous literary works for its rhetoric and conventions. Rapidly, however, the two become entangled for the tradition which Hone relied upon records previous conflicts of language and class.

Hone's self-defence was literary in that he knew his trial would be published, and he was already an experienced writer of trial literature. During the course of any major trial, the participants understood that their speeches were being recorded in shorthand and that an edited version of the transcript could be sold as a pamphlet. Radicals would frequently take advantage of the trial as a public forum to express political ideas that had no direct bearing on the charges against them. The intensely dramatic situation of a political trial made their words all the more vivid and all the more avidly read. Hone published each of his three trials singly and in a collected edition in 1818. *The Times* published a great deal of the proceedings in transcript, and thousands of people attended the trials themselves or waited in the streets. This degree of excitement is not hard to understand. The publication of political trials combined the suspense and the thrill of criminal literature with a contest of ideas that were then receiving a great deal of public attention. They were intellectual thrillers, if you will. The odds were uneven, either the state or the individual was seriously threatened, and the outcome was momentous. The plot of a poor, self-educated character defending himself against the state had the potential excitement of the battle of David and Goliath. When such writers could credibly portray themselves as defending that treasure of British liberty, the freedom of the press, they had a good deal of narrative clout on their side.

Hone was fully aware that trials were exciting vehicles of political education. Before his trial he had published several broadsheets and pamphlets concerning important trials: *The Trial of Lord Cochrane of Guildford, August 17, 1816;*

The Report of the Coroner's Inquest on Jane Watson; The Case of Elizabeth Fenning; and *Hone's Interesting History of the Memorable Blood Conspiracy*. Although such titles appear to be sensationalist fare, Hone applied the familiar format to discuss politically sensitive issues. Lord Cochrane was a radical member of Parliament, Jane Watson had been shot by a soldier who was accused of murder, and the *Blood Conspiracy* discusses the government's practice of rewarding informers who had encouraged victims to commit a crime. Hone thus performed within the recognizable genre of trial literature with a degree of flexibility. His awareness of the status of trial literature as a genre is most evident in his writing a parody of one. After publishing *The Noble Lord's Bite and his Dangerous Condition*, Hone wrote *Another Ministerial Defeat. The Trial of the Dog for Biting the Noble Lord*. The dog's name is 'Honesty'.

A self-defended trial is both actually and metaphorically a literary event, analogous to the act of writing a book. Several other writers, Cobbett, Wooler, and Carlile among them, also chose to defend themselves. It was a long and arduous act, demanding a great deal of authorial skill in the midst of extreme pressure. Defendants had to invent themselves as characters while standing in front of their audience, one that would soon pronounce judgement. Compared to the judge and jury, literary critics and readers might appear tame. The two characters portrayed by the defendant and the prosecution contend for control of the plot and its interpretation. Moving rhetoric, convincing narration, and effective characterization must be maintained in order to control the thoughts and reactions of the jury. In Hone's trials especially, literary tradition plays a distinct part, contributing to his defence as evidence, as rhetoric, and as a point of reference for imagery and allusions. Accused of blasphemous libel, Hone bases his defence on the existence of a vast quantity of parodies which had never been judged blasphemous. Each day of the three trials, Hone walked into the courtroom with an armful of books from which he recited parodies and other adaptations of biblical language for non-sacred purposes. Describing himself during the first trial, he stated, 'He had his books about him, and it was from them that he must draw his defence. They had been the solace of his life'.[25] As well as using parodies as evidence, Hone's rhetoric relies heavily on the literature he had read as a child. To a remarkable degree he speaks within the recognizable traditions, rhetoric, and conventions of books which had a reputation as the classics of popular literature. Thus, he defends himself not only by considering the legality of his action but by asserting the strength of his audience's literary traditions.

Hone's own satirical pamphlets sometimes function as a literary tradition in the course of the trials. Hone's major subject as a writer was the government's unwarranted suspicions of the lower and middling classes. Inevitably, several of the figures discussed or present during the trials had already been satirized in one or more of Hone's pamphlets. *The Political Litany,* one of the pamphlets for which Hone was tried, satirizes Lord Sidmouth, the Secretary to the Home Office who was responsible for Hone's prosecution. So does *Bartholomew Fair Insurrection or the Piebald Poney Plot,* where Hone mocks Sidmouth for believing the misguided advice of an informer. Cruickshank's illustration of Sidmouth on the title-page, riding a hobby horse and waving noise-makers, depicts what Hone considered to be the ferocious attention which Sidmouth gave to the lower orders. The previous existence of Hone's pamphlets and broadsheets alters the nature of his self-defence. When Hone exclaims, 'A parody was never seized before. Why was his parody now attacked? Was it because Lord Sidmouth was the only good Secretary for the Home Department' (3rd, 174), Hone's characterization of Sidmouth in *Bartholomew Fair* extends the absurdity of Hone's meaning. Hone had also caricatured Lord Ellenborough, the notorious Judge who presided at two of Hone's trials. In the inverse of the usual state of things, the real people mentioned or present during Hone's trials allude to quasi-fictional characters. By referring to government officials, Hone refers to characters which he had to some extent invented.

As a literary artifact, Hone's three trials waver between allegory and farce. Once, even Lord Ellenborough smiles.

[25] *The Three Trials of William Hone,* ed. William Tegg, 1876, 1st, 23.

Other factors besides Hone's previous satires contribute to the intermittent and sometimes grim comedy. An air of distortion pervades the trials. Prosecuted on ex-officio information, Hone could hardly be considered a danger to the state. He had withdrawn the parodies from sale on 22 February, several months before he was charged and ten months before he was tried. Only by relying on bloated rhetoric could the Attorney-General maintain that the state was threatened: 'The pamphlet before the jury was so injurious in its tendency, and so disgusting in its form, that any man, on the first reading, would start (he had almost said) with horror from it; it was like an infecting pestilence, which every man shunned that valued his safety' (1st, 65). The prosecution more than once must prove what is obviously untrue. Hone adds to the distorted air of the trial by confessing to seditious libel: 'if there was ridicule, those who rendered themselves ridiculous, however high their station, had no right to cry out because they were ridiculed. He *intended* to laugh at them.' (2nd, 126.) Inappropriately charged with blasphemy, Hone was probably the only radical in history who could legitimately defend himself by claiming that he had attacked the state. According to Hone, the parody of scriptural language was not intended to ridicule the church but to make his criticism of the state more emphatic:

> *Spare us, good Prince.*
> From an unnational debt; from unmerited pensions and sinecure places; from an extravagant civil list; and from utter starvation,
> *Good Prince, deliver us.*
> From the blind imbecility of ministers; from the pride and vain-glory of warlike establishments in time of peace,
> *Good Prince, deliver us.*
> From all the deadly sins attendant on a corrupt method of election; from all the deceits of the pensioned hirelings of the press,
> *Good Prince, deliver us.* (2nd, 78)

And so on. In considerable length and brave detail, Hone discusses the validity of the *Litany's* supplications. The Attorney-General's claim, most succinctly stated during the first trial, that 'it has nothing of a political tendency about it' is hardly convincing (1st, 2). By charging Hone on religious grounds for reasons that were recognizably political, the prosecution cannot avoid sounding hypocritical and dishonest.

Both the Judge and the Attorney-General repeatedly claim that all parodies of scriptural language are by nature libellous, although neither can point to a trial in which one was judged to be so. Ellenborough maintains that Hone cannot refer to previous parodies as evidence without first proving their innocence, a difficult proposition as none were judged illegal. Hone points out that if all religious parodies are libellous then those which favoured the administration should also be charged, including a parody of the Te Deum, translated into five languages, and distributed among the armies fighting Napoleon at the expense of the government:

> Oh, Emperor of France! we curse thee.
> We acknowledge thee to be a Tyrant.
> Thou murdering Infidel! all the world detest thee.
> To thee all nations cry aloud,
> BONEY, BONEY, BONEY! (1st, 42)

Despite a good deal of intimidation, neither Hone nor the three juries could be made to believe that a traditional and accepted genre had suddenly become criminal or that the main object of Hone's parodies was to ridicule the church. The court's attempt to prove the unprovable falls into Hone's skilful and satirical hands.

In the course of the three trials, the parodies themselves become relatively insignificant by no longer being the cause for argument but rather the objects around which more important arguments are made. In order to prove Hone's guilt, the court must prove that Hone, his reading audience, and their literary tradition are criminally indecent. At every possible occasion, the Attorney-General and the Judge assert an unbridgeable gulf between what the court assumes to be normal and the deviance of Hone's standards. Some such comments were conventional, such as the Attorney-General's claim that the inexpensive price of the pamphlets demonstrates that they were intended to have a dangerous effect upon the ignorant. To maintain the alleged difference between Hone's audience and the standards of the court, his audience must be portrayed as class specific and as incapable of moral control:

> If any of you, gentlemen, be fathers, and wish your children to hold in reverence the sacred subjects of Christian belief, read these publications of the defendant, and say if you would put them into the hands of those children you love. If you would not put them into their hands, would you into those of the lower classes of society, which are not fit to cope with the sort of topics which are artfully raised for them? (1st, 4)

These standard comments gain a sharper and more dangerous edge during Hone's trial because a great number of parodies and humorous pieces are described as illegal or indecent in the course of the trial. Not only the specific parodies but any literature that could be described as 'improper' was under threat. Moreover such comments were directed at an author whose language and writing were based on that allegedly vulgar tradition, without the intermediary of a lawyer. Hone must bear the insult and defend himself against it. The Judge, during his summation to the jury, describes the language and traditions of the court as essentially different from Hone's. According to Ellenborough, Hone necessarily defended himself because no lawyer 'would outrage decency and propriety so far as to exhibit such disgusting parodies and prints' (3rd, 193). The prosecution attempts to prove Hone's criminality by asserting ever stricter concepts of propriety. Even laughter becomes revolutionary: 'If the social bonds of society are to be burst asunder by the indecent conduct of a rabble, the Court may as well discontinue its proceedings' (2nd, 75). The concept which the Judge and the Attorney-General apply to define legal culture cannot describe the genre under discussion or the literary and social world as Hone knew it to be.

Hone's practice as publisher and the genre of parody in themselves contradicted notions of refinement. To an unusual extent, Hone's style and practice as a publisher was not class specific. To refute the Attorney-General, Hone argues that the inexpensive price of the parodies did not indicate the class composition of the audience but simply the standard price for that many sheets. He says that the parodies were sold to the 'uneducated' and to 'persons of high standing in that Court — to Magistrates of the City of London — to Members of Parliament, and even to his Majesty's Ministers' (2nd, 85). The scriptural language on which the parodies are based presents a model of language that could include an audience of such various social classes and language skills. Religious language contradicts the notion that an inseparable gulf exists between the language of different classes. As in the originals of the Catechism, the Litany, and the Athanasian Creed, the parodies imply that people are united in their beliefs and aspirations and that class is insignificant. The parodies convey the implication of an undifferentiated audience both in their language and in the analogy between the readers and a congregation. By naming the people who wrote such parodies, Hone disproves the court's argument that only disreputable people are capable of such an act. He points out that parodies had been written by respected and deeply religious people. Martin Luther, Dr Boys, Lord Somers, and Bishop Latimer had written them without anyone suspecting that they intended to ridicule religion. More recently the government had sponsored the publication of parodies and had rewarded those who wrote them. John Reeves, founder of the Association for preserving Liberty and Property against Republicans and Levellers, had been rewarded with the government office of Printer of the Prayer Book, despite having published a parody of the Catechism (1st, 36). The *Anti-Jacobin* had published many parodies in the 1790s and a collection of its writings had been sponsored by Pitt and other Cabinet ministers. Canning's parody, 'The New Morality: or the installation of the High Priest', famous for its attack on 'C---dge and S--th-y, L---d and L--be, and Co.', especially offended Hone because Canning, who was famous for his sarcastic eloquence, was a member of the Cabinet which was responsible for Hone's prosecution.

Unable to assert vulgarity by the price, the character of the author, or the class of the audience, the prosecution relies upon the prevalent assumption that English had changed significantly. Hone could not rely upon earlier parodies because they were now 'too indecent for the ears of any persons in these times' (3rd, 164). Such an idea might characterize the refined language, but from Hone's perspective language had not fundamentally changed. Because Hone determines the texts which he and the prosecution will consider, the discrepancy between the Judge's concept of modern, proper language and language as Hone knew it becomes starkly apparent. Hone recites a song in which religion is represented as a woman, and sectarianism as two men fighting over her. One sectarian is a sceptic who argues:

> That all the books of Moses
> Were nothing but supposes;
> That he deserved rebuke, sir,
> Who wrote the Pentateuch, sir;
> 'Twas nothing but a sham.
> 'Twas nothing but a sham.

> That as for father Adam,
> With Mrs. Eve, his madam,
> And what the serpent spoke, sir,
> 'Twas nothing but a joke, sir,
> And well-invented flam,
> [And well-invented flam.]

(1st, 32 and 2nd, 104)

The song concludes with religion leaving both of the men fighting among each other. The language throughout is simple and innocent enough, although not solemn and respectful. During the second trial, when Hone reaches this point in reciting the song, Lord Ellenborough forbids him to continue:

LE: That is such mischievous matter that I shall prohibit its being read. No person, under pretence of explaining one libel, shall offend the ears of public decency by the recital of such profanations. . . .

H: I pledge myself that the few lines of the song I have not read have a perfectly moral tendency.

LE: I will not hear them. It would deserve severe punishment if it were a modern publication.

H: My Lord, it has been published over and over again of late years, and no notice taken of it.

LE: I am sorry for it: mischievous people are to be found at all times.

H: The Rev. Mark Noble, the author, is a beneficed clergyman of the Church of England, and, I venture to say, has no sense of the impropriety. (2nd, 104-5)

In such debates, the notion of a recognizably vulgar language spoken by disreputable people fails to account for either the literature or the people who wrote it. The notion of a modern, monolithic language of propriety disregards the republication of earlier works, the diversity of the ways in which people speak, and the continuance of traditions and values that do not accord with hegemonic ones. Hone reveals that the concept of vulgarity is not identifiable with a particular class, that 'crude' language does not define the sensibility of the speaker, and that English had not become a language that is significantly different from its earlier forms. No wonder Hone admired Tooke's work. On very different terrains, they formulated similar arguments.

Especially during the last two trials, the contest between Hone and the prosecution becomes a drama of class conflict enacted in the public forum of the court. The social condescension evident in the tone and gestures of the prosecution has greater scope than that of a personal insult, because behind it lies the disregard of a class and a culture. When Hone argues that vast quantities of literature exist that the prosecution's comments do not take into account, Judge Abbot (presiding during the first trial) replies that it ought not to exist: 'I don't care what the common people have had for centuries. If the publication be profane, it ought not to be tolerated.' (1st, 44.) Hone refers here to a broadsheet of a Christmas carol that was printed with the claim that the carol had been miraculously found under a stone in Jerusalem. When Hone recites a verse saying that he had heard it often as a child, he explains that it might be considered 'ludicrous' but not profane:

> The first good joy our Mary had,
> It was the joy of one;
> To see her own child, Jesus,
> To suck at her breast bone. (1st, 45)

The Attorney-General *'here manifested great uneasiness'*. Hone comforts him by stating that the carol had been sung for centuries and that millions of copies had been published with 'no effect upon the most ignorant' (1st, 45).

To withstand the prosecution's assessment of his language, Hone retaliates by defining a language of corruption that contrasts sharply with his own. Gillray and Canning have greater linguistic freedom because they serve the state. When Hone points out that Gillray published cartoons based on scripture while receiving a pension, the Judge replies:

ABBOT: But, if you can prove that he, being pensioned, published those things, will that form a defence for you?
HONE: My Lord, I have no pension. (1st, 58)

Such a remark is typical of Hone's apparent innocence, disguising a confident appraisal of the relation of language to class. What the court portrays as decent language, Hone portrays as a superficial refinement that protects the state. Canning, whose parliamentary eloquence frequently justified repressive legislation, represents for Hone the utmost of hypocrisy and rhetorical glitter (3rd, 168). To contrast himself with such speakers, Hone emphasizes his solitary position and portrays the verbal ease of Canning, Sidmouth, and company as a fluency derived from corrupt co-operation. Hone, the poor, uneducated, honest man, defending himself against the combined resources and talents of the state, must vindicate himself, his publications, the literature of his class, and its language.

The third trial differs from the others in that Hone defends himself not merely by discussing the works of his class, but by speaking according to them. His accurate portrayal of himself as a poor man without resources becomes a matter of portraying himself according to the narratives that he had read as a child. He sounds, acts, and imagines himself to be an early protestant Dissenter such as Foxe, Bunyan, or Lilburne. It is this literary culture which steers Hone through his final trial. Exhausted by having spoken for six hours one day, and seven the next, Hone is described as 'exceedingly ill and exhausted' as the trial begins (3rd, 138). Previously, he had never spoken to a group of more than ten people. The unfamiliarity of the situation and its relentless repetition appear to have been nightmarish. As he described it later,

'The third day I spoke like a man in a dream. I spoke and felt carried out of myself by the subject but I knew not what I said'.[26] His defence accords with this description by being exceptionally personal, imaginative, vehement. Part of the excitement in reading it lies in the evident danger that Hone might not have sufficient strength to continue and that his vehemence might degenerate into hysteria. Hone maintains the coherence and control that his imagination grants him throughout a long and often eloquent defence. By relying on a unified tradition, Hone discovers a means of understanding his situation and a determinedly political, vulgar language.

References and allusions shift from contemporary London to the late seventeenth century. During the first two trials, Hone defends himself as a representative of the population: 'I say, on behalf of the whole people of England, that to those who may be placed in my situation, it is a great grievance' (2nd, 94). The antagonism between himself and members of the government is considered in class terms, according to contemporary political perspectives. Thus Hone states that if Canning had been 'in the humble situation of him (the defendant) in society, he would this day, instead of sitting in the Cabinet, have been standing before his lordship and the jury' (2nd, 93). On both days, he frequently mentions political conflicts and practices which infringed on the civil liberties of himself and his audience. Hone mentions these during the third trial as well but with less frequency and less intensity. He characterizes his predicament primarily as one of a religious persecution in response to which he pleads for charity and tolerance. The religious significance of the number three and the spiritual meaning of the word 'trial' gather rhetorical momentum. Canning's exemption from punishment is now portrayed as a spiritual failing: 'Mr. Canning ought to have been a willing witness for him on the present occasion; he ought to come into the witness box to confess his own sins' (3rd, 163). Hone no longer claims an identity as a representative citizen but as a solitary figure

---

[26] *Some Account of the Conversion of the Late William Hone*, ed. F. W. Rolleston, 1853, p. 41.

allied with God against the worldly power and spiritual tyranny of Sidmouth, Ellenborough, and Canning:

> If Providence ever interfered to protect weak and defenceless men, that interference was most surely manifested in his case. It had interposed to protect a helpless and defenceless man against the rage and malice of his enemies. He could attribute his defence to no other agent, for he was weak and incapable, and was at the moment a wonder unto himself. (3rd, 153-4)

Even several references to contemporary events contribute to the pervasive air of earlier forms of political conflict. The recent publication of the Stuart papers reminds Hone of an earlier tyrranical age: 'The Stuarts must be excused and spoken gently of; they must not be talked of as the tyrants, the hypocrites, the bloody-minded persecutors they really were. Such language was unacceptable to courtly taste.' (3rd, 184.) A bill to prohibit preaching among the Dissenters also bridged the past and the present: 'Lord Sidmouth had before tried his hand at persecution, when he brought in his bill against the Dissenters. The same noble lord left him to stand three days in that Court.' (3rd, 184.) While considering the sanctity of the Athanasian Creed, Ellenborough and Hone discuss the Act of Uniformity passed in 1662 (3rd, 185). Thus, restraints on liberty are frequently defined in the combined religious and political terms of earlier conflicts, even when contemporary events are discussed. Throughout the trial, Hone repeatedly turns the present into the past by a play upon two similar words: 'My prosecutors, my persecutors, are unrelenting' (3rd, 159).

Rather than being the representatives of the state with fearsome powers, Hone's antagonists become allegorical figures whose strength is limited by their evil natures. As he describes them in Bunyanesque terms, Hone guides the narrative, for ultimately, as in any allegory, description controls the plot: innocence is victory. Hone's ability to imitate *Pilgrim's Progress* skilfully seems in itself a source of courage. It enables him to appropriate Christian's story and to perceive his opponents within a controlled sphere of meaning:

It was hoped, he had no doubt, by certain very grave members of the Cabinet (my Lord Sidmouth and my Lord Liverpool), that William Hone could not stand the third day — that he would sink under his fatigues and want of physical power. "He can't stand the third trial," said these humane and Christian Ministers; "we shall have him now; he must be crushed." (Great shouts of applause.) Oh no! no! he must not be crushed; you cannot crush him . . . There is nothing can crush me, but my own sense of doing wrong . . . but when I have done no wrong, when I am right, I am as an armed man; and in this spirit I wage battle with the Attorney-General, taking a tilt with him here on the floor of this Court. The consciousness of my innocence gives me life, spirits, and strength, to go through this third ordeal of persecution and oppression. (3rd, 163–4)

As in Bunyan's descriptions, characters occupy two worlds; spiritually evil, they are politically and socially coercive. The victorious cry of 'we shall have him now' echoes that of Apollyon's as he almost defeats Christian who, like Hone, fights his enemy with a sword and is almost crushed to death before he regains the strength that derives from his innocence:

Then said Apollyon, 'I am sure of thee now,' and with that he had almost pressed him to death, so that Christian began to despair of his life. But as God would have it, while Apollyon was fetching his last blow thereby to make full end of this good man, Christian nimbly reached out his hand for his sword, and caught it saying, *'Rejoice not against me, O mine enemy! when I fall I shall arise.'*[27]

The specificity of the allusion is striking but of less importance than the diffuse and central position of *Pilgrim's Progress* in the third trial as a whole. By relying on *Pilgrim's Progress*, Hone finds a language and an imagery which enable him to make sense out of an intense and dangerous situation, a language which his audience was apt to recognize and apparently appreciated ('Great shouts of applause'). The biblical allusions, the colloquial language, and the allegorical imagery of the third trial fabricate a new fiction — an entire imaginative portrayal which finally reduces the Judge and others to the status of characters in a setting which Hone defines.

[27] *Pilgrim's Progress*, ed. Roger Sharrock, 1965, pp. 93–4.

Although *Pilgrim's Progress, The Tryal of John Lilburn*, and the *Book of Martyrs* contribute individually to the rhetoric and imagery of Hone's trial, they also contribute collectively, as a tradition formed by a common history and language. Throughout the third trial, Hone's language approaches that of a late-comer to the culture of early protestant dissent. Such expressions as 'he who runs may read' and 'we hoped to throw a grain into the earth which might become a great tree' are self-consciously old-fashioned, even by nineteenth-century standards (3rd, 147, 160). The stark simplicity of Hone's vocabulary, its concreteness, an abundance of metaphor, the frequent biblical references, and a dependence on sincerity for rhetorical power are not the features of formal, early nineteenth-century language, or even of the predominant language of Hone's first trial. Metaphors of being caught, trapped, and crushed (3rd, 148, 167, 183) occur with exceptional frequency in the third trial and recall Christian's extreme vulnerability. Images of violent assault also often appear in Lilburne's and Foxe's texts. Lilburne imagines himself as 'ensnarred', trapped, or knocked upon the head.[28] In Foxe's book, the vulnerability of the Martyrs is more literal, but metaphors of physical threat are also commonplace. Although it was not a current political problem, the aggressive acts of religious persecution evoke Hone's most indignant language. His sensitivity to persecution, a word which appears relentlessly in the third trial, presumably was prompted by his early reading of the *Book of Martyrs*. After giving an account of torture for atheism in Poland, Hone continues, 'Who, O Who (cried Mr. Hone, raising his voice to a tone of the utmost vehemence), who were the blasphemers? Who were the Atheists? Were they not the bloody-minded men who called themselves Christians, rather than the defenceless man whom they put to death.' (3rd, 175.) This pitch of excitement cannot be accounted for by the legal problem of Hone's defence. His outrage has significance because of his fictive portrayal of his trial in sixteenth or seventeenth-century terms. It is an instance of the subject suiting the language, of religious

[28] *The Tryal of Lieutenant Colonel John Lilburn*, ed. Theodorus Verax, 2nd edn., 1710, pp. 13, 21, 24.

persecution being described in a speech that often reverts to earlier forms of discourse. In the third trial, Hone interweaves colloquial with biblical language much as Bunyan does in *Pilgrim's Progress*: 'When in the King's Bench, he was shunned as a pestilence, even by those who were, or pretended to be, formerly his friends — by those whom, as David said of Jonathan, his heart loved' (3rd, 154). John Lilburne similarly defines himself by absorbing scriptural language into his own: 'to their [the jury's] Consciences, and to their Judgements, I leave both this Matter, and the constant Series of all my Actions in this my Pilgrimage, and Vale of Tears here below' (p. 116). By speaking in terms that would be anachronistic if they were less persuasive, Hone discovers a vernacular language that is not vulgar and that the prosecution fails to acknowledge.

By its reversion to a style of language which Hone had learned by reading old books, his third defence suggests how little contemporary modes of discourse had to offer him. The possibility of an uneducated man or perhaps of anyone successfully opposing a judge such as Ellenborough while speaking according to the prosecution's understanding of language, is unlikely indeed. To accord with the Judge's standard of propriety, Hone could not have quoted any previous parodies of religious works. Even language based on scripture is designated as inappropriate. In the second trial, the Attorney-General states: 'The Scriptures should be looked upon with a sacred eye, and never used for secular purposes' (2nd, 131). Theories of language and books of rhetoric also argued that biblical language was unsuitable for contemporary usage. The third defence as a whole can be seen as a reply to the Attorney-General's comment, as a *tour de force* of an answer revealing the centrality of the Bible as a model of vernacular discourse. To erase biblical language from literary works would leave many blank spaces, as Hone points out. For the self-educated, its erasure would be more drastic, for the Bible was often the only text from which they learned to read and write, as it was for Hone. More formally educated readers did not have a text which so singly contributed to their learning of the written language. Hone's third defence demonstrates his explicit reply to the Attorney-

General's comment, 'He on all occasions made frequent use of the language of Scripture. That proceeded from his intimate acquaintance with it.' (3rd, 175.)

From a seemingly neutral, moral language of scripture which the state was attempting to claim for its own purposes, Hone forms a language that can politically protect him. In the course of his three trials, he discovers an alternative tradition and brings it forward by his enactment of its language. Because few texts were written in a vernacular language after the Restoration, books by protestant Dissenters occupied a dominant place in the literature of Hone's class. The isolation of the audience with a few radical texts was an irony of the supremacy of the refined language. Read by children as well as adults, Foxe's *Book of Martyrs* and *Pilgrim's Progress* had powerful effects because their impact was not dissipated by many other texts written at calmer moments. The meagre supply of books helped to construct and maintain a coherent popular tradition that vividly portrayed antagonism towards the state and the strength of vernacular English. In the nineteenth century, a plethora of books designed ('calculated' was the term) for children and for the lower classes would correct this oversight of the refined tradition. For different reasons, William Cobbett also opposed the tradition of radical protestantism. To refute Malthusian attitudes towards the poor, Cobbett wrote his *History of the Protestant "Reformation"*,[29] in which he argues that pre-Reformation Catholics had treated the poor with greater humanity than either the modern church or state. He reduces the Protestants to a group of greedy men who disguised their worldly motives by claiming to be moral. He denounces their reputation as the defenders of political liberty and the text which glorified them, the *Book of Martyrs.* Hone's trial demonstrates how valuable such a tradition could be. By relying on biblical language and its variant, the language of radical protestantism, Hone reveals that his audience certainly did have a political, moral, and literary heritage.

Written during the Marian persecutions and the aftermath

---

[29] Published in series from 1824 to 1826, unpaginated, paras 248-52.

of the Civil War, Foxe's, Lilburne's, and Bunyan's texts were each written by people who had been persecuted by the state. Each portrays trials which were self-defended, and each encodes a vernacular English of considerable political dignity. John Foxe fled arrest in 1554 during the reign of the Catholic Queen Mary and wrote his book more safely in Germany. Returning during the reign of Queen Elizabeth, Foxe was persuaded to have his book, initially written in Latin, translated into English. From its initial appearance until the nineteenth century, it was a major text for readers who were informally educated. Eighteenth-century rewritings of the text made some editions more refined — martyrs burned more decorously.[30] John Bunyan believed the book to be second only to the Bible and is rumoured to have had it with him while in gaol writing *Pilgrim's Progress*.[31] Hone claimed to have been deeply impressed by the martyrs' 'fortitude under torture, and the triumph of their deaths' (Hackwood, p. 36). John Lilburne fought in the Civil War and opposed Cromwell after it was won. Believing in manhood suffrage, Lilburne was one of the levellers after whom the Association for preserving Liberty and Property against Republicans and Levellers was named. In 1649, he was tried for high treason for publishing two pamphlets which criticized Cromwell for the abuse of civil liberties. *The Tryal of John Lilburn* was the only book which affected Hone as strongly as *Pilgrim's Progress:*

Since "The Pilgrim's Progress," no other book had so riveted me; I felt all Lilburne's indignant feelings, admired his undaunted spirit, rejoiced at his acquittal, and detested Cromwell as a tyrant for causing him to be carried back to the Tower, after the Jury had pronounced him to be free of charge. This book aroused within me new feelings, and a desire of acquainting myself with Constitutional Law, which in a few years afterwards, I had an opportunity of acquiring. (Hackwood, p. 40)

Hone believed that reading Lilburne's trial influenced decisions which he made a 'few years' later, a time which would include his employment as a law clerk and his membership of the London Corresponding Society.

---

[30] *Foxe's Book of Martyrs*, ed. G. A. Williamson, 1965, p. x.
[31] Monica Furlong, *Puritan's Progress: A Study of John Bunyan*, 1975, p. 86.

John Bunyan was prosecuted by the state and similarly to his character Faithful, he defended himself. Convicted for not attending divine service, Bunyan was not released for twelve years because he refused to promise not to 'call the people together'. In a 'Relation of my Imprisonment', he protests against being suspected of holding seditious meetings under the guise of religion.[32] He also questions the legality of his trial. The procedure was so informal that Bunyan did not know he was being tried until the moment before he was sentenced: 'Now, and not till now, I saw I was indicted' (p. 118). Having been prosecuted and having fought in the Civil War, probably with the New Model Army, Bunyan was describing the very 'real' world of civil resistance in *Pilgrim's Progress* when he depicted Faithful's trial at Vanity and Christian's combat with his king. Christian's battle with Apollyon depicts resistance to the state. Before fighting Apollyon, Christian and the king discuss loyalty: 'How is it then that thou hast ran away from thy king?' (p. 90.) Whatever Bunyan's intentions, when Hone read *Pilgrim's Progress*, he read it as a book which described the world in which he lived: 'I read in it continually, and read it through repeatedly. I read it without the least conception of the Allegory, forgetting, too, that the narrative was a dream — I supposed it to be real and literal. I earnestly desired to become a man that I might travel and find the places described.' (Hackwood, p. 29.) To read the book this way familiarizes readers with a morally valid imprisonment, with citizens fighting kings, with the condemnation of the aristocracy, and, arguably, with the dream that had vast political implications, of a heavenly city on earth.

An anonymous writer recognized the radical potential of Bunyan's book and added a third part which parallels the original but which transforms it into a more spiritual book. A sixteenth edition of the third part was printed in 1755 and many others followed. Its main character Tender Conscience travels through the same places as Christian and encounters roughly similar people. Where Christian encounters Apollyon, Tender Conscience is wounded by

---

[32] 'A Relation of my Imprisonment', in *Grace Abounding to the Chief of Sinners*, ed. Roger Sharrock, Oxford, 1962, p. 121.

arrows shot from Beelzebub's castle. Beelzebub does not appear, he is not a king, and he does not accuse Tender Conscience of disloyalty. When Tender Conscience arrives at Vanity, the lower classes are the only ones which are actively hostile: Tender Conscience was 'molested on all Hands by the ruder sort of People, and unpitied of them that according to their Age and Stations ought to have shewn more Wit and Humanity'.[33] Initially given a 'correct certificate' which he surrenders to the Interpreter, Tender Conscience then receives the 'King's Royal Pass' which allows him to enter heaven. At every stage of the journey, Tender Conscience must demonstrate that he has the right ticket given to him by his social superiors. In the original *Pilgrim's Progress*, the main text does not state that Christian dies although a note explains the fact. He crosses a river and enters the Celestial City, which is described as resembling Heaven: it was '*as if* Heaven itself was come down to meet them' (p. 202). In the third part, Tender Conscience clearly dies and heaven is clearly distinguished from an earthly city: 'There came a bright cloud and covered them all, and they were carried up in the Cloud, through untracked paths of Air' (pp. 114-17). The dichotomy between earthly and spiritual worlds is completed in the third part except at moments which endorse class structure and the authority of the state. Its anonymous author foresaw and attempted to avert the potential of *Pilgrim's Progress* to encourage lower-class radicalism: '*Pilgrim's Progress* is, with the *Rights of Man*, one of the two foundation texts of the English working-class movement: Bunyan and Paine, with Cobbett and Owen, contributed most to the stock of ideas which make up the raw material of the movement from 1790-1850.' (E. P. Thompson, p. 31.)

The immense popularity of Bunyan's book ensured that Hone's audience would be moved by references to its language and ideology as the applause recorded in the third trial suggests. The text provided Hone with a cast of characters and a means of describing them that prophesied the outcome of the trial. Hone relies upon *Pilgrim's Progress* in

[33] *The Pilgrim's Progress*, 29th edn., 3 pts, 1755, p. 185. The 16th edn. of the 3rd pt.

order to establish a means of aligning himself with the audience against the prosecution. The central text of a culture became the central means of forming a political and cultural alliance. In contrast, the *Tryal of John Lilburn* could not be a text shared between Hone and his audience. It was not widely read and only two editions had been printed, the last in 1710. Hone had read it merely by chance. At a young age, he came upon the book by reading a page used for wrapping. Then he tracked down the title and eventually a copy. An accurate record of Lilburne's defence for high treason, the *Tryal* records the dialogue between Lilburne and the prosecution. Had he hunted for one, Hone could not have found a better model for his own defence. As Lilburne put it, 'I have several times been arraigned for my Life already' (p. 3). While *Pilgrim's Progress* enables Hone to define himself in relation to his audience, the *Tryal of John Lilburn* helped him to respond to the argument and tactics of the prosecution. The record of Lilburne's trial appears to have served as a map of strategy and resistance which guided Hone in his replies to the Judge.

Structural similarities in the two trials encouraged similar exchanges and types of behaviour. Both Lilburne and Hone defended themselves for three successive days and inevitably became increasingly exhausted. Both were indicted according to procedures which had been designed to protect the state from physical violence, although they had only written pamphlets: Hone by ex-officio information and Lilburne by Oyer and Terminer. Not allowed a lawyer, Lilburne defended himself before thirty-two judges. Lord Keeble was by far the most prominent and behaves much as Ellenborough does during Hone's trial. The court clearly had its own traditions, and we can take it for granted that Ellenborough learned from his predecessors. Nor is it surprising that Hone's political beliefs should be similar to Lilburne's since Hone claims the *Tryal* initiated a serious interest in 'Constitutional Law'. Initially, both Lilburne and Hone refuse to plead because they cannot read their indictments. Lilburne's was written in Latin and Hone could not afford a copy (p. 13; 2nd, 94). Both state that their trials are unjust because the obscurity of the law encourages tyranny and because

Parliament was publicly supporting the prosecution (pp. 24, 30; 3rd, 154, 163). Both protest that the form of prosecution is inappropriate to their offence (p. 8, 2nd, 91). The trials parallel each other in part because Hone learned a great deal from the *Tryal* and because repressive governments rely on old techniques.

Over and over again similarities in the trials can be found, not only in what Lilburne and Hone say, but in what they believe, what they do, how they see themselves and the Judges, and how they defeat the prosecution's arguments. Both claim that no lawyer would dare to defend them or even to visit them in prison (p. 26; 3rd, 154). Both request that the court grant them more time to prepare their defence and, in both instances, the court refuses (p. 105; 3rd, 146). Both accuse the court of attempting to defeat them by sheer exhaustion (p. 102; 3rd, 163). Both accuse their Judges of taking advantage of their authority to confuse them with their superior learning (p. 24; 3rd, 147). The Judges respond to the defendants in similar ways which, in turn, provokes a similar response from the defendant. Both Judges argue that the defence is inadmissable (p. 120; 3rd, 146). Both interrupt the defendants repeatedly until the defendants become exasperated and finally insist that the Judges no longer interrupt them (p. 108; 3rd, 148). Both defeat the Judges' attempts to deprive them of their defence by responding with imagery:

LILBURNE: Give me but leave to speak for my Life, or else knock me on the head, and murther me where I stand. (p. 21)

HONE: If that is your lordship's decision against me, then I have no defence to this information, and I am ready to go with your lordship's tipstaff wherever your lordship may think proper to send me. (2nd, 87)

Neither Keeble nor Ellenborough can reply to such a remark. Both defendants claim that their Judges have no legal authority except that of announcing the sentence which the jury decides upon:

LILBURNE: You that call yourselves Judges of the Law, are no more but *Norman* Intruders, and indeed and in Truth, if the Jury please, are not more but Cyphers, to pronounce their Verdict. (p. 107)

HONE: Gentlemen, it is you who are trying me to day. His lordship is no judge of me. You are my judges, and you only are my judges. His lordship sits there to receive your verdict. (3rd, 148)

Like Lilburne, Hone describes his accusers as Pharisees and asks the jury to remember the first commandment (pp. 100, 104; 3rd, 158). Both appeal to the jurors as Christians who are more tolerant and charitable than the state, a portrayal which gains much credit because of the Judges' behaviour:

LILBURNE: I leave it to the Consciences of my *Jury*, believing them to be a Generation of Men, that believe in God the Father. (p. 116)

HONE: He appealed to them as men, as Christians, as men and brethren, to consider what he had said . . . He trusted they would, in the spirit of justice and Christian charity, examine his case. (3rd, 186)

Such a list could go on, but this might suffice. The difficulty lies in making sense of a bizarre number of similarities, of several different kinds, without resorting merely to Hone's unusual susceptibility to print and his exceptionally vivid memory. (One writer claims that it was photographic.[34]) Parallels could be drawn between any two self-defended trials, such as T. J. Wooler's, Thomas Spence's, or Richard Carlile's because the situation was a stringent one which called for certain types of behaviour. They could not match, however, the number and range of similarities between Lilburne's and Hone's. Despite Lilburne's exceptional audacity (he can take one's breath away), he and Hone share a similar style of language and behaviour which denies the two-hundred-year interval between trials. It is as if reading Lilburne's text taught Hone how to manage the dialogue, as if he had read it for that purpose the day before.

The rhetorical and political similarities of the two trials — this accumulation of like bits and pieces — is granted greater coherence by the underlying concern for the adequacy of

---

[34] Louis James, *Print and the People, 1819–1851*, 1976, p. 71.

unrefined English. Hone and Lilburne, and Foxe and Bunyan as well, identify the existence of a hegemonic language, disregard it in their own modes of speech, and defend the political and moral capacity of the vernacular. In Foxe's *Book of Martyrs*, the translation of the Bible and the administration of the sacraments in English are essential to the conflict between the Catholic monarchy and the martyrs. Scholars who translated the Bible or who defended the English service, such as Tyndale and Latimer, burn heroically at the stake as does a nineteen-year-old apprentice caught reading the Bible and an illiterate fisherman whose son read it to him (pp. 244, 258). The advocacy of the vernacular here has its most violent effects: 'Sir John Shelton standing by as Taylor was saying the psalm *Misere* in English, struck him on the lips — Ye knave,' said he 'speak Latin. I will make thee' (p. 241). Many narratives contain debates about English or portray reading or speaking English as essential to the Martyrs' fate. Bunyan portrays Faithful and Christian as politically effective citizens whose moral integrity determines their language and distinguishes them from the wealthier citizens of Vanity: 'They naturally spoke the language of Canaan; but they that kept the Fair were men of this world; so that from one end of the Fair to the other, they seemed barbarians to each other' (pp. 127-87). Vulgar language is vindicated by Faithful's and Christian's ability to live according to their own meaning despite great opposition.

Unlike Hone's trial where the prosecution relentlessly attempts to prove the criminality of Hone's language, in Lilburne's trial the prosecution does not aggressively maintain a distinction between Lilburne's language and its own. The assumption that all participants share a discourse is striking after the cultural antagonism of Hone's trial. Keeble thus commands Lilburne to restrain his speech, but he does not protest against his very manner of speaking. Moreover, he makes the command in the simple, metaphoric, and powerful language that Lilburne is equally capable of speaking: 'Your distemper will break out, your heart is so full of boyling Malice and Venome' (p. 43). Lilburne raises the topic of a hegemonic language himself when he objects to the writing of the law in languages which he and others cannot read, Latin and French. His description of the Judges as *'Norman* Intruders' is one instance of his mockery of the Judges for speaking the language of oppression (cited earlier). As Thomas Paine did in the *Rights of Man,* Lilburne considers English to be the language of freedom that was made subordinate by a foreign conquest. Referring to himself as having an 'affectionate and compassionate *English* Spirit within me' and to justice as 'the Common and just Liberties of *England'*, Lilburne spars with the Judges on the basis of their knowing a politically corrupt language (pp. 117, 116). The jury and Lilburne himself can be coyly innocent by comparison, as when Lilburne asks his Judges to translate the Latin text of the statute by which he was charged: 'Say if you please, to do me the Favour but to *English* it, and explain it for the Jury' (p. 117). Despite significant changes in language practice over two hundred and fifty years, Foxe, Lilburne, Bunyan, and Hone defend their vernacular language as the agent and the guardian of political liberty. By relying upon these texts, Hone's discourse encompasses their history, and he speaks with the strength of memory.

Hone appears not only to rely on a particular tradition but to verge on being overtaken by it. Lilburne's and Faithful's trials are brought closer to Hone's by the frequent comment that he is being tried for his life. Sentences for blasphemous libel were less drastic, as Hone knew, and he explains that ill health would probably result in his death before his release. At an emotive and literary level, however, Hone's claim that 'I am here on trial for my life' accords with his drama of religious persecution (3rd, 159). Whenever Hone's sensitivity and imagination are alert, he perceives himself in terms of early radical protestantism. And the reverse is true. Even issues which Hone thought were crucial during the first two trials and in his later writings are unimportant in the third. As he concludes his defence, he states briefly that 'the liberty of the press is attacked through him' (3rd, p. 187). His statement is one of information, without force. His heart is not in it because the statement has no bearing on the fiction that he has established. His later description of the trial, 'I felt carried out of myself. I knew not what I said' (cited earlier), seems true in a way that one might not expect, as if Hone were speaking not according to how he was in his own time but according to his imaginative grasp of the trial which was informed by certain texts.

By speaking according to the language of Lilburne, Foxe, and Bunyan, Hone disengages himself from the constraints on vulgar discourse. He enters a fiction, a fictive seventeenth-century version of his nineteenth-century trial. As a.tactic it worked exceedingly well, enabling Hone to discipline his rhetoric and confirm his courage despite antagonism and fatigue. But his language cannot be described as merely a tactic, or as a matter of literary influence. By a great effort of the imagination, Hone wrenches his discourse from the constraints imposed by contemporary, hegemonic language on to another terrain where vernacular language had achieved its greatest freedom and power.

Chapter VI

Variations of the
Languages of Men:
Rustics, Peasants, and Plough-boys

An unusually festive sign of the dominance of conservative
rhetoric was William Cobbett's return from the United States
in 1800. For five years England had been grateful for the
pamphlets which he had written. Cobbett's dislike of
America, his intense longing for England, and his ignorance
of political tensions existing there had contributed to his
ability to write virulent pamphlets. Many of these were also
published in England, some with slight adaptations. George
Canning, then Under-Secretary of State, published one of his
pamphlets in 1796 (*PR*, xv (1809), 909), not long after
Cobbett had begun his new career with the writing of
Observations on the Emigration of Dr Joseph Priestley
(1794). While liberally-minded periodicals such as the *Monthly
Review* accused him of vulgarity, conservative ones praised
his verbal strength and his audacious logic.[1] Both *Anti-
Jacobins*, especially, gave him a good deal of attention.
Cobbett warmed to the praise and was proud of his singular
position as England's spokesman in a Francophile and
democratic America.[2] He imported Hannah More's work
and the *Liberty and Property* series, he wrote a laudatory
preface to his American publication of Burke's *Letter to a
Noble Lord*, and incorporated Polwhele's abuse of Mary
Wollstonecraft into the preface of *A Bone to Gnaw*. Five
years of mutual support and high esteem were celebrated

---

[1] *Anti-Jacobin; or, Weekly Examiner*, 4th edn., i (1797), 211; i (1798),
332-3; ii (1798), 301. *British Critic*, vi (1795), 587-97. *Gentlemen's Magazine*,
lxv (1795), 47-8. *Anti-Jacobin Review and Magazine*, i (1798), 7-17; i (1798),
342-9; i (1798), 725-8; Appendix i. 836-40. *Monthly Review*, series 2, xvi
(1795), 118-19.
[2] *Letters from William Cobbett to Edward Thornton, Written in The Years
1797 to 1800*, ed. G. D. H. Cole, 1937.

soon after Cobbett arrived when he dined with Windham, Canning, Pitt, Frere, Ellis, and others.[3]

The more essential experience, however, occurred several days later as Cobbett looked over the valley at Farnham and considered his present status. He defined his allegiance then:

From that hill I knew that I should look down into the beautiful and fertile valley of Farnham. My heart fluttered with impatience, mixed with a sort of fear, to see all the scenes of my childhood; for I had learnt before, the death of my father and mother. . . . But now came rushing into my mind, all at once, my pretty little garden, my little blue smock-frock, my little nailed shoes, my pretty pigeons, that I used to feed out of my hands, the last kind words and tears of my gentle and tender-hearted and affectionate mother! I hastened back into the room. If I had looked a moment longer, I should have dropped. When I came to reflect, *what a change*! I looked down at my dress. What a change! What scenes I had gone through! How altered my state! I had dined the day before at the Secretary of State's in company with Mr. *Pitt*, and had been waited upon by men in gaudy liveries! I had had nobody to assist me in the world. No teachers of any sort. Nobody to shelter me from consequence of bad, and no one to counsel me to good, behaviour. I felt proud. The distinctions of rank, birth, and wealth, all became nothing in my eyes; and from that moment (less than a month after my arrival in England) I resolved never to bend before them.[4]

Such an experience was being analysed and granted aesthetic value by Wordsworth and Coleridge. The influence of the past on the present, through the agency of a familiar landscape, resulting in a moral commitment was an important subject to the poems of the *Lyrical Ballads* and to its Preface.

There is more than one irony here. While Wordsworth and Coleridge were defining the rustic, Cobbett was more interested in writing for the propertied classes. Although he was not 'bought', he was well supported by Windham who provided him with the funds to start the *Porcupine* (1800) and the *Political Register* (1802). It took a short time for Cobbett's unwillingness to bend to develop into an anti-ministerial and anti-corruption stance in which he defended the interests and culture of his origins before a well-educated

[3] *The Diary of the Right Hon. William Windham, 1784–1810*, ed. Mrs Henry Baring, 1866, p. 430.

[4] *A Year's Residence in the United States of America* (1818), 1828, 3 pts, pp. 34–5.

audience, and considerably longer to develop into his directly addressing, encouraging the articulacy, and defending the political interests of the non-propertied. As Paine had done with *Rights of Man*, Cobbett activated a new reading audience when he published his 'Address to Journeymen and Labourers' on 2 November 1816. The week following he altered his political position from household to male suffrage. Meanwhile, Wordsworth and Coleridge had also changed their political stance since their joint and muted presentation of it in the Preface to *Lyrical Ballads*. Such changes of mind were not unusual. One major result, however, was three various and seminal definitions of the vulgar audience. The Preface, Cobbett's *A Grammar of the English Language* and the *Biographia* variously define the audience's relation to English society by the competence of its language.

During the turn of the century, the radical literati were especially frightened by the increasing restraints on written expression. For the first time a classically educated radical was prosecuted for publishing a seditious work, and the acts of 1798 were severe. The arrest and conviction of Gilbert Wakefield made clear that the literati were no longer exempt from prosecution. When Wakefield wrote the third edition of his *Reply to the Bishop of Landaff* (1798), his publisher had already been found guilty of seditious libel. The publisher, Joseph Johnson, had published most of the works of the radical literati, such as those of Hazlitt, Godwin, Horne Tooke, Wollstonecraft, Wordsworth, Blake, and Coleridge, and also edited the *Analytical Review*. Until the prosecution of Wakefield's pamphlet, Johnson had managed to steer clear of prosecution by referring books which he believed were too risky to other publishers. His arrest and conviction must have discomforted several of the writers whose work he published. Possibly, Wordsworth's and Coleridge's choice of a less well-known and provincial publisher was partially due to Johnson's arrest. In the new edition of his *Answer* Wakefield says why he did not expect the pamphlet to have been prosecuted. The first reason is that of his reputation for despising violence and for faith in intellectual argument.

Other reasons pertain to his having addressed his pamphlet to a small, intellectual audience:

2. a respectable *type* and *paper*, not adapted to writings of a *seditious* tendency. . . .
3. no window exhibition of the pamphlet by the purveyor of *Pig's-meat* at the Cock and Swine [a reference to Spence] !
4. A scholastic mode of composition, inter-larded after a pedantic fashion with quotations from the Greek and Roman authors.[5]

Such comments indicate that authors expected themselves to be protected by well-known conventions which distinguished their work from the writing of less well educated and poorer radical writers. Wakefield's sentence of two years' imprisonment was an official notification that such distinctions could no longer be trusted. In addition, his death soon after his release in 1801, due to physical debilitation, pointed out that the dangers of conviction were much greater than those of imprisonment.

Comments on the extent of prosecution and alarm reveal how ready the literati were to consider themselves as a distinct group, for none mentions the previous arrests of such figures as Paine, Eaton, or Spence. Wakefield's arrest struck with the energy of a new and unexpected event. The common banner of the 'swinish multitude', which Wakefield used in his pamphlet, proved to have its limits as radical writers relied on the social status of themselves, of their audience, and of learning to safeguard themselves from prosecution. John Aikin discussed the significance of Wakefield's arrest in the *Annual Register* of 1801. His comment presupposes that the literati were previously unworried about prosecution: 'It is not unreasonable to conclude, that a victim of the Liberty of the press, of name and character sufficient to inspire a wide alarm, was really desired'.[6] William Godwin's discussion of alarm in *Thoughts Occasioned by the Perusal of Dr. Parr's Spital Sermon* likewise pays no attention to the non-literati authors.

---

[5] *A Reply to some parts of the Bishop of Landaff's Address to the People of Great Britain,* 3rd edn., 1798, vii.
[6] 'A Tribute to the memory of Gilbert Wakefield', *Annual Register,* xliii (1801), 383.

Although Godwin had attended Paine's trial and had been outraged by it, he talks about persecution as if it had not previously existed:

If they [despotism and intolerance] are not thus checked, I am persuaded that the contempt, the scurrilities and the obloquy which are now circulated, will speedily be exchanged for those more formidable adversaries of discussion, imprisonment and pillory, banishment, and what its promulgators will denunciate an ignominious, death.[7]

Disregarding the fate of such writers as Paine, Spence, and Eaton, Godwin urges the existence of a distinct philosophical realm which would be free from the intolerance of political debate and the threat of prosecution.

The greater vehemence of intellectual arguments paralleled greater legal pressures: 'It is a serious thing to say, that men must neither argue nor write, till they have first subdued the free-born nature of their souls to the trammels of some fortunate and highly patronized creed, which is to be received as orthodoxy' (p. 79). Godwin describes the sudden fervour of arguments opposing his own book, *Enquiry concerning Political Justice*, which had been received more calmly when published eight years before. Such narrowness of orthodoxy is evident in the Blagdon controversy which lasted from 1800 to 1803. Hannah More was charged with the terminology and vehemence employed against 'Jacobins' for educating children in the Mendip Valley: 'For three successive years the *Anti-Jacobin Review* seldom missed an issue in its attack on Hannah More'.[8] Such denunciations reveal a rhetoric growing out of control and attacking its own allies. Radicals, of course, were more vulnerable to the vehemence of critics and the fear of the law. Mary Wollstonecraft was attacked with greater hatred than anyone. Kelvin Everest describes the political pressures on Coleridge during this period, including his dread of being considered an atheist. The *Anti-Jacobin* had already accused him of being a revolutionary of the Frankish sort:

---

[7] 1801, p. 79.
[8] M. G. Jones, *The Charity School Movement; A Study of Eighteenth Century Puritanism in Action*, Cambridge, 1938, p. 172.

Ye five wandering Bards that move
In sweet accord of harmony and love,
C---dge, and S--th-y, L--d, and L--be & Co.
Tune all your rustic harps to praise LEPEAUX.[9]

Already, he had been spied on when visited by John
Thelwall, an event which he found less amusing in 1797 than
when describing it in the *Biographia*. David Erdman and E. P.
Thompson fully discuss the emotional complexity with
which Coleridge thought about political issues.[10] Nor was
Wordsworth invulnerable to the pressures of slander and
persecution. In 1809 he read a magazine article that
reminded him of Wakefield's trial of 1799. Immediately,
he wrote to his publisher: 'This has made me look to myself,
and therefore I beg that, if my Pamphlet be not published,
you would take the trouble of reading it over to see whether
it may not be made a handle for exercising upon my Person
a like act of Injustice'.[11] He authorized his publisher to alter
the *Conventions of Cintra* in any way and to any extent that
would lessen the likelihood of prosecution. If Wordsworth
was worried by the memory of Wakefield's trial in 1809,
he was surely more worried by it in 1800, a year after the
event. Tooke's printer was also troubled by Wakefield's
arrest. The passages which he left blank in the second volume
frequently referred to Wakefield. For thirty years, the printer
had printed Tooke's work without qualms, even after
Tooke's arrests for sedition and high treason (*Diversions*,
ii, Errata). When Alexander Stephens published the omitted
passages in his biography, he suspected that readers would be
disappointed that the remarks were not more inflammatory,
a matter of not recognizing the heat when the burning was
over (ii. 345).

---

[9] Cited from the *Anti-Jacobin* of July 1798 by Kelvin Everest in *Coleridge's Secret Ministry: The Context of the Conversation Poems, 1795–1798*, 1979, p. 40. William Hone refers to the poem, written by George Canning, during each of his three trials.

[10] 'Coleridge as Editorial Writer' and 'Disenchantment or Default? A Lay Sermon' in *Power and Consciousness*, ed. Conor Cruise O'Brien and William Dean Vanech, 1969.

[11] *The Letters of William and Dorothy Wordsworth. The Middle Years, Part One, 1806–1811*, ed. Ernest de Selincourt, 2nd edn. revised by Mary Moorman, 1969, p. 340.

Many of the evasions of the Preface to *Lyrical Ballads* can be accounted for by the frightened temper of 1800. To write a clear argument in favour of the intellectual capability of the lower and middle classes and to criticize roundly an élitest tradition of literature might well have been considered risky and certainly would have lessened the numbers of those who were willing to listen to an aesthetic argument. Despite its hesitancies, the Preface clarifies the contextual thought of the poetry to a greater extent than had previously been the case. The Advertisement to the *Lyrical Ballads* had briefly countered conventional theories of language. The alleged dichotomy between primitive and refined language was challenged by the 'Rime of the Ancyent Marinere', the language of which 'has been equally intelligible for these three last centuries'.[12] The dichotomy between literary and vernacular language was challenged as well. The experimental nature of the poems lies primarily 'with a view to ascertain how far the language of conversation in the middle and lower classes of society is adapted to the purposes of poetic pleasure' (p. 116). Although the poems were allegedly written to oppose conventions of language, readers did not recognize them as exceptionally challenging. Critics had little objection to the poems or the nature of the experiment as they understood it. As their responses to the first edition testify, the desire for a simpler poetic language was prevalent in the 1790s and others besides Wordsworth and Coleridge believed that artificiality was detrimental to the writing of good poetry. The two critics who discussed colloquial language considered it as part of the existing tradition of conversational poems such as *The Task*.[13] Curiously, none of the critics identifies the language of the poems with the class terms used in the Advertisement, although the *Analytical and Monthly Reviews* cite the passage in which they occur. The experimental use of lower and middle-class language does not appear to have offended

---

[12] 'Advertisement to the Lyrical Ballads', *Prose Works of William Wordsworth*, i. 117.

[13] 'Robert Southey, *Critical Review*, October 1798, xxiv 197–204' and 'From an unsigned review, *British Critic*, October 1799, xiv 364–5', in *Coleridge: The Critical Heritage*, ed. J. R. de Jackson, 1970, p. 59.

the taste or challenged the critical assumptions of most reviewers. Rather, the *Anti-Jacobin* praised the author for his 'classical and accomplished' mind.[14]

The primitive language of the 'Ancyent Marinere' received more rigorous treatment. Charles Burney, writing anonymously for the *Monthly Review*, criticized the poem for wilfully adopting primitive language: 'None but savages would have submitted to eat acorns after corn was found'.[15] The chief pleasure of reading ancient poetry could not be repeated by modern imitations, that of unexpectedly reading 'so many beautiful thoughts in the rude numbers of barbarous times' (p. 56). Burney thus recognizes the challenge to ideas about language conveyed by the diction of Coleridge's poem. By choosing to write in a 'primitive' language, Coleridge implies that it is fully capable of expressing poetic feeling and that no essential difference exists between the sensibility of the poet and that of the savage. The experiment countered prevalent ideas about the nature of civilized language, and, more specifically, those of Lord Monboddo in *Of the Origin and Progress of Language*. Whereas the Advertisement states that the language of Coleridge's poem has remained steadily intelligible 'for these three last centuries', Monboddo claimed that 'the languages spoken in the several nations of Europe only three hundred years ago, are so different from the present, that if we can understand them at all, it is only by the help of learned critics' (i. 479).

In the second edition of the *Lyrical Ballads*, Wordsworth blunts the challenge of the 'Ancyent Marinere' because he did not want its unconventionality to deter readers from reading the rest of the volume. Previously, he had written to his publisher and considered excluding the poem altogether: 'If that Volume should come to a second Edition, I would put in its place some little things which would be more like to suit common taste'.[16] Instead Wordsworth placed the

---

[14] 'Unsigned notice, *Anti-Jacobin,* April 1800 v. 334', ibid., p. 59.

[15] 'Charles Burney, *Monthly Review*, June 1799, xxix. 202–10', ibid., pp. 55–6.

[16] *The Letters of William and Dorothy Wordsworth. The Early Years, 1787–1805*, 2nd edn. revised by Chester L. Shaver, Oxford, 1967, p. 264.

poem less prominently at the volume's conclusion and wrote a preamble discussing its weaknesses. Coleridge's wounded feelings are one instance of the hazards of defying convention during this period.[17]

Despite Wordsworth's apprehension, the second edition with its Preface is far more radical than the first. Whereas the Advertisement states minimally that the language of the lower and middle classes might be suitable for poetry, the Preface presents a theory of language that redefines the language and mentality of 'vulgar' speakers. While conservative theories had justified social fragmentation by distinguishing the refined from the vulgar language, the Preface states that the language and the sensibilities of various classes are fundamentally alike and that society is 'naturally' unified. Vanity only, not fundamental difference, motivates class distinction. A letter which Coleridge wrote in September 1800 discusses several ideas which appear in the Preface and discusses them as deriving from his study of Tooke's theory of language. The issue of concern here is not which of the ideas in the Preface were Coleridge's, but the relation of Tooke's ideas to Coleridge's letter and to similar ideas in the Preface. The Preface will be discussed as a 'joint production' of the two poets.[18]

Although Wordsworth only mentions Tooke once in a letter expressing suspicions of his character (*Early Years*, p. 137), Coleridge refers to him on several occasions and expresses several different opinions of him. Coleridge's persistent interest in Tooke is evident in his poem of 1796, in his letter to Godwin in 1800, in passages in his *Notebook*, from 1806 and 1809, and in his only published and signed acknowledgement of Tooke in *Aids to Reflection* of 1825.[19] Coleridge's concern there with the confusion of words with ideas and with the imposition of unclear language is a major topic in the *Diversions*, his letter of 1800, and the Preface.

---

[17] Thomas MacFarland, *Romanticism and the Forms of Ruin: Wordsworth, Coleridge, and The Modalities of Fragmentation*, Princeton, 1981, pp. 100–1.

[18] *Collected Letters of Samuel Taylor Coleridge*, ed. Earl Leslie Griggs, 1959–71, 6 vols., i. 627.

[19] *The Notebooks of Samuel Taylor Coleridge*, ed. Kathleen Coburn, 1957–73, nos. 2784 and 3587.

He states that his primary intention in writing *Aids to Reflection* is

To direct the Reader's attention to the value of the Science of Words, their use and abuse . . . and the incalculable advantages attached to the habit of using them appropriately, and with a distinct knowledge of their primary, derivative, and metaphysical senses. And in furtherance of this Object I have neglected no occasion of enforcing the maxim, that to expose a sophism and to detect the equivocal or double meaning of a word is, in the great majority of cases, one and the same thing. Horne Tooke entitled his celebrated work, Ἔπεα Πτερόεντα, Winged Words: or Language, not only the *Vehicle* of Thought, but the *Wheels*. With my convictions and views, for ἔπεα, I should substitute λόγοι, i.e., words *select* and *determinate*, and for πτερόεντα, ζώοντες that is, *living* Words.[20]

Even in 1825, when Coleridge disagreed with Tooke on many counts, the *Diversions of Purley* continued to be basic to his understanding of language and a starting point for his own work. Recent commentators have interpreted a later comment of Coleridge's as an adequate assessment of his opinion of the radical philosopher: 'It shows a base and unpoetical mind to convert so beautiful, so divine a subject as language into the vehicle or make-weight of political squibs.'[21] Coleridge was skilled at insults, and the vividness of his statement here betrays his earlier admiration for Tooke as both a radical and a scholar. His eulogistic poem of 1796 praises Tooke highly for what the statement of 1830 claims to despise, the political implications of the *Diversions*. In the interim, Coleridge met him and apparently saw him often 'at one time' (*Table Talk*, p. 90). On first meeting him in 1800 he was somewhat disappointed by the man but not with his work:

He is a clear-headed old man, as every man needs must be who attends to the real import of words; but there is a sort of charletannery [sic] in his manner that did not please me. He makes a mystery & difficulty out of pain & palpable things—and never tells you any thing without first exciting & detaining your Curiosity. But it were a bad Heart that could not pardon worse faults than these in the Author of the Epea Pteroenta. (*Letters*, i. 559–60)

[20] 1836, xi–xii.
[21] *Omniana of S. T. Coleridge*, Oxford, 1917.

More importantly, Coleridge wrote two letters about Tooke's theory. They reveal that he studied the *Diversions* and *A Letter to J. Dunning* with unusual intensity and in relation to the *Lyrical Ballads*.

The second reference, written in October 1800, is a quick and playful one: 'The endeavour to finish Christabel . . . for the second volume of the Lyrical Ballads threw my business terribly back — & now I am sweating for it—/Dunning Letters &c &c—all the hell of an Author' (i. 634). A letter to Godwin written a month earlier more fully considers Tooke's theory:

I wish you to write a book on the power of words, and the processes by which human feelings form affinities with them — in short, I wish you to *philosophize* Horn Tooke's System, and to solve the great Questions — whether there be reason to hold, that an action bearing all the *semblance* of pre-designing Consciousness may yet be simply organic, & whether a *series* of such actions are possible — and close on the heels of this question would follow the old 'Is Logic the *Essence* of Thinking?' in other words — Is *thinking* impossible without arbitrary signs & — how far is the word 'arbitrary' a misnomer? Are not words &c parts & germinations of the Plant? And what is the Law of their Growth? — In something of this order I would endeavor to destroy the old antithesis of *Words & Things*, elevating, as it were, words into Things, & living Things too. All the nonsense of vibrations etc you would of course dismiss. (i. 625-6)

Coleridge's suggestion that Godwin write the book does not indicate a lack of serious interest on his own part. Coleridge had evidently given the *Diversions* a great deal of thought and he would continue to consider the 'great Questions' which he raises here. His concentration appears from his having already subsumed questions which pertain more to Hartley within the project of philosophizing 'Horn Tooke's System'. Hartley and Tooke are so thoroughly assimilated here that the questions raised by the two thinkers are considered to be Tooke's. Discussions of free will, the relation of free will to consciousness, and 'the nonsense of vibrations' do not appear in Tooke's study of etymology. Before writing to Godwin, Coleridge had already decided that the language portrayed by the *Diversions* was the language of Hartley's depiction of consciousness. His desire to integrate the theories of Hartley and Tooke is the desire to find an alternative to the theories of mind and language which would merge the extreme dichotomies of conservative linguistic thought. His method of doing so was to establish a parallel between the evolution of language and an individual's psychological relation to words.

Horne Tooke's theory of language begins by claiming that only the nouns and verbs represent an operation of the mind. Tooke defines nouns, and verbs to some extent, as the operation of receiving 'impressions, that is to have Sensations or Feelings'. Because all words evolve from nouns and verbs in discernible patterns of syntax, they are not 'arbitrary' or consciously invented as Monboddo and others had claimed. Types of words result from the tendency of language to devise new forms for more effective communication. They are 'parts & germinations of the Plant'. By assigning the origins of different types of words to the 'growth' of language, Tooke reopened the question of the relation of language to the mind. Tooke's theory is applicable to Hartley and to the study of psychology because the nouns in linguistic evolution could be considered as analogous to the 'signs of things'. If sensation and feeling are the basis of vocabulary and of all modes of thought, then experience and perception become reputable forms of knowledge and can no longer be described as essentially different from rationality and abstraction. Within this framework, the 'old antithesis of Words and Things' is abolished, and thought is possible without language. Sensation and feeling are in themselves a form of thinking.

Tooke referred to the accumulated meanings gathered by words as the 'force' of words. Coleridge's term in the letter, the 'power' of words refers to an analogous phenomenon in an individual psyche: their power lies in the accumulated meanings which they gather during a person's lifetime. If meaning were uncontrolled, if words gathered considerable power, an individual's actions would then be determined by thoughtlessly responding to overbearing signs. The Preface likewise discusses the danger of a word gathering idiosyncratic meaning due to the singularity of a person's experience, what it calls 'particular' associations. It warns more seriously, however, of the distortion of meaning that can result from one's knowing only the contemporary usage of a word. 'Arbitrary' refers, as it does throughout the Preface, to what is socially imposed and socially divisive, as in 'arbitrary taste'.

I am sensible that my associations must have sometimes been particular instead of general, and that, consequently, giving to things a false importance, sometimes from diseased impulses I may have written upon unworthy subjects; but I am less apprehensive on this account, than that my language may frequently have suffered from those arbitrary connections of feelings and ideas with particular words, from which no man can altogether protect himself. (*Prose Works*, i. 152)

Wordsworth and Coleridge defend themselves from the possible charge of employing 'arbitrary' language by claiming that poets are more apt than readers to be 'acquainted with the various stages of meaning through which words have passed, or with the fickleness or stability of relations of particular ideas to each other' (i. 152). Their fear of the fickleness of vocabulary is one of not having freed themselves from society's ability to distort vocabulary and thereby to determine meaning.

In the Preface and in Coleridge's letter, depth of feeling, freedom of the will, and sound vocabulary depend upon each other and are essentially interrelated. To alter one's language weakens the will by interfering with the relation of language to thought. Words are so synonymous with feeling that for a poet to alter words at the suggestion of critics amounts to a betrayal of the emotions that can leave the poet 'utterly debilitated' (i. 152). If one believes, as Coleridge puts it in his letter, that the 'processes by which human feelings form affinities' with words can actually determine thought, then words become extremely important. Freedom of the will then depends upon the extent to which individuals are dominated by the social and psychological distortions of their vocabulary. Tooke had discussed the possibility of social dominance through distorted and vague meanings, what he called 'verbal imposture', and the Preface describes a similar danger to unconsciously held meanings. Although no one can achieve a vocabulary entirely without 'false association', one must strive to free one's self from intellectual imposition by understanding the meaning of words. Without carefully considering vocabulary, people are enslaved both by their own past as it is encoded in their language, and by their own society which determines contemporary usage. The Preface thus portrays a society that aggressively interferes with the integrity of its members and that intrudes upon the process of thinking.

Rustics are credited with speaking a pure language because theirs is less buffeted by the pressures and demands of society. Without newspapers, without current political debates, without sensationalism, and without fashion, rustics speak a language that has not been distorted by the ephemeral significance of words. At its simplest, the following passage means that the rustic does not suffer the risk of 'arbitrary' connections between words and ideas:

Such men hourly communicate with the best objects from which the best part of language is originally derived; and because, from their rank in society and the sameness and narrow circle of their intercourse, being the less under the action of social vanity they convey their feelings and notions in simple and unelaborated expressions. Accordingly such a language arising out of repeated experience and regular feelings is a more permanent and far more philosophical language than that which is frequently substituted for it by Poets. (i. 124)

The relation which the passages discusses between language and thought is more complex than this, however. Rustics speak a 'permanent' and 'philosophical' language because they constantly engage in the act of mind from which all language originates, that of receiving impressions from ordinary objects. John Horne Tooke's theory of language is crucial here for he proved that all vocabulary, even the particles which were said to be the 'glory' of the grammatical art, represented the act of receiving impressions from common objects. Somewhat mystically, the passage means that rustics speak a pure language because they live among and are surrounded by the origins of words, as if they were standing in a landscape of language.

The meditative and experiential thought which the Preface claims is the basis of all language is expressed by the poems in a language that in itself stems from meditation and experience: 'I have at all times endeavoured to look steadily at my subject' (i. 132). Thus the Preface considers language within the same construct as former theories of language. The nature of the mind and the proper subject of language are assumed to be the same because they are aligned by the nature of language. In the Preface, the basis of language in 'sensations or feelings' becomes the proper mode of poetic thought which in turn becomes the proper subject of poetry. The poet's task is to trace 'the fluxes and refluxes of the mind when agitated by the great and simple affections of our nature' (i. 126). Without the redefinition of language in the *Diversions*, Wordsworth and Coleridge would not have been able to align the mind and language in this way. They would not have been able to advance the argument any further than Priestley, who could advocate an aesthetic theory but could not base it on a philosophy of language. By applying Hartley to Tooke, as Coleridge did in his letter, the Preface can align the nature of mind, the nature of language, and the subject of poetry into a single, self-confirming theory.

Although the Preface disagrees sharply with conventional theories, it does not emphasize the nature and the extent of its disagreement. Writing after collaborating on the Preface, Coleridge wrote to Sir Humphrey Davy that he wanted to write an essay on poetry that would 'in reality be a disguised System of Morals & Politics' (*Letters*, i. 632). The Preface is such a work, one that mutes its own incisiveness with tactical evasion. Arguments begin *in medias res* and then stop short of conclusions, as others have noted. The conventional distinctions between vulgar and refined speakers is not mentioned. Rather, the two figures of the rustic and the artificial poet embody the Preface's redefinition of vulgar and refined language. The personification of the rustic makes the Preface's argument more palatable by his nostalgic value as a representative of the pastoral tradition. His distance from the city precludes the danger of his reminding readers of the current political turmoil. Arguments against the concept of the refined language are subsumed in the discussion of the poets who pride themselves on their dissimilarity from the main body of the population: they 'think that they are conferring honour upon themselves and their art in proportion as they separate themselves from the sympathies of men, and indulge in arbitrary and capricious habits of expression in order to furnish food for fickle tastes and fickle appetites of their own creation' (i. 124). Rather than discuss language as manifesting intellectual operations which distinguish one class of people from another, Wordsworth and Coleridge assume that 'mere native English' is the basis of everyone's language. Accordingly, the classical languages are not mentioned. The casual phrase 'the very language of men' disregards the unusualness of the concept (i. 130). Wordsworth and Coleridge advocate a spoken language and make striking claims for its dignity and importance without fully portraying the ideas and the social assumptions which the phrase was refuting.

Instead of identifying and attacking a particular theory, Wordsworth and Coleridge merely allude to conventional theories of language. They appropriate a given theory's vocabulary by duplicating its diction and by altering that diction's meaning. 'Permanent', the 'language of flesh and blood', 'universal', 'artificial' and 'arbitrary' were terms used by Harris, Monboddo, Johnson, and others to establish the value of the refined language. In Johnson's *Dictionary*, the more 'permanent' language is written and differs from the language of the 'laborious and mercantile' classes, which is 'in great measure casual and mutable'. The 'permanent' and 'philosophical' language described in the Preface and employed in the poems themselves, portrays commonly experienced perceptions and emotions. 'Universal' does not refer to archetypical and neoplatonic ideas but to 'the great and universal passions of men' (i. 144). According to Monboddo, the 'arbitrary' or 'artificial' language was the conscious invention of an intellectual élite for the purposes of art and science. The language of 'flesh and blood' had not been improved and was the language of appetite and need (cited earlier). For Wordsworth and Coleridge, 'arbitrary' and 'artificial' are negative terms which depict a separation from nature and from the commonality of human experience that results from social vanity, as in 'false refinement or arbitrary innovation' (i. 124). Purity of language does not result from avoiding common diction or from being endowed with a refined sensibility but from living apart from social pressures and under the moral influence of beauty. Wordsworth and Coleridge adhere to the 'language of men' because by doing so they will keep readers in the company of 'flesh and blood' (i. 130).

The inverted terms are effective in that they work in two distinct and related ways. They refer to a recognizably philosophic vocabulary and to ordinary words that were invariably associated with a particular social class. Read naïvely, their meaning is still inverted. Universality, permanence, and philosophy were not associated with the activities or language of rustics. As Coleridge sometimes does in his early poetry, he inverts terms by applying them to a social class which employed those terms to define their social inferiors. When Coleridge describes an aristocrat as a 'Smooth Savage' in 'Religious Musings' (1. 68), he defamiliarizes the term 'savage' and reveals that the word in itself subsumes complex ideas about social relations. By confronting his readers with a glaring exception to the normal use of a term, Coleridge points out that its habitual usage disguises an unconsidered meaning, one that helps to fix the relation between social classes. Words here are exceptionally active agents, contributing by their vagueness and by their associations to social fragmentation. The equivocation of the Preface's terminology suggests a relation between ideas which are consciously held and debated as philosophy and those which are unconsciously assumed to justify certain forms of social behaviour. The 'artificial' poet behaves in ways which are socially divisive, and a philosophy which praises the artificiality of civilized language perpetuates such behaviour.

In a sentence which appears at the beginning and at the end of the Preface, Wordsworth and Coleridge stress the scope and significance which they wish their ideas about poetry to have. They want to encourage the writings of a poetry that is 'important in the multiplicity and quality of [mankind's] moral relations' (i. 120, 158). The emphasis on social behaviour in the Preface adds a new component to the poetry and alters the manner in which the poems are to be read. The Preface controls the content of the *Lyrical*

Ballads by refusing to allow readers to engage with the poetry in a manner which would support conventional assessments of class. The Indian woman, the idiotic child, and the narrator of 'The Thorn' could be understood as characters who were essentially different from refined readers and who were of interest precisely because of that difference. Without the Preface, they could be interpreted according to the concept of uncivilized speakers as portrayed here by Hugh Blair:

In the infancy of all societies, men are much under the dominion of imagination and passion. They live scattered and dispersed; they are unacquainted with the course of things; they are, every day, meeting with new and strange objects. Fear and surprise, wonder and astonishment, are their most frequent passions. Their language will necessarily partake of this character of their minds. They will be prone to exaggeration and hyperbole. They will be given to describe every thing with the strongest colours, and most vehement expressions; infinitely more than men living in advanced and cultivated periods of society, when their imagination is more chastened, their passions are more tamed, and a wider experience had rendered the objects of life more familiar to them. (*Lectures*, i. 81-2)

The Preface argues against such an assessment of the poem's characters. Wordsworth and Coleridge are not reasonable men viewing the lives of the vulgar to see how emotive and excitable people think, but are attempting to redefine the relation of language to thought, which will in turn, refute false means of social differentiation. The Preface thus maintains that readers can learn about their own minds by examining the language of the Indian Woman and an idiotic child. It maintains that what had been defined as the vulgar language warrants serious study because by considering it the literati could learn about their own minds: 'The principal object then which I proposed to myself in these Poems was to make the incidents of common life interesting by tracing in them, truly but not ostentaciously the primary laws of our nature.' (i. 122.) 'The primary laws of our nature' is yet another phrase which mutes the extremity of its statement. Readers and the poems' characters are quietly said to have a similar sensibility that is manifested by their sharing a common language.

In this unusual domain of directing an argument against both ideas about language and their bearing on social fragmentation, the Preface and the *Diversions* are especially alike. The two works not only share certain ideas but also an impetus around which those ideas are formed. Both have an ostensibly political intent. Isolated ideas or even several ideas in the Preface can be compared to those of other theorists: to Blair, Beattie, Dennis, Condillac, Herder, Rousseau, or Michaelis. Coleridge read extensively and undoubtedly he considered his own ideas in the process of reading both English and continental writers. But because ideas about language in England had a specific relation to social structure only an English theorist could delineate what was simultaneously a philosophical and a social problem. The Preface vindicates the vernacular as did several European theories. It also considers the difficulty of achieving intellectual freedom when society imposes ideas through the associations of vocabulary, and it responds specifically to theories which had defined language, the mind, and society in relation to each other. The *Diversions of Purley* and the Preface discuss the problem of language in an exceptionally cogent way, as a complex philosophical and political subject.

The political thought behind the Preface would have had a clearer and sharper edge if Wordsworth and Coleridge had named Horne Tooke. To acknowledge an intellectual debt to an 'acquitted felon' would have been bold of them, but it would have considerably diminished their audience and provoked a good deal of vehement discussion. Although other writers praised Tooke and developed his work, they did so only after divesting the *Diversions* of its political content. For the poets, already identified as radicals, to have extended the political aspects of his work would have provoked an immediate and unconsidered response to their ideas. The Preface was thus obscured to forestall another type of obscurity.

Nor did it end at that point, for the obscurity of 1800 enabled Coleridge to distort his literary autobiography. While the *Biographia* claims to be a record of intellectual growth, it omits any discussion of the value of radical thinkers whom Coleridge once learned a great deal from. Both John Horne Tooke and John Thelwall are slighted in the process. The intellectual excitement of Coleridge's letters to Thelwall during the late 1790s and the eulogistic poem which Coleridge addressed to him suggest that Thelwall deserved more mention than as 'myself and friend' who were trailed by a spy.[22] E. P. Thompson in his essay 'Disenchantment or Default' gives an account of the 'Spy Nozy' episode in which Coleridge makes a funny little story out of Thelwall's political harassment. Coleridge slights Thelwall in order to portray himself as a character who is entirely detached from radical politics. Even being trailed by state informers does not worry him. Coleridge talks about politics solely in the form of 'anecdotes and digressions', as he describes it in the title of chapter ten. Political life is an insignificant matter of time, places, and circumstance that is distinct from intellectual life. Coleridge thus relies on the conventional distinction between literature and politics as a rhetorical strategy to persuade readers that the tumultuous history of the 1790s had no bearing on the development of his thought. Writing in the margins of his own copy of the book, Thelwall exclaims that Tooke deserved more credit. The following comment appears besides the famous passage where Coleridge distinguishes the fancy from the imagination:

It is curious how freely persons of a certain cast of mind will borrow from those they affect to despise. What reader acquainted with the Diversions of Purley will not fail to discover that the fountain of all this reasoning is in that book — which indeed has given a new impulse to the grammatical speculations of mankind. Yet Coleridge in his conversation affects an utter contempt for Tooke & his grammatical philosophy.[23]

By ignoring some thinkers and naming others, Coleridge portrays himself according to conventional assessments of refined or philosophical thinkers. He thereby demonstrates

---

[22] Carl Woodring in *Politics in the Poetry of Coleridge*, Madison, 1961, discusses their friendship.

[23] Cited by Norman Fruman in *Coleridge, the Damaged Archangel*, 1972, p. 98. Fruman also vindicates Horne Tooke from Coleridge's charge of plagiarism recorded in *Table Talk*, p. 88.

his credentials as a thinker who, by definition, was disengaged from political concerns.

The *Biographia* attempts to recover literary tradition, and Coleridge himself, from some of the buffetings it had experienced during the 1790s and which would reappear soon after the *Biographia* was published. The expansion of the reading audience, the evident artistry of Paine, Cobbett, and Hone and such writings as the *Diversions* and the Preface placed new strains on concepts of literature by challenging received notions concerning the relation of language to thought, the nature of the reading audience, and the capability of the vernacular language. In writing the *Biographia*, Coleridge hoped to redefine and to settle his political quarrel with the literati. In the introduction to the second volume, he discusses his desire to rid the Preface of the intense controversy which followed its publication. From the start, he disavows his contribution to the Preface by referring to it as solely Wordsworth's work:

From this preface . . . however mistaken its direction might be deemed, arose the whole long-continued controversy. For from the conjunction of perceived power with supposed heresy I explain the inveteracy and in some instances, I grieve to say, the acrimonious passions, with which the controversy has been conducted by the assailants.[24]

By 'correcting' the Preface, by refuting its democratic theory of the mind and language, Coleridge intended to depoliticize the text and to reduce it to merely an aesthetic argument. If he had entirely succeeded, Coleridge would have redeemed himself from the stigma of his former radicalism and established himself as a member of a somewhat strengthened literati. Although it could be argued that this was the eventual effect of the *Biographia*, Coleridge's intentions were not achieved when the book was published.

Coleridge was not willing to change his mind completely. With considerable ambivalence, he attempts to maintain some of the advances of a radical critique of literature while denying that those advances have any political significance. He thus asks his readers to accept ideas which criticize their

---

[24] *Biographia Literaria,* ed. J. Shawcross, Oxford, 1907, 2 vols., ii. 7.

own status. The respect he accords to the non-learned and his criticism of the literati can be remarkably strong:

There appears to have existed a sort of secret and tacit compact among the learned, not to pass beyond a certain limit in speculative science. The privilege of free thought, so highly extolled, has at no time been held valid in actual practice, except within this limit; and not a single stride beyond it has ever been ventured without bringing obloquy on the transgressor. The few men of genius among the learned class, who actually did overstep this boundary, anxiously avoided the appearance of having so done. Therefore the true depth of science, and the penetration to the inmost centre, from which all the lines of knowledge diverge to their ever distant circumference, was abandoned to the illiterate and the simple. (i. 95–6)

The context, however, is vapid. Religious mystics such as Behemn and Foxe did not constitute a threat to orthodoxy in 1817. Coleridge thus brings a radical critique to solve a relatively insignificant problem, while evading a more genuine and much greater difficulty.

Coleridge's refutation of the Preface similarly depends on denying the context of its argument. Coleridge criticizes the Preface without mentioning the theories of language and the social assumptions that it opposed. He defines a language of 'good sense and natural feeling' based on the vernacular, as if such a language had always been acknowledged (ii. 41). To prove the value of such a language, he relies on a seventeenth-century commentator:

It is an excellent remark of Dr. Henry More's ... that 'a man of confined education, but of good parts, by constant reading of the Bible will naturally form a more winning and commanding rhetoric than those that are learned; the intermixture of tongues and artificial phrases debasing *their* style' (ii. 31).

Here, Coleridge evades the complexity of an articulate lower class by discussing that articulacy only in relation to the Bible. Moreover a theory of language from the late eighteenth century which concurred with More's comment would be difficult to find, excepting John Horne Tooke's. According to conventional theories of language a relatively uneducated person could not achieve 'a winning and commanding rhetoric'.

The thesis which the Preface argues, that language is a democratic vehicle of expression, is taken for granted as Coleridge counters the figure of the rustic with that of 'any other man of common sense':

A rustic's language, purified from all provincialism and grossness, and so far reconstructed as to be made consistent with the rules of grammar (which are in essence no other than the laws of universal logic, applied to psychological materials), will not differ from the language of any other man of common-sense, however learned or refined he may be, except as far as the notions, which the rustic has to convey, are fewer and more indiscriminate. (ii. 38–9)

In the Preface the figure of the rustic embodied the 'language of men' and indicated the extent to which Wordsworth and Coleridge believed that 'native' English had the same worth and scientific value that had previously been granted to the classical languages. Coleridge assumes here what the Preface argued with some care, while also strategically twisting the argument. He maintains that a rustic's language is not essentially different from anyone else's, once it has been 'reconstructed'. Whereas the Preface had argued that refined language was basically the same as vulgar language, once it was purified of artificiality, Coleridge claims that the weaknesses of the vulgar language distinguish the two. Coleridge bypasses the Preface's concern with artificiality altogether, by discussing the rustic's language in comparison with that of 'any other man of common-sense', a language that was not recognized by conventional theories. Ultimately, when set against eighteenth-century theories, the difference between the 'man of common-sense' and the 'language of men' is less great than Coleridge claims. Both stress the competency of vernacular English, both disregard the dichotomies of conventional assessments of language, and both advocate a language of 'good sense and natural feeling'.

As early as 1802, Coleridge recognized that he disagreed with Wordsworth's 'daring Humbleness of Language' and stated that he hoped to write a theory of poetry that would be an 'arbitrator between the old and the New School' (*Letters*, ii. 836). The *Biographia* negotiates between élitist and more democratic theories in that it favours a vernacular language while reasserting the denunciation of vulgar speakers. The rustic of the Preface was to some extent a philosophic construct who embodied a refutation of conventional theories of language. By disregarding the rustic as a representative of a theoretical argument, by taking the rustic literally, Coleridge differentiates his ideas from those of the Preface without acknowledging their common base. He ignores theory and rigorously examines the cultural life of 'peasants'. By doing so, he re-established a firm, binary division between social classes. The language of peasants is shown to be influenced by arbitrary factors. It varies 'according to the accidental character of the clergyman, the existence or non-existence of schools; or even, perhaps, as the exciseman, publican, or barber, happened to be, or not to be, zealous politicians, and readers of the weekly newspaper *pro bono publico*' (ii. 42). Peasants are portrayed as having no culture or language worth mentioning except that which is accidental and which descends from a superior social stratum. Peasants are passive vehicles who if they share in 'the best part of language', do so because they have been given it:

The best part of human language, properly so called, is derived from reflection on the acts of the mind itself. It is formed by a voluntary appropriation of fixed symbols to internal acts, to processes and results of imagination, the greater part of which have no place in the consciousness of uneducated man; though in civilized society, by imitation and passive remembrance of what they hear from their religious instructors and other superiors, the most uneducated share in the harvest which they neither sowed or reaped. (ii. 39–40)

('Fixed symbols' refers to words indicating moral and intellectual ideas, and Coleridge's rhetoric echoes that of Lord Monboddo who described such ideas as expressing 'the *reflex act* of the mind upon itself' (i. 160).) Many questions are left unanswered here but the dismissive force of the passage is stridently clear. And all the more so, as Coleridge compares the language of peasants to that of 'brute creation' and 'uncivilized tribes' (ii. 39, 40). Language, culture, and morality are thus reclaimed as the province of a limited number of civilized people. Unlike the debate in the 1790s, however, the grounds of the debate are shifted from the nature of language itself to the effects of deprived cultural conditions.

In the *Biographia* the political and recognizably radical theories of language in the Preface and the *Diversions* are dissipated while Coleridge benefits from their reassessment of the nature of language. Coleridge is not restrained by the necessity of excluding either feeling or a wide range of vocabulary and metaphor from his prose style. But the refutation of eighteenth-century theories is divested of its political motive by arguing against the rustic, by excluding the *Diversions* from the discussion, and by ignoring the concept of refinement. By a powerful act of omission, Coleridge denies that there was any political motive to the Preface's discussion of language. The political challenge to literature and theories of language was eventually muted by the former radical's denial that such a challenge existed. If the legal and intellectual constraints of 1800 had not already muted the Preface, Coleridge would not have been able to do this. Nor would he have been able to maintain the bluff of the *Biographia* — that the political excitement of the 1790s had no bearing on his intellectual and poetic growth.

The *Biographia* suffered from its two-year delay in publication. Finishing the book in 1815, Coleridge formulated his ideas and his rhetorical strategy during the quiet interlude of the Napoleonic War. Arguments could be displaced and the history of his youth could be slightly altered because the issues raised in the 1790s were in abeyance: 'We have enjoyed an intermission, and long may it continue' (i. 130). Such statements were drastically out of place with the resurgence of political activity in 1817. More than any other individual, William Cobbett disrupted the attempt of the *Biographia* to set old problems aside. On 2 November 1816, Cobbett published the famous eighteenth number of his *Political Register*, 'An Address to Journeymen and Labourers'. By doing so, Cobbett was engaged in a parallel, and yet deeply antagonistic effort to Coleridge. Both the *Biographia* and the 'Address' were partly motivated by the necessity of dispersing the vehemence of previous rhetoric. Coleridge's defence of Southey, his attack on Jeffrey, his frequent pleas for tolerance, his attempt to distinguish himself from a school of poetry castigated as Jacobin — a good part of the book — is motivated by the attempt to recover from the 'Cerberean whelps of feud and slander' (i. 126). If Coleridge had succeeded, he would have defined himself in relation to a new audience, 'ad clerum' as he defines it in the Statesman's Manual of 1816.[25] By disavowing his political self, he hoped to gain the position of a philosopher talking to his fellows.

The acuteness of the turmoil of 1817 did not allow for such detachment. In two articles in the Quarterly Review published in October 1816 and January 1817, Southey described the situation as more precarious than the threat of invasion. He refuted the arguments of Cobbett's 'Address' and stated that 'poets and philosophers' could no longer look on as 'indifferent observers'.[26] Like the Biographia, Cobbett's 'Address' was also an attempt to create a new audience by recovering from the vehemence of previous rhetoric. While Coleridge denied the peasants a place in English culture, Cobbett grants 'Journeymen and Labourers' an essential place in civilization. The Biographia might have been received with less annoyance if Cobbett's success had been less dramatic.

Having written vast amounts of political material during the previous twenty years, Cobbett was knowledgeable in the ways of its workings. The major strategy of the 'Address' is to supply a definition of its readers and to contrast it with previously existing ones. The war provided the means of granting a new status to the audience: 'As it is the labour of those who toil which makes a country abound in resources, so it is the same class of men, who must, by their arms, secure its safety and uphold its fame.' Labourers are granted a fundamental position in the development and security of civilization: 'without the assistance of their hands, the country would be a wilderness, hardly worth the notice of an

[25] In Lay Sermons, Collected Works of Samuel Coleridge, ed. R. J. White, gen. ed. Kathleen Coburn, Princeton, 1972, 15 vols., vi. 36.

[26] Unsigned, 'Parliamentary Reform' and 'The Rise and Progress of Popular Disaffection', Quarterly Review, xvi. 225–78 and 511–52. The first article appears in the October issue although Southey discusses Cobbett's 'Address to Journeymen and Labourers' which was published on 2 November. Despite the discrepancy of the dates, Southey discussed the 'Address' in detail by quoting various passages and alluding to the title.

invader.' The strength of this initial formulation allows Cobbett to dismiss other rhetorics which define his audience as opposed to the interests of England: 'With this correct idea of your own worth in your minds, with what indignation must you hear yourselves called the Populace, the Rabble, the Mob, the Swinish Multitude' (*PR*, xxxi (1816), 546). The sense of wholeness and moral purpose of his loosely Johnsonian air denies previous definitions of his audience which excluded it from social participation on moral grounds.

Cobbett could imitate a range of political styles because he had previously written in most of them. Political language of the 1790s informs his earlier writings. He can sound like Burke, Paine, Hannah More, or the *Liberty and Property* series because of the idiosyncratic status those writings had for him. With the exception of Paine's work, which has been discussed, Cobbett was writing in America from the basis of his memory and of conservative pamphlets. Cobbett was not in England, except for a few months, between 1785 and 1800. The rhetorics of More, Burke, and others struck him with special vividness because he was writing from an isolated and antagonistic position with few other allies except the printed word. To an unusual degree, conservative writings were disembodied voices — clear and vivid statements without a context except for Cobbett's nostalgia and pride. At the age of twenty-eight, Cobbett was only 'beginning to read, and even to talk, as well as to write upon politics', and the political material of the 1790s was his training ground for the defence of his country (*PR*, vi. (1804), 517). In 1816, this training left him with a remarkable ability either to subsume previously antagonistic styles within his own use of language or to imitate them as if he were a mocking bird.

In the 'Address', various types of political rhetoric are either contained within his own style or explicitly discussed. The Report of the Board of Agriculture, Malthusians, tax-makers, revolutionaries, and an exponent of domestic quietude are represented by the styles of language in which they argue. Cobbett organizes his 'Address' by characterizing these positions and arguing against them. His discussion of the tax-makers culminates with his mimicking the rhythm and tone of condescension:

The writers and speakers, who labour in the cause of corruption, have taken infinite pains to make the *labouring classes* believe, that *they* are *not taxed*; that the taxes which are paid by the landlords, farmers and tradesmen, do not affect *you*, the journeymen and labourers; and that the tax makers are *very lenient* towards *you*. But, I hope, you see to the bottom of these things now. (xxxi. 547–8)

Rhetoric from the 1790s, especially that of Burke, the *Liberty and Property* Series, and the earlier Cobbett, are also appropriated. Cobbett employs a style that had previously castigated all reformers as revolutionaries. Unlike the reader, a revolutionary 'would ride upon the shoulders of some through rivers of the blood of others, for the purpose of gratifying his own selfish and base and insolent ambition' (p. 569). Such an argument was powerful because it had previously been used to threaten the audience with their own potential violence. Cobbett diminishes the power of 1790s rhetoric by contrasting it with the needs and identity of his audience.

Ignorance, confusion, and the status of social outcasts are exchanged in the course of the 'Address' for information explaining the cause of misery, recognition by the author, and the possibility of social participation. The choices are between adhering to two types of imagery, Cobbett's or the opposition's. Responding to the suggestion that encouraging emigration was a solution to widespread poverty, Cobbett answers:

No: you will not leave your country. If you have suffered much and long, you have the greater right to remain in the hope of seeing better days. And I beseech you not to look upon yourselves as the *scum*; but, on the contrary, to be well persuaded, that a great deal depends upon *your exertions*. (p. 565)

Before the war, the virulence of conservative imagery which defined the audience as savage could not be countered by images which described it as political but not revolutionary. The pig allegories in particular suffered from the inability to disclaim violence while also advocating a clear political argument and strategy. Cobbett's ability to coordinate his two intentions is one measure of the difference between radical writings of the 1790s and of 1817. He wanted both to halt the machine-breaking of the countryside and to stimulate political activity by urging his audience to attend public meetings and to sign petitions. He keeps these intentions distinct by the clarity of his image of the audience, the moral certainty of his language, and his reinterpretation of the French Revolution.

The fundamental lesson of the French Revolution is not the violence of the people but the oppressiveness of government. The hatred for the French, which was effectively deployed by the *Liberty and Property* series against the reformers, was, according to Cobbett, due to England's traditional hatred of a tyrannical state: 'It is notorious, that that government was a cruel despotism; and that we and our forefathers always called it such' (p. 551). Cobbett makes a firm distinction between England and France in order to argue against those who had prophesied that reform in England would result in a French revolution, as Cobbett had prophesied himself twenty years earlier. Because the tradition of English liberty is in itself a means of order, the English reformers will behave differently:

It was the misfortune of the French people, that they had no great and settled principles to refer to in their laws or history. They sallied forth and inflicted vengeance on their oppressors; but, for want of settled principles, to which to refer, they fell into confusion; they massacred *each other*; they next flew to a military chief to protect them even *against themselves*; and the result has been what we too well know. Let us, therefore, congratulate ourselves, that we have great constitutional principles and laws, to which we can refer, and to which we are attached. (p. 568)

This is the *coup* of Cobbett's 'Address'. He writes the swinish multitude into a dignified and traditional, particularly Burkean, social fabric. Cobbett's style is not usually extensively composed of other people's rhetorics, although he always takes full advantage of his ability to mock the language of his enemies. The strategy of his 'Address' was to adopt styles for the purpose of encouraging an audience which those styles once successfully opposed. Cobbett's prose is essentially an act of healing, of transforming previously domineering and antagonistic images and styles into a resource of self-knowledge and a basis of action.

The effect of the 'Address' was momentous. Before it was published, Cobbett attempted to recall it, fearing that it might stimulate rather than diminish the machine-breaking in the North. Selling for two pence, the 'Address' could reach an audience that had not been specifically addressed with radical material since the 1790s. By extracting the main article from the *Political Register* and publishing it separately, Cobbett evaded the stamp duty which added four and a half pence to every paper sold. Six thousand copies had been sold before Cobbett's son arrived at the printers to stop the publication of the cheap edition. Cobbett announced that anyone could reprint it and claimed that it sold two hundred thousand copies in two months. The petitions sent to Parliament in 1817 were promoted by Cobbett's 'Address'. Cobbett decided to continue publishing a cheap edition of the *Register*, his *Weekly Political Pamphlet*. Cobbett prided himself on stopping the violence of the countryside, on ending the hold of Hannah More's and other religious tracts, and on awakening political consciousness.[27] The pamphlets were published for six months before the passage of the habeas corpus Suspension Bill caused Cobbett to flee to the United States. From America, he wrote the articles in his *Register,* which discuss the relation of grammar to class, and *A Grammar of the English Language,* first published in New York (1818) and then in London a few months later (1819). Five thousand copies were sold in two weeks; five hundred thousand by 1822; and one hundred thousand by 1834. The figures are remarkably high for a grammar that was probably never used by a school. In a little over two years, Cobbett had reactivated the audience, extended its boundaries, and enabled it to learn how to write.

All appeared to happen in a remarkably short time, but since the 1780s Cobbett had had a peculiarly political/ grammatical history. Each step of his political career accompanied a change in his audience and in his understanding of language. Cobbett did not come fully into his own until the progression was completed by his advocating male suffrage, by his learning to write for every segment of society, and by his writing a grammar of the 'vulgar' language. Although Cobbett's political career seems exceptionally fickle, his development was simultaneously direct and wayward. It was geographically wayward if nothing else. Cobbett learned about language and politics in France, Canada, and America before he settled in England and had to reformulate his knowledge there. Unlike an English university graduate, he learned about language and politics in a variety of circumstances and places and without the privilege of any directed and intensive study. More so than Wordsworth or Coleridge, more so than anyone, Cobbett fully disclosed his political thought in detail and without restraint while editing newspapers from 1797 to 1835. Compared to other writers, who had stable situations in which to think and who guarded themselves more carefully, Cobbett's changes of mind are not all that exceptional.

Although he altered his opinions, Cobbett's direction did not deviate. The language with which he describes his intentions as a radical in 1818 echoes that of his earlier promise as a Tory in 1800.

To my mind no emotions are more pleasing than those which are awakened by the recollection of my coarse red coat and my little blue smock-frock; and, I now derive great satisfaction from the hope, that, by these my exertions, many a private soldier, and many a plough-boy, will be enabled to shine amongst those who are destined to root out from the minds of men the base and blasphemous notions, that wisdom and talent are confined to what is called high-birth, and that the few possess a right divine to rule, oppress and plunder the many. (*PR*, xxxiv (1818), 269)

From refusing to bend before the aristocrats, Cobbett extended his initial promise to that of enabling his audience not to bend either. Not only did he enlarge his audience to include all men, and sometimes women, but he taught it how to write and to disregard the claims of its intellectual inferiority. Once Cobbett believed that people similar to his younger self were politically competent, once he learned to address an audience composed of the social class to which he once belonged, his ideas altered less drastically, and he wrote such fully effective pieces as *A Grammar of the English Language*, 'The Last 100 Days of British Freedom', and *Rural Rides*. Even Coleridge, the master critic, noted with some alarm and with extremely mixed praise, that Cobbett's writing in 1819 was better than it ever had been (*Letters*, iv. 979). Memory was so basic to both his creativity and his politics that he achieved his greatest capacity as a writer once he learned to address an audience that coincided with his image of his youth. Cobbett had been both soldier and plough-boy, and his grammar written for 'Soldiers, Sailors, Apprentices, and Plough-boys' was the pivotal text, the one in which Cobbett taught his audience to be similar to himself.[28]

As a soldier stationed in Canada, Cobbett began his long, and convoluted political/grammatical career. Knowing the written language led him over and over again into political quarrels that were often waged with leading grammarians and theorists. From the start, politics and language are welded together in Cobbett's own life. Because he knew how to write, Cobbett became clerk of his regiment, a post which exposed him to information that would not otherwise have been available to him. Upon discovering that his officers were appropriating funds designated for soldiers, he decided to charge them with corruption. After he had returned to England in 1791, he wrote *The Soldier's Friend* and initiated his suit. Realizing that his accusations would not be tolerated, Cobbett fled to France, to study the language of a country in the midst of revolution. From there he soon went to the United States and taught English to French *émigrés* who had fled a rebellion of slaves in St. Domingo. Living in Philadelphia, he wrote an English grammar for French students that was also published in Paris and that was frequently reprinted, *Le Tuteur Anglais*. During one of his classes, a pupil reported enthusiastically on the arrival of Joseph Priestley, and Cobbett retaliated with the pamphlet which initiated his career, *Notes on the Immigration of Joseph Priestley*. He later claimed not to have been interested

[28] *A Grammar of the English Language* (1818), 2nd edn., 1819, title-page.

in politics at the time but to have risen in anger to defend his country: 'I was actuated, perhaps, by no very exalted notions of either loyalty or patriotism; the act was not much an act of refined reasoning, or of reflection; it arose merely from feeling, but it was that sort of feeling, that jealousy for the honour of my native country . . .' (*PR*, vi (1804), 451). Cobbett claimed to be addressing an audience he scorned, the American Francophile democrats who criticized England as virulently as one might expect of those emerging from revolution. In contrast to the English pamphlet war, radical pamphleteers accused the more conservative Cobbett of vulgarity. They were delighted by his errors and his unrefined expressions: 'the bustle was over', 'perverse fellow', 'I have done all that laid in my power', 'why do I pursue in this odious comparison', and, the most telling, 'my father learned me to read'.[29] Soon Cobbett hated yet another radical grammatical Francophile, Noah Webster, who attempted to formulate a democratic variant of English. Cobbett accused Webster, among other things, of being a 'language-maker', a variant of the phrase 'constitution-maker' applied to Thomas Paine.[30] Leaving America in 1800, with arguments and lawsuits tumbling about his ears, Cobbett quitted an audience which he often abused in order to return to his beloved England.

Beginning his short-lived paper, the *Porcupine*, Cobbett addressed himself to the unfamiliar audience of 'persons of property, rank, and respectability' and wrote in an ostensibly refined style.[31] After having been roundly accused of vulgarity in America, Cobbett was apt to have felt constrained before his new and more imposing audience. He might have studied Samuel Johnson's prose in order to accustom himself to writing in a style that was more appropriate for the English upper classes. A series of articles evaluating Johnson's writing, signed 'Atticus' and published in the *Porcupine*, appear to have been written by Cobbett.

---

[29] *The Imposter Detected, or a Review of some of the writings of Peter Porcupine by Timothy Tickletoby*, Philadelphia, 1796, pp. ix–x. *Plum Pudding for the humane, chaste, valiant and enlightened Peter Porcupine*, Matthew Carey, 2nd edn., Philadelphia, 1799, p. 38.

[30] 'Gazette Selections, March 1797', *Porcupine's Works*, v. 151.

[31] Cited from the *Porcupine* by M. C. Pearl, p. 53.

Not only is the style similar to Cobbett's, but Cobbett imitated Johnson's prose on other occasions when he wanted to sound serious and dignified. Moreover, Cobbett examines passages of the *Rambler* in his *Grammar* where he makes the same assessment of the *Rambler's* prose that Atticus made seventeen years earlier: 'its general tendency is to spread a gloom over life and to damp all enterprise, private as well as public' (*Grammar*, p. 54). If Cobbett had not written the articles, he had learned their lessons well. By 1807, Cobbett directed his prose towards another audience which the *Edinburgh Review* defined as 'that most important and most independent class of society which stands just above the lowest' (xx (1807), 386). Now an advocate of household suffrage, Cobbett also announced his disregard for the refined language by arguing that knowing the classical languages had no special advantages to a knowledge of English. In a series of letters published in the *Political Register*, he challenges 'the *learned* gentlemen of two universities' to convince him that Greek and Latin merit their special status: 'If I do not *fairly* beat them in the controversy . . . I will then beg their pardon, and will allow, that to be able to speak, or write, in a language which people do not understand is a proof of learning.' (*PR*, xi (1807), 36). From January to June, Cobbett printed thirty-eight of the letters that he received in reply which vary in tone from arrogant, parodic, humble, to proud. One praises the classical languages for making the language and thought of the higher orders distinguishable from that of their social inferiors (p. 570). Another, carefully and proudly written, explains that people can learn English grammar as the writer did, by studying Hugh Blair's *Lectures in Rhetoric and Belles Lettres* (p. 480). Cobbett considered the literati to be successfully routed. His sensitivity to the suppression of his audience and the intensity of opinions expressed in the letters suggest the seriousness of his challenge.

The penultimate stage of Cobbett's political/grammatical transformation was his advocacy of household suffrage and his involvement with Tooke's political circle. The *Edinburgh Review* in 1807, and even *The Times* in 1816 (no. 9992), define Cobbett's inconsistency by describing his new admiration of John Horne Tooke: 'Horne Tooke is branded through many volumes, as a republican, Jacobin, and demagogue. He is even accused pretty distinctly of having been guilty of high treason; and yet we find in the late Number (vol. xi, p. 872), a most gracious and polite invitation to him to come forward for the public service.' (x. 392.) It was a well-chosen sign, for Cobbett later acknowledged that he became more radical after reading Tooke's and Hardy's trials for high treason: 'This reading *cured* me' (*PR*, xxi (1812), 165). Cobbett had other reasons for admiring Tooke besides his conduct during his trial. Cobbett's political opinions and his literary style were similar to the old leader's. Like Tooke, Cobbett wanted to return England to its former condition in the early eighteenth century when the constitution was less obstructed by corruption. Oddly enough, both demonstrated their allegiance to former times by wearing old-fashioned clothes, although Cobbett did not do so until later in his career. Tooke dressed as an old-style gentleman and Cobbett as a prosperous farmer. Both frequently reiterated their faith in king, church, constitution, and even the social hierarchy while also favouring extensive reforms and household suffrage. Both were libertarians who dreaded the possible extention of state power through public education. Cobbett admired Tooke for his ideas concerning political economy and for his plain-dealing language, two subjects of great importance to Cobbett:

During the short time that he was in Parliament, he uttered more good sense, upon subjects of Political Oeconomy, than I have ever heard of being uttered in that House for the last 30 years. He dealt not in fine-spun stuff that has no other effect than that of puzzling plain men, and that always has its rise in a want of clear notions in the speaker or writer. He saw the thing clearly himself; and he communicated his knowledge to others, in a way that no man of common sense could fail to understand. (*PR*, xix (1811), 193)

Tooke's concise, fierce, and demotic prose is more similar to Cobbett's than that of any other contemporary writer.

Until 1817, when he began to advocate male rather than household suffrage, Cobbett was closely associated with

Tooke's political circle, and especially with the leading radical member of Parliament during much of this time, Sir Francis Burdett. J. Anne Hone describes Tooke as the leader of what was basically an independent radical party which continued after his death in 1812 but with a less coherent leadership.[32] After the more broadly-based political activity of the 1790s, Tooke and Burdett concentrated upon electing a radical candidate for Westminster. At his notoriously drunken Sunday dinners, Tooke provided a consistent meeting-place for radicals and intellectuals for almost twenty years. An impressive number and variety of people attended either occasionally or for long periods: Thomas Hardy, Joel Barlow, Thomas Paine, John Thelwall, Thomas Holcroft, William Godwin, Lord Erskine, Henry Hunt, Samuel Rogers, Sir James MacKintosh, Gilbert Wakefield, and Richard Porson, among others. Hazlitt apparently attended for he describes Tooke's conversation during the dinners with evident pleasure; Southey wanted to attend in 1808 but feared he would lose his pension; Coleridge found the democrats there repugnant.[33] Sir Francis Burdett and William Bosville were exceptionally intimate with Tooke, Burdett so much so that he was called Tooke's 'puppet'. From 1807-16, Burdett, Bosville, and Cobbett co-operated extensively with each other to return a radical candidate to Westminster and to wage other political campaigns.

A political crisis of 1810 depicts the extent of their association. John Gale Jones was arrested for advertising a debate concerning two recent discussions in Parliament. With the word 'strangers', his handbill refers to journalists who reported the debates. The handbill read: 'Which was a greater outrage upon the public feeling, Mr. Yorke's enforcement of the standing order to exclude strangers from the House of Commons, or Mr. Windham's recent attack upon the liberty of the press?' (PR, xv. 481.) Because he was arrested by the House, Jones could be (and was) confined to

---

[32] For the Cause of Truth: Radicalism in London, 1796–1821, Oxford, 1982, p. 220.

[33] 'The Late Mr. Horne Tooke', Complete Works, xi. 49. Grigg's Letters, ii. 720. Geoffrey Carnall, Robert Southey and his Age: The Development of a Conservative Mind, Oxford, 1960, p. 84.

the Tower without trial and for an unspecified length of time. Burdett came to his defence in an open letter which was printed in Cobbett's *Political Register*, 'Sir Francis Burdett to his Constituents; denying the power of the House of Commons to imprison the People of England' (*PR*, xvii (1810), 421). It was actually written by Cobbett. Burdett, then a member of the House, was also committed to the Tower. William Cobbett expected similar treatment for publishing the letter but instead was arrested on an outstanding indictment for an article which protested against flogging in the navy. Cobbett was terrified. Unlike writers who guarded themselves constantly, Cobbett was fearless until suddenly afflicted with the urge to save himself and run. He offered to stop writing the *Register*, if the administration dropped the charges. He had proceeded so far as to write a farewell article, but no one knows if the administration rejected his offer or if he withdrew it. At his trial Cobbett defended himself before Lord Ellenborough (some say disastrously) and received a sentence of two years at Newgate with sureties and fines amounting to £6,000. Burdett lent Cobbett £2,000 and Bosville gave him £1,000. Burdett presided at the public dinner, attended by six hundred people, to celebrate Cobbett's release in 1812.[34]

Cobbett continued to work closely with Burdett until shortly after he fled to the United States, where he denounced him virulently in 'The Last 100 Days of British Freedom'. Whereas Tooke had written a letter to *The Times* in 1807 disclaiming the frequently repeated charge that Burdett was his puppet, Cobbett seizes the honour himself by describing Burdett as created 'by our generosity, by the exertion of *our talent*, by our words put into his mouth; by our writings transcribed by him; by, in short, *our own* talent' (*PR*, xxxiv (1818), 414). Cobbett's recent biographer, George Spater, supports Cobbett's claim that all of Burdett's major public speeches including those in Parliament, were written by Cobbett (p. 172). One could find something beguiling in these political and literary machinations, in Burdett's tendency to speak words that certain other people

[34] George Spater, *William Cobbett: The Poor Man's Friend*, 1982. 2 vols., i. 237-8.

wrote. He was, as well as everything else, the character F in the *Diversions of Purley*. After Tooke's death, Burdett apparently transferred himself, or rather the self that appeared in print, to William Cobbett. It was a strangely appropriate transferral of the most famous radical Member of Parliament from the previous writer of a radical theory of language, to the future writer of a radical grammar. Politics and language could not have been more entangled.

Cobbett's *Grammar* emerges out of this radical tradition and his complex relation to it. Although Cobbett implies that his is a single mind opposing a monolithic tradition, the *Grammar* was an original contribution to a group of recent works that were aware of the political implications of language theory. Cobbett knew of Priestley's, Tooke's, and Webster's writings, not only as a series of texts but as the work of writers whom he sometimes scorned and sometimes greatly admired. Tooke and Webster more directly than Priestley appear to have contributed significantly to Cobbett's *Grammar*, although he mentions neither by name. Like Coleridge, Cobbett tended to describe his enemies more fully than his allies and to ignore writers that he once learned a great deal from. In the midst of denouncing Burdett, Cobbett is not apt to have praised his mentor.

Cobbett both relies on the *Diversions* and criticizes it as a 'learned' argument. He alludes to Tooke with the occasional remark that he will not proceed further with the discussion because 'such an examination would be more curious than useful' (*Grammar*, p. 68). The expression, or one similar to it, accompanies ideas that are recognizably Tooke's, such as the part of speech of the word 'that', the etymology of pronouns, the syntax of 'it' as an impersonal verb (as in 'it rains'), and compound verbs formed by prepositions. Despite the repeated disclaimers, the number of references to the *Diversions* suggests that Cobbett studied it with some care and was reminded of it repeatedly while writing his grammar. The *Grammar's* structure implies the same by the division of the book into two parts, etymology and syntax. Etymology obtains a much more prominent position in Cobbett's *Grammar* of 1818 than in his earlier one for French speakers. Cobbett defines the parts of speech as pertaining solely to a word's function in a particular sentence, as do Hazlitt and Webster. Etymology explains 'what are the relationships of words, how words grow out of each other, how they are varied in their letters in order to correspond with the variation in the circumstances to which they apply' (p. 16). This close relation of etymology or the parts of speech with syntax was one of the major discoveries of Tooke's work. A word does not have an identity as a particular part of speech but only as it is applied in each instance: 'Mind, therefore, that it is the *sense in which the word is used,* and *not the letters of which it is composed*, that determines what is the part of speech to which it belongs.' (p. 73.) The syntactical variation of Tooke's concept of abbreviation was ellipsis, an aspect of grammar that is considered in Cobbett, Webster, and Hazlitt but not by the more conventional grammarians, Murray and Lowth. Like Webster, Cobbett explains the subjunctive as an elliptical form of the future, and not as the necessary accompaniment of a conditional conjunction: 'the subjunctive is necessarily always used when a *sign* is *left out*: as "Take care that *he come* tomorrow . . . and that *all things be* duly prepared for his entertainment". Fill up with the *signs* and you will see the *reason* for what you write.' (p. 148.) The 'to' of the infinitive is also explained by ellipsis.

More than one might expect, Cobbett's grammar is formulated out of a 'learned' argument. The informal diction of the text and Cobbett's critique of learning disguise his familiarity with the details of the grammatical debate. Cobbett accurately identifies the characteristics which were said to distinguish the refined language. Sometimes in his attempt to correct Lowth or Murray, however, he writes a prescriptive grammar of his own. Cobbett includes a long list of verbs which he intends to make regular, including to dare, to burst, to swell, to mow, to load, to spring. No one would now say 'having durst' or 'having loden' as Lowth recommended. Some would say 'having mown' and not 'mowed'. And no one would say 'having springed' as Cobbett recommends. Cobbett argues that these irregular verbs were formed by contraction, as Lowth maintains in his grammar. Moreover, as previously argued, several grammarians advocated making verbs irregular in order to make English more similar to the classical languages. Perhaps their arguments had had effect, and refined speech had generated an increasing number of irregular verbs. The border between arguments based on grammatical texts and those based on Cobbett's observation of contemporary patterns of speech is not easy to discern. The language which Cobbett's grammar advocates depends partly on 'learned' texts which considered the nature of refined and vulgar language and partly on an allegedly vulgar language that Cobbett believed to be truer to the language of his own social class. There is no means of knowing how precisely the two coincided.

All grammars were composed of previous works on language with varying degrees of original contributions from the author. Although Cobbett extensively criticizes Lowth and Murray, he relies upon them as well. The more unconventional aspects of his grammar were preceded by the writings of Tooke and Webster. Not only did they contribute to Cobbett's understanding of the details of language usage but to the political critique which distinguishes Cobbett's text. Before Cobbett, Tooke discussed language as embedded in political conflict. Tooke's critique of erudition, his awareness of 'imposture', and even his informal and sometimes aggressive tone might have encouraged Cobbett to discuss language in a similar manner. Although Cobbett discusses the political implications of language more exhaustively than Tooke, he probably was encouraged by his work. Cobbett's reading of Webster's *Dissertations on the English Language* (1789) is more speculative as fewer traces of it are visible in the *Grammar*. Cobbett was in America, preparing his English grammar for French speakers soon after the *Dissertations* was published. As he also knew of Webster 'the language-maker', he is apt to have read his work or at least known of it, although he would not have agreed with much of it at this time. Webster did his utmost to publicize his ideas through lecture tours, articles, and essays. Even in the 1790s, Cobbett might have appreciated Webster's description of Lowth's students:

They read Lowth's Introduction, or some other grammatical treatise, believe what they read ... and attempt to shape their language by his rules. Thus they enter the world with such phrases as mean, averse from, if he have, he had gotten and others which they deem correct; they pride themselves, for some time in their superior learning and peculiarities; till further information, or the ridicule of the public, brings them to use the language of other people. (Webster, vii)

By 1817, Webster's critique of refinement and his attempt to formulate a democratic variant of English are fully compatible with Cobbett's understanding of language. By relying on Tooke and possibly Webster, Cobbett was encouraged to conceive of a grammar that was perfectly formed to counter an understanding of language that divided the population into two unbridgeable social classes.

Cobbett's unique contribution to the practice of language was to formulate a vernacular, written language which was suitable for public discourse. Although such a language existed in a number of literary texts and was discussed in a few radical theories, it did not exist in a form which was readily available to be learned. Unlike grammars addressed to 'gentlemen designed merely for Trade' or for 'young Ladies', Cobbett's grammar was written to teach labourers how to write for the specific purpose of their political defence. Writing it was a more complex act than teaching punctuation and syntax. Cobbett intended his grammar to counter the refined language at every level of its effectiveness. It provided an alternative to modes of education which did not teach the vulgar how to write; it formulated a language by making it available to be learned; and it provided an antidote to the psychological inhibitions perpetuated by the concept of the refined language. Cobbett's articles of 1817, discussed in the first chapter, indicate the extent to which Cobbett believed in the intellectual suppression of his audience. An ignorance of grammar not only prohibits the audience from written discussion but also inhibits thought: 'It creates a dependence, a diffidence, it cripples; it benumbs'. With a grammar, Cobbett hoped to counteract a social system which, from multiple and diverse angles, aligned learning with class so as to exclude his audience from the social and intellectual participation that writing brings.

Appropriately, the *Grammar* has the air of an initiation ceremony, even a puberty rite, during which Cobbett accompanies his readers through an important and dignified transition. Written in the form of letters to his fourteen-year-old son, Cobbett's *Grammar* educates its readers in becoming adult men. Women are excluded from the relation of teacher to student which is overwhelmingly one of father to son. By concentrating on 'My Dear Little James', Cobbett affectionately addresses his readers while concentrating on their future as active citizens:

In a confident reliance on your attentiveness, industry, and patience, I have a hope not less confident of seeing you a man of real learning, employing your time and talents in aiding the cause of truth and justice, in affording protection to defenceless innocence, and in drawing down vengeance on lawless oppression; and, in that hope, I am your happy as well as affectionate father. (p. 11)

The serious respect which he grants to his audience depends on his relation to them as a teacher and a father. Cobbett, at times, catches the tone which Hannah More hoped conservative pamphleteers could convey to their readers: 'I want something which will give the idea of a tall man stooping'.[35] The paternal tone is radicalized by Cobbett's desire for his audience to change as Cobbett brings his representative son into the adult world of public expression and social responsibility.

Cobbett's *Grammar* alerts its readers to certain moral dangers by teaching them to recognize the 'language of corruption'. Cobbett appropriates the phrase 'the corrupt language' which formerly characterized vulgar discourse in order to portray his contempt for those who speak the refined language. Grammarians and politicians are equally culpable in that they rely upon a language which sacrifices clarity and understanding for the self-aggrandisement of its speakers and the subordination of others. Lowth, Murray, Blair, Members of Parliament, and the Royal family speak the language of 'corruption'. The distinguishing features of refinement are briefly dismissed. Harmonious sounds, variations in sentence length, and the careful placing of prepositions 'might be very well if we were to *sing* our

[35] Cited from a letter of 24 March 1817 in Charlotte M. Yonge's *Hannah More*, Eminent Women Series, 1888, p. 94.

writing' (p. 183). Accent does not matter as long as the speaker is saying something worthwhile (p. 15). Delicacy is not a fundamental criterion of diction: 'the best words are those, which are familiar to the ears of the greatest number of persons' (pp. 71–2). The language of corruption is ambiguous and inaccurate, primarily because meaning is disregarded. Hugh Blair's prose in *Lectures in Rhetoric and Belles Lettres* has the dubious honour of being frequently quoted:

'These two paragraphs are extremely worthy of MR. ADDISON, and exhibit a style, which *they,* who can successfully imitate, may esteem themselves happy'. It ought to be *those* instead of *they*. But, this is not the only fault in this sentence. Why say '*extremely* worthy'? *Worthiness* is a quality which hardly admits of *degrees*, and, surely, it does not admit of *extremes*. Then again, at the close: 'to *esteem*' is to *prize*, to *set value on*, to *value highly*. How, then, can men '*esteem* themselves happy?' How can they *prize themselves* happy?' ... My Dear James, let chamber-maids and members of the House of Commons, and learned Doctors, write thus: be you content with plain words which convey your meaning: say that a thing is *quite worthy* of a man; and that men may *deem* themselves happy. (p. 111)

Relentlessly, Cobbett demonstrates the fallibility of the literati. Passages from Johnson's *Rambler* and Watts' *Logic* reveal that even the writer of a dictionary and a treatise on logic did not always write English accurately. Cobbett also criticizes a King's speech and one by the Prince Regent in a letter titled 'Errors and Nonsense in a King's Speech' (p. 173). Readers of the *Grammar* might have been intimidated by Cobbett's expectation of them to write more accurately than Hugh Blair, Samuel Johnson, members of parliament, and George III. Cobbett's intention here is not solely to demonstrate that the great can make mistakes but to discredit political and cultural authorities by the inaccuracy of their language. Correctness has overwhelming significance here for it establishes the equality of those who are 'plain English scholars' with members of a political and literary élite (p. 94). Cobbett thus counters intellectual subordination with grammatical minutiae. In the Introduction to his grammar, Cobbett reiterates his faith in the class system while his grammar portrays the cost of intellectual suppression and equips his readers to defy it. Cobbett was at his most radical while considering ideas about language. Grammar, as he deploys it, becomes a mighty leveller.

In order to train his students to be independent thinkers, Cobbett demystifies the written language and teaches his readers methods of self-education. Cobbett understood that the more difficult language was described as being, the more authority his readers would grant to himself and to other skilled writers. Cobbett did not want to perpetuate the literati as a class. He tells his readers that they already know the language and that his position is to extend a skill that they already have: 'I need not tell you, that I *was working* means the same as I *worked*, only that the former supposes that something else was going on at the same time.' (p. 135.) Cobbett's casual diction and his direct address to readers minimize any self-consciousness or embarrassment that readers might feel while attempting to learn the language. Such passages contrast sharply with the implications of the language used in Murray's text where, according to the text, readers have no previous relation to the language: 'To produce the agreement and right disposition of words in a sentence many rules are necessary. The following, with annexed observations, comprise the chief of them.' (p. 87.) Murray's text thus presents language as intricate, mysterious, and foreign. After studying the book thoroughly, readers will remain ignorant of some of the rules. Cobbett, however, accompanies his readers throughout the process of learning, anticipating confusion and training his readers to deal with it intelligently rather than surrender to despair: 'Read again paragraphs 60 and 61, Letter VI. Think well upon what you find there; and when you have done that, proceed with me.' (p. 100.) Cobbett's manifest energy of mind, as well as his promptings, encourage his readers to think actively and energetically. Confusion is portrayed as the same as any difficulty that can be overcome by thought and exertion:

You ought to proceed in your study, not only with diligence, but with *patience;* that, if you meet with difficulties, you should bear in mind, that, to enjoy the noble prospect from Port's-Down Hill, you had first to climb slowly to the top; and that, if those difficulties gather about you and impede your way, you have only to call to your recollection any one of the many days that you have toiled through briers and brambles and bogs, cheered and urged on by the hope of at last finding and killing your game. (p. 10)

Whereas Cobbett had accused Murray of writing a text that 'inculcates passive obedience and softly promotes the čause of corruption', Cobbett writes his own variant of a grammar that duplicates the writer's chosen relation of the citizen to the state. Whereas Murray's encourages readers to acquiesce in what they do not understand, Cobbett's teaches his readers to recognize confusion and to insist that the proceedings make sense.

Grammars could be said to encourage obedience by the unwavering attention that they require from their readers. Cobbett, however, interrupts the enclosed relation of teacher and pupil:

A verb is called active when it expresses an *action*, which is produced by the nominative of the sentence: as, 'Sidmouth *imprisoned* Benbow'. It is passive, when it expresses an action, which is received, or endured, by the person or thing which is the nominative of the sentence, as, 'Benbow is *imprisoned*'. It is neuter, when it expresses simply the state of being, or of existence, of a person or thing: as 'Benbow *lies* in irons'. (p. 46)

Cobbett's examples are simultaneously very funny and very serious. Explaining active, passive, and neuter verbs becomes incongruously trivial when set against the more pressing problem of Benbow's arrest. This belittling of the text by the teacher adds greatly to the pleasure of reading it. Despite their humour, such examples focus the reader's attention on the political conflict which, according to Cobbett, was their motive for learning to write. By employing, quite literally, the language of his *Political Register*, Cobbett confirms his code of values while also ensuring that his readers will be familiar with the language they are studying. Whereas conventional ideas about language disregarded the 'particular', the political circumstances of the present are of supreme importance in Cobbett's text. To use political material to explain the language implies, as Cobbett intended it to, that political conflict is the very essence of language.

Cobbett recognizes no other purpose to language except 'to *inform*, to *convince*, or to *persuade*' (p. 181). Language does not exist to express one's self or to demonstrate one's sensibility but to influence the actions of others and to participate in public life: 'The actions of men proceed from their *thoughts*. In order to obtain the co-operation, the concurrence, or the consent of others, we must communicate our thoughts to them. The means of communication are *words*; and grammar teaches us *how to make use of words*' (p. 9). Clarity is the essential virtue of language because it is the only democratic means of exchanging ideas. As in Paine and Tooke, obscurity in the grammar is the *modus vivendi* of oppression. Repeatedly, Cobbett requests his readers to consider their meaning, claiming that language will then make an almost natural sense.

I will not fatigue your memory with more examples relating to the *times* of verbs. Consider well what you *mean*; what you *wish to say*. Examine well into the true meaning of your words; and you will never make a mistake as to the times. '*I thought to have heard* the Noble Lord produce something like proof.' No! my dear James will never fall into the use of such senseless gabble! You would think of *hearing* something; you would think of *to hear,* not *to have heard*. You would be *waiting to hear*, and not, like these men, be *waiting to have heard*. (p. 137)

Clarity is not merely a matter of syntax but of enabling one's self to negotiate in a society that was apt to interfere with one's meaning. Corruption not only relies upon obscurity to defend itself but to obscure the statements of others: 'Grammar, perfectly understood, enables us, not only to express our meaning fully and clearly, but so to express it as to enable us to defy the ingenuity of man to give our words any other meaning than that which we ourselves intend them to express.' (p. 14.) It is not difficult to see how thoroughly Cobbett's grammar is a defence against oppression. Not only does it teach his readers the language of the *Political Register* in the hope of creating more writers like himself, but it formulates a language to recover his audience from having been overwhelmed by the language of a hostile governing class. The hope that burns behind the grammar, the wonder of what will happen when oppression ends, is that 'vulgar' writers will be able to create their precise meaning and then keep that meaning virginally intact. Correct grammar, at this point, becomes synonymous with the possibility of maintaining perfect integrity. 'Meaning' becomes synonymous with autonomy.

Cobbett's and Coleridge's work is comparable because they both responded with an acute sensitivity to the problems raised by conventional assessments of language. Coleridge's desire to write 'ad clerum' was part of his effort to address an audience which he hoped would judge his work according to the values granted to the refined language. Cobbett's desire to create a working-class audience that could defend itself politically, effectively disrupted some of the political effects of the concept of refinement. The *Biographia* and *The Grammar* thus strove against each other. The two texts cannot be simply described, however, as engaged in a conflict of élitism vs. radicalism. Both were written by authors who had formerly espoused very different positions and who were invalidating their own earlier arguments. Cobbett's *Grammar* carries the signs of his conservatism in his paternalistic tone and in his continuing faith in class hierarchy. He seems to have believed that one could drastically alter the culture (by teaching subordinate classes how to write in their own defence) without altering class hierarchy except to purify it. The *Biographia*, which is a deeply apologetic text, criticizes the literati despite Coleridge's keen awareness of the antagonism that such criticism would provoke. It argues against the Preface's radical theory of language in a manner that is overburdened with complexity and that reveals Coleridge's dread of judgement from those whom he criticizes. Writing for vastly different audiences, Cobbett and Coleridge both wanted to define an audience that could create itself anew, despite the confusion generated by political hysteria, and both attempted to do so by redefining the nature of language. The vehemence against unorthodox opinions is a major subject of their works and also a major motive for writing them. In the Preface, the 'Address to

Journeymen and Labourers', the *Biographia*, and *The Grammar*, society is portrayed as an antagonistic distorter of meaning which must be resisted if political integrity or creative freedom is to be maintained. It is a group of works which strongly indicts English intellectual life at the turn of the century. The *Biographia*, as much as the 'Address' and the *Grammar*, struggles to regain dignity and standing after a painful debate.

Cobbett's *Grammar* and Coleridge's *Biographia* also constitute the last stages of what had once been an alliance between radicals and the literati. Because the concept of vulgar and refined language restricted creative writers as well as the 'vulgar', the two groups temporarily shared an interest in replacing conventional theories of language with theories that allowed a greater range of expression. The *Diversions of Purley* and the Preface emerge from this alliance. The experimentation of such writers as Thomas Paine, Thomas Spence, William Hone, and William Cobbett accompanies such major innovations in style as the writings of Blake, Hazlitt, Wordsworth, and Coleridge. Spence's attempt to make English a language that was more available to labourers parallels Wordsworth's and Coleridge's efforts to vindicate the language of rustics. The creative and political necessity of rediscovering a written vernacular language was hardly the concern of only a literary avant-garde but also of social classes that were demanding to be admitted into what had been defined as 'civilization'. While the literati gained a greater flexibility of style and more extensive resources of expression, the writings of the audience gained tremendously in both quality and number. After the war, radical writers could no longer be outdone by such writings as the *Liberty and Property* series and Hannah More's Cheap Repository Tracts. Imitators of Hone and Cobbett were remarkably unsuccessful. Hone's ability to defend himself against three charges of libel vindicated the capacities of the vernacular language as well as those of the accused. The differences between *Politics for the People* and Cobbett's *Political Register* are vast and immediately telling. Whereas a political vernacular was rarely achieved during the 1790s, after the war even the mechanics of it were explained and published.

By this time, as the audience achieved such gains, the alliance between radicalism and creativity no longer existed. Matching the vehemence of those who once denounced the Preface, Coleridge denounced the vulgar language and those who spoke it with his depiction of the 'peasants'. Cobbett despised the term, which he called new and 'fashionable', because it described a class without culture, morals, or value (*Taking Leave*, p. 6). Others turned against a population that had previously held their political support. Southey had written his radical poem *Wat Tyler* in a radically vernacular language. Deciding not to publish it in the 1790s, the Poet Laureate was dismayed when Richard Carlile and William Hone published it in 1817. A few months earlier, Southey had written his two essays in the *Quarterly Review* which argued that the suppression of plebeian radicalism was insufficiently severe.

Such contradictions were obvious and commented upon. The non-literati recognized that they had not only lost previous allies but that their new enemies had managed to turn their previous radicalism into forms of obeisance to conventions that derided the vulgar. The rustic could be and was turned against them. One of William Hone's parodies for which he was charged concludes with an angry depiction of the various metamorphoses of once radical writers. (Readers should know that 'Derry Down Triangle' was Hone's nickname for Castlereagh, leader of the House of Commons who was alleged to have countenanced the use of a torture device called the 'triangle' after the Irish Rebellion of 1798. Sherry was paid to the Poet Laureate. Sackbut and psaltery were medieval musical instruments.)

And COLERIDGE shall have a Jew's Harp, and a Rabbinical Talmud, and a Roman Missal: and WORDSWORTH shall have a Psalter, and a Primer, and a Reading Easy: and unto SOUTHEY's Sack-but shall be duly added: and with Harp, Sack-but, and Psalry, they shall make merry, and discover themselves before Derry Down Triangle, and HUM his most gracious Master, whose Kingdom shall have no end. (*Trials*, 3rd, p. 145)

Such a passage suggests the greater force of radical expression since the 1790s and also the complexity and anger with which that gain was finally won. Hone's attack on the refined poets could be matched by an infinitely greater number of passages denouncing the vulgar language. As a vernacular written language came into existence, it was accompanied by a long history of denunciations, a kind of screaming shadow of abuse, in newspaper articles, in critical essays of literary reviews, in the *Biographia,* in parliamentary discussions, and in political trials. Although radicals had a more effective language, which would be needed, they still did not have the means of disarming the literati and the state from using language against them.

Selected Bibliography

Unless otherwise stated the place of publication is London. Eighteenth- and nineteenth-century titles have been shortened and their capitalization altered.

PRIMARY SOURCES

Manuscripts

Association Papers: Original Letters from various authors relating to the Association. BL, Add. MSS 16919–16928. Letters from various other associations. BL Add. MSS 16929–16931.

William Cobbett: Correspondence with J. Wright and others, 1800–10. Correspondence with William Windham, 1800–6, BL Add. MS 37853 ff. 1–242.

William Hone Papers: BL Add. MS 40120. Letters to Francis Place, BL Add. MS 37949.

Francis Place Papers: BL, Add. MSS 27808–27813.

Printed Material

Adams, John Quincy, *An Answer to Pain's Right of Man,* 1793.

Annual Register

Annual Review

Anti-Jacobin Review and Magazine

Anti-Jacobin; or, Weekly Examiner

Ash, John, *Grammatical Institutes,* 1760, EL no. 9.

Association for preserving Liberty and Property against Republicans and Levellers.

—— *Association Papers addressed to all the Loyal Associations,* 1793.

—— *Liberty and Property preserved against Republicans and Levellers. A Collection of Tracts* [1795].

—— *Proceedings of the Association for preserving Liberty and Property against Republicans and Levellers* [1793].

Bamford, Samuel, *Passages in the Life of a Radical,* 1844.

Beattie, James, *The Theory of Language,* 1788, EL no. 88.

Bewick, Thomas, *A Memoir of Thomas Bewick by Himself,* ed. Montague Weekly, 1961.

Binns, John, *Recollections of the Life of John Binns,* Philadelphia, 1854.

Blair, Hugh, *Lectures on Rhetoric and Belles Lettres* (1780), Edinburgh, 1820, 2 vols.

Boswell, James, *Boswell's London Journal, 1762–1763*, ed. Frederick A. Pottle, New York, 1950.
——, *Life of Johnson*, ed. R. W. Chapman, 3rd edn., 1970.
British Critic
[Henry Brougham with Francis Jeffrey], 'Don Pedro Cevallos on the French Usurpation of Spain', *Edinburgh Review*, xiii (1808), 215–34.
Buchanan, James, *The British Grammar*, 1762, EL no. 97.
——, *Linguae Britannicae vera Pronunciatio*, 1757, EL no. 39.
Bunyan, John, *Grace Abounding to the Chief of Sinners*, ed. Roger Sharrock, Oxford, 1962.
——, *The Pilgrim's Progress*, ed. Roger Sharrock, 1965.
——, *The Pilgrim's Progress*, 29th edn., 1755, 3 pts, 16th edn. of the 3rd pt.
Burke, Edmund, *The Correspondence of Edmund Burke*, vol. vi, ed. Alfred Cobban and Robert A. Smith, Cambridge, 1967.
——, *Reflections on the Revolution in France*, ed. Conor Cruise O'Brien, 1969.
Burnett, James [Lord Mónboddo], *Of the Origin and Progress of Language*, 1774–1792, EL no. 48, 6 vols.
Butler, John, *Brief Reflections upon the Liberty of the British Subject*, Canterbury [1791?].
Campbell, George, *The Philosophy of Rhetoric* (1776), a new edition, New York, 1855.
Clare, John, *Sketches in the Life of John Clare written by Himself*, ed. Edmund Blunden, 1931.
Cobbett, William, *Cobbett's Political Register*, 1802–1835, 89 vols.
——, *A Grammar of the English Language in a Series of Letters*, 2nd edn., 1819.
——, *A History of the Protestant "Reformation" in England and Ireland*, 1824–6.
——, *Letters from William Cobbett to Edward Thornton, Written in the Years 1797 to 1800*, ed. G. D. H. Cole, 1937.
——, *Mr. Cobbett's Taking Leave of his Countrymen*, 1817.
——, *The Porcupine*, 1800–1.
——, *Porcupine's Works*, 1801, 12 vols.
——, *Le Tuteur Anglais, ou Grammaire Regulière de la Langue Anglaise*, Philadelphia, 1795.
——, *A Year's Residence in the United States of America* (1818), 1828.
[Cobbett, William], *Important Considerations for the People of this Kingdom*, 1803.
——, *The Soldier's Friend*, 1792.
Coleridge, Samuel Taylor, *Aids to Reflection* (1825), 1836.
——, *Biographia Literaria* (1817), ed. J. Shawcross, Oxford, 1907, 2 vols.

——, *Collected Letters of Samuel Taylor Coleridge*, ed. Earl Leslie Griggs, Oxford, 1959–71, 6 vols.

——, *Notebooks of Samuel Taylor Coleridge*, ed. Kathleen Coburn, 1957–73, 3 vols.

——, *Samuel Taylor Coleridge: Poems*, ed. John Beer, Everyman's Library, 1974.

——, 'The Statesman's Manual' in *Lay Sermons, Collected Works of Coleridge*, ed. R. J. White, gen. ed. Kathleen Coburn, Princeton, 1972, 15 vols, vol. vi.

——, *Omniana of S. T. Coleridge*, Oxford, 1917.

Complete Collection of State Trials, initially compiled by William Cobbett and continued by T. B. Howells, 1818–20, 34 vols.

Condillac, Étienne Bonnot de, *An Essay on the Origin of Human Knowledge, being a Supplement to Mr. Locke's Essay on Human Understanding*, trans. Mr Nugent, 1756.

Cooper, Thomas, *The Life of Thomas Cooper* (1872), Leicester, 1971.

A Dialogue between Mr. Worthy and John Simple [1792].

Eaton, Daniel Isaac, *Politics for the People: or, a Salmagundy for Swine*, 1793–5, Greenwood Reprint, New York, 1968, 2 vols.

——, *Trial of Daniel Isaac Eaton, July the tenth, 1793* [1793].

Edgeworth, Richard and Maria, *Practical Education*, 2nd edn., 1801, 3 vols.

Edinburgh Review

Fell, John, *An Essay towards an English Grammar*, 1784, EL no. 16.

Fenning, Daniel, *A New Grammar of the English Language*, 1771, EL no. 19.

Fisher, Anne, *A New Grammar*, 1750, EL no. 130.

Foxe, John, *Foxe's Book of Martyrs*, ed. G. A. Williamson, 1965.

Gentleman's Magazine

Gilchrist, James, *Philosophic Etymology; or a Rational Grammar*, 1816.

Godwin, William, *The Enquirer: Reflections on Education, Manners, and Literature*, 1797.

——, *Enquiry concerning Political Justice* (1793), ed. K. Codell Carter, 1971.

——, *Thoughts Occasioned by the Perusal of Dr. Parr's Spital Sermon*, 1801.

Great Britain. Report of the Departmental Committee appointed by the President of the Board of Education, *The Teaching of English in England*, 1921.

Hansard's Parliamentary Debates. Initially compiled by William Cobbett and titled *The Parliamentary History of England*, 1803 to the present.

Hanway, Jonas, *A Comprehensive View of Sunday Schools*, 1786, 2 pts.

Harris, James, *Hermes; or, a Philosophical Inquiry concerning Language and Universal Grammar*, 1751, EL no. 55.

Hartley, David, *Observations on Man, his Frame, his Duty, and his Expectations* (1748), 6th edn. 1834.

Hazlitt, William, *The Complete Works of William Hazlitt*, ed. E. P. Howe, 1930–4, 21 vols.

The History of Thomas Hickathrift, ed. G. L. Gomme, 1885.

Holcroft, Thomas, *Memoirs of the Late Thomas Holcroft written by himself*, ed. William Hazlitt, 1816, 3 vols.

Hone, William, *Another Article for the Quarterly Review*, 1824.

——, *Aspersions Answered: An Explanatory Statement*, 3rd edn., 1824.

——, *The Every-Day Book and Table Book; or, the Everlasting Calendar of Popular Amusements*, 1837, 2 vols.

——, *Facetiae and Miscellanies with one hundred and twenty engravings by George Cruikshank*, 1827.

——, *The Reformists' Register and Weekly Commentary*, 1817.

——, *The Three Trials of William Hone* (1818), ed. William Tegg, 1876.

[Hone, William] , *Another Ministerial Defeat. The Trial of the Dog for Biting the Noble Lord*, 1817.

——, *The Apocryphal New Testament*, 1820.

——, *Hone's Interesting History of the Memorable Blood Conspiracy* [1816].

——, *The Man in the Moon*, 16th edn., 1820.

——, *Official Account. Bartholomew Fair Insurrection; and the Pie-Bald Poney Plot*, 1817.

——, *Official Account of the Noble Lord's Bite and his Dangerous Condition*, 1817.

——, *The Political House that Jack Built*, 1819.

Howell, James, trans., *An Exact History of the Late Revolution in Naples*, 1650.

Hunt, Henry, *Memoirs of Henry Hunt, Esq., Written by Himself in his Majesty's Jail at Ilchester*, Dolby, 1820, 3 vols., vol. i.

Hunt, Leigh, 'The Late Mr. Horne Tooke', *Leigh Hunt's Political and Occasional Essays*, ed. Lawrence H. Houtchens and Carolyn W. Houtchens, 1962, pp. 131–41.

The Imposter Detected: a Review of some of the writings of Peter Porcupine, by Timothy Tickletoby, Philadelphia, 1796.

Ingram, James, *Inaugural Lecture on the Utility of Anglo-Saxon Literature*, Oxford, 1807.

Janeway, James, *A Token for Children*, 1797.

Johnson, Samuel, *A Dictionary of the English Language, 1755*, 2 vols.

——, *Selected Poetry and Prose*, ed. Frank Brady and W. K. Wimsatt, 1977.

[Jones, Sir William], *Principles of Government in a Dialogue between a Scholar and a Peasant*, 1782.

Lackington, James, *Memoirs of the First Forty-Five Years of the Life of James Lackington*, 2nd edn., 1792.

A Letter to William Paley from a Poor Labourer, 1793.

Lilburne, John, *The Tryal of Lieutenant Colonell J. Lilburn*, ed. Theodorus Verax, 2nd edn., 1710.

Lovett, William, *The Life and Struggles of William Lovett*, 1876.

Lowth, Robert, *Lectures on the Sacred Poetry of the Hebrews*, trans. G. Gregory, 1787, 2 vols.

——, *A Short Introduction to English Grammar*, 1762, EL no. 18.

Mackintosh, Sir James, *Memoirs of the Life of the Right Honourable Sir James Mackintosh*, ed. Robert James Mackintosh, 1835, 2 vols.

——, *Vindiciae Gallicae*, Dublin, 1791.

Mathias, Thomas James, *The Pursuits of Literature*, 2nd edn., 1797.

Mill, James, 'Tooke's Diversions of Purley', *Literary Journal*, i (1806), 1–16.

Monboddo, Lord, see Burnett, James.

Monthly Review

[More, Hannah], *Cheap Repository Tracts; Entertaining, Moral and Religious*, 1798, 3 vols.

——, *The Riot; or Half a Loaf is Better than no Bread*, signed Z [1795].

——, *The Shepherd of Salisbury Plain*, signed Z, undated, 2 pts.

——, *The Two Shoemakers*, signed Z, undated.

——, *Village Politics addressed to all the Mechanics, Journeymen, and Day Labourers in Great Britain by Will Chip*, 1793.

Murray, Lindley, *English Grammar*, 1795, EL no. 106.

——, *English Grammar*, 1808, 2 vols.

Nottingham Journal

Paine, Thomas, *The Writings of Thomas Paine*, ed. M. D. Conway, 1894–6, 4 vols.

[Paine, Thomas], 'Mr. Dunlap', signed Comus, *Pennsylvania Packet; or, General Advertiser*, 16 Mar. 1779.

Paley, William, *Reasons for Contentment; addressed to the Labouring Parts of the British Public*, 1793.

[Parkinson, James], *An Address to the Hon. Edmund Burke from the Swinish Multitude*, signed Old Hubert, undated.

——, *A Sketch by Old Hubert: Whilst the Honest Poor are Wanting Bread* [1795?].

——, *The Village Association; or, the Politics of Edley*, signed Old Hubert [1793?].

——, *A Vindication of the London Corresponding Society* [1796?].

Parr, Samuel, *A Discourse on Education and on the Plans pursued in Charity-Schools* [1786].

Peel, Frank, *The Rising of the Luddites, Chartists and Plug-Drawers*, 4th edn., reprinted in 1968.

Percy, Thomas, *Reliques of Ancient English Poetry* (1765), 6th edn., 1823, 4 vols.

Place, Francis, *The Autobiography of Francis Place*, ed. Mary Thrale, Cambridge, 1972.

Plain Answers to Plain Questions in a Dialogue between John Bull and Bonaparte [1803].

Polwhele, Richard, *The Unsex'd Females*, 1798.

Priestley, Joseph, *A Course of Lectures on Oratory and Criticism*, 1777, EL no. 126.

——, *A Course of Lectures on the Theory of Language and Universal Grammar*, 1762, EL no. 235.

——, *The Rudiments of English Grammar*, 1761, EL no. 210.

Quarterly Review

Rickwood, Edgell (ed.), *Radical Squibs and Loyal Ripostes: Satirical Pamphlets of the Regency Period, 1819-1821*, Bath, 1971.

Rogers, Samuel, *Recollections*, ed. William Sharpe, 2nd edn., 1859.

Sheridan, Thomas, *A Dissertation on the Causes of the Difficulties which Occur in Learning the English Tongue*, 1761, EL no. 40.

——, *A General Dictionary of the English Language*, 1780, 2 vols., EL no. 50, 2 vols.

[Shelley, P. B.], *A Letter to Lord Ellenborough occasioned by the Sentence which he passed on Mr D. I. Eaton*, 1894.

[Southey, Robert], 'Parliamentary Reform', *Quarterly Review*, xvi (1816), 225-78.

——, 'The Rise and Progress of Popular Dissaffection', *Quarterly Review*, xvi (1817), 511-52.

——, *Wat Tyler; a Dramatic Poem. A New Edition with a Preface Suitable to Recent Circumstances*, 1817.

Spence, Thomas, *The Case of Thomas Spence, Book-Seller* [1792].

——, *Dhe impórtánt Triál öv Tóm'is Sp'ens For a Pól'it'ik'al Pámfl'et 'entitld 'Dhē Rēstorr öv Sosiēte tw its nāteüral Stat'*, 3 pt., 1803.

——, *The Grand Repository of the English Language*, 1775, EL no. 155.

——, *The Important Trial of Thomas Spence* [1801].

——, *Pig's Meat; or Lessons for the Swinish Multitude*, 1793-6, 3 vols.

——, *The Restorer of Society to its Natural State*, 1801.

——, *The Rights of Infants*, 1797.

——, *Spence's Recantation of the End of Oppression* [1795].

[Spence, Thomas], *A Supplement to the History of Robinson Crusoe*, 2nd edn., Newcastle, 1782.

Stewart, Dugald, 'On the Tendency of Some Late Philological Speculations', *The Collected Works of Dugald Stewart*, ed. Sir William
Hamilton, Edinburgh, 1835, 10 vols., vol. v.

Thelwall, John, *An Appeal to Popular Opinion against Kidnapping and
Murder*, 1796.

——, *Poems chiefly written in Retirement*, 2nd edn., 1801.

——, *Prospectus of a Course of Lectures*, 1796.

——, *The Tribune; a Periodical Publication consisting chiefly of the
Political Lectures of J. Thelwall*, 1795-6, 3 vols.

[Thelwall, John], *The Peripatetic*, signed Sylvanus Theophrastus, 1793,
3 vols.

Tooke, John Horne, 'A Letter to John Dunning Esq.', ΕΠΕΑ
ΠΤΕΡΟΕΝΤΑ, *or the Diversions of Purley*, ed. Richard Taylor,
1860.

——, ΕΠΕΑ ΠΤΕΡΟΕΝΤΑ *or, the Diversions of Purley*, 1798 and 1805,
EL no. 127, 2 vols.

Trimmer, Sarah, *Reflections upon the Education of Children in Charity
Schools*, 1792.

Tuckerman, Henry T., *Characteristics of Literature illustrated by the
Genius of Distinguished Writers*, 2nd series, Philadelphia, 1851.

Wakefield, Gilbert, *The Defence of Gilbert Wakefield* [1799].

——, *Reply to Some Parts of the Bishop of Landaff's Address to the
People of Great Britain*, 3rd edn., 1798.

Walker, John, *A Rhetorical Grammar*, 1785, EL no. 266.

Webster, Noah, *Dissertations on the English Language*, 1789, EL no.
54.

——, *A Grammatical Institute of the English Language*, 1783 and 1784,
EL nos. 89-90, 2 vols.

——, *A Letter to the Governors, Instructors, and Trustees of the Universities*, New York, 1798.

——, *A Philosophical and Practical Grammar of the English Language*,
New Haven, 1807.

Windham, William, *The Diary of the Right Hon. William Windham,
1784-1810*, ed. Mrs Henry Baring, 1866.

Wooler, Thomas J., *The Black Dwarf*, 1817-24, 12 vols.

——, *A Verbatim Report of the Two Trials of T. J. W., Editor of the
Black Dwarf*, 1817.

Wordsworth, William, *The Letters of William and Dorothy Wordsworth*,
ed. Ernest de Selincourt, 2nd edn., *The Early Years, 1787-1805*,
revised by Chester L. Shaver, 1967; *The Middle Years, 1806-1811*,
revised by Mary Moorman, 1969.

——, *The Prose Works of William Wordsworth*, ed. W. J. B. Owen and
J. W. Smyser, Oxford, 1974, 3 vols.

A Wurd or 2 of good counsil to abowt hafe a duzzen diffrant sorts o fokes. By Nichalas Noboddy, Birmingham, 1792.

SECONDARY SOURCES

Aarsleff, Hans, *From Locke to Saussure: Essays on the Study of Language and Intellectual History*, Minneapolis, 1982.

——, *The Study of Language in England 1780-1860*, Princeton, 1967.

Abrams, M. H., *Natural Supernaturalism: Tradition and Revolution in Romantic Literature*, New York, 1973.

Adamson, John William, *English Education, 1789-1902*, Cambridge, 1930.

Aldred, Guy A., *Richard Carlile, Agitator: His Life and Times*, Glasgow, 1941.

Aldridge, Alfred Owen, *Man of Reason: The Life of Thomas Paine*, 1960.

——, 'Thomas Paine: A Survey of Research and Criticism since 1945', *British Studies Monitor*, v (1975), 3-29.

Alston, R. C., *A Bibliography of the English Language from the Invention of Printing to the Year 1800*, Leeds, 1965-71, 11 vols.

——, English Linguistics, 1500-1800 (A Collection of Facsimile Reprints), Menston, 1967.

Altick, Richard, *The English Common Reader: A Social History of the Mass Reading Public, 1800-1900*, Chicago, 1957.

Aspinall, Arthur, 'The Circulation of Newspapers in the Early Nineteenth Century', *Review of English Studies*, xxii (1946), 29-43.

——, *Politics and the Press, c.1780-1850*, 1949.

Barrell, John, *English Literature in History, 1730-80: An Equal, Wide Survey*, gen. ed. Raymond Williams, 1983.

Baugh, Albert, *History of the English Language*, 1951.

Beattie, Arthur, *William Wordsworth: His Doctrine and his Art in their Historical Relations*, University of Wisconsin Studies in Language and Literature, no. 24, 2nd edn., Madison, 1927.

Bergheaud, Patrice, 'De James Harris à John Horne Tooke: Mutations de l'analyse du langage en Angleterre dans la deuxième moitié du XVIIIe siècle, *Historiographia Linguistica*, vi (1979), 15-45.

Birrell, T. A., 'The Political Register: Cobbett and English Literature', *English Studies*, xlv (1964), 214-9.

Black, Eugene Charlton, *British Extraparliamentary Political Organization, 1769-1793*, Cambridge, Mass., 1963.

Blakely, Dorothy, *The Minerva Press, 1790-1820*, 1939.

Boulton, James T., *Arbitrary Power; an Eighteenth-Century Obsession*, University of Nottingham Inaugural Lecture, Nottingham, 1966.

——, (ed.), *Johnson: The Critical Heritage*, 1971.

——, *The Language of Politics in the Age of Wilkes and Burke*, Westport, 1975.

Brailsford, H. N., *Shelley, Godwin and their Circle*, 1913.

Brewer, John, *Party Ideology and Popular Politics at the Accession of George III*, Cambridge, 1976.

Burke, Peter, *Popular Culture in Early Modern Europe*, 1978.

——, 'Religion and Crisis in Seventeenth-Century Naples' unpublished paper, delivered at the University of Birmingham, 28 Jan. 1980.

——, 'The Virgin of the Carmine and the Revolt of Masaniello', *Past and Present*, no. 99 (1983), 3–21.

Cameron, Kenneth Neil, *The Young Shelley: Genesis of a Radical*, 1951.

Campbell, Theophila Carlile, *The Battle of the Press as Told in the Story of the Life of Richard Carlile*, 1899.

Carnall, Geoffrey, *Robert Southey and his Age: The Development of a Conservative Mind*, Oxford, 1960.

Chard, Leslie, *Dissenting Republican: Wordsworth's Early Life and Thought in their Political Context*, 1972.

Clark, Henry Haden, 'Thomas Paine's Theory of Rhetoric', *Transactions of the Wisconsin Academy*, xxviii (1933), 307–41.

Clark, Mary Elizabeth, 'Peter Porcupine in America: The Career of William Cobbett, 1792–1800'. Unpublished Ph.D dissertation, University of Pennsylvania, 1939.

Cloyd, E. L., *James Burnett, Lord Monboddo*, Oxford, 1972.

Cohen, Murray, *Sensible Words; Linguistic Practice in England, 1640–1785*, Baltimore, Maryland, 1977.

Cole, G. D. H., *The Life of William Cobbett*, 1924.

Cone, Carl B., *The English Jacobins: Reformers in Late Eighteenth Century England*, New York, 1968.

Culler, Jonathan, *Ferdinande de Saussure*, Modern Masters, New York, 1976.

Cruse, Amy, *The Englishman and his Books in the Early Nineteenth Century*, 1930.

Davenport, Allen, *The Life, Writings, and Principles of Thomas Spence* [1836].

Duff, Gerald, *William Cobbett and the Politics of Earth*, Salzburg Studies in English Literature, Romantic Reassessment, gen. ed. James Hogg, Salzburg, 1972.

Emsley, Bert, 'James Buchanan and the Eighteenth-Century Regulation of English Usage', *PMLA*, xviii (1933), 1154–66.

Emsley, Clive, *British Society and the French Wars, 1793–1815*, 1979.

Erdman, David, *Blake; Prophet against Empire*, 3rd edn., Princeton, 1977.

——, 'Coleridge as Editorial Writer', *Power and Consciousness*, ed. Conor Cruise O'Brien and William Dean Vanech, 1969.

Evans, Michael Kent, 'Coleridge on the Evolution of Language', *Studies in Romanticism*, xx (1980), 163–83.

Everest, Kelvin, *Coleridge's Secret Ministry: The Context of the Conversation Poems, 1795–1798*, New York, 1979.

Flugel, Ewald, 'The History of English Philology', *Flugel Memorial Volume*, University Series, Stanford, 1916.

Foner, Eric, *Tom Paine in Revolutionary America*, 1976.

Formigari, L., Language and Society in the Late Eighteenth Century', *Journal of the History of Ideas*, xxxv (1974), 275–93.

Foucault, Michel, *The Order of Things; An Archaeology of the Human Sciences*, 1977.

Frost, Michael Brian, 'The Development of Provided Schooling for Working Class Children in Birmingham, 1781–1851', unpublished M. Litt. dissertation, University of Birmingham, 1978.

Fruman, Norman, *Coleridge: The Damaged Archangel*, 1972.

Furlong, Monica, *Puritan's Progress: A Study of John Bunyan*, 1975.

Ginter, Donald, 'The Loyalist Association Movement', *Historical Journal*, ix (1966), 179–90.

Goodwin, Albert, *The Friends of Liberty: The English Democratic Movement in the Age of the French Revolution*, 1979.

Gramsci, Antonio, *Letters from Prison*, trans. Lynne Lawner, 1975.

Hackwood, Frederick William, *William Hone: His Life and Times*, 1912.

Halévy, Elie, *England in 1815*, trans. E. I. Watkin, 2nd edn., 1949.

Heath, William, *Wordsworth and Coleridge: A Study of their Literary Relations in 1801–1802*, Oxford, 1970.

Hepworth, Brian, *Robert Lowth*, Twayne's English Author Series, Boston, 1978.

Holyoake, George Jacob, *The Life and Character of Richard Carlile* [1870].

Hone, J. Anne, *For the Cause of Truth: Radicalism in London, 1796–1821*, Oxford, 1982.

——, 'William Hone (1780–1842), Publisher and Book-Seller: An Approach to Early Nineteenth Century London Radicalism', *Historical Studies*, xvi (1974), 55–70.

Hopkins, Mary Alden, *Hannah More and her Circle*, New York, 1947.

Howell, Wilbur Samuel, *Eighteenth-Century British Logic and Rhetoric*, Princeton, 1971.

Ikegami, Yoshihiko, *Noah Webster's Grammar: Traditions and Innovations – A Critical Study on Early English Grammars Published in the United States*, The Proceedings of the Dept. of Foreign Languages and Literatures, College of General Education, University of Tokyo, Tokyo, xix, no. 2, 1971.

Jackson, J. R. de, (ed.), *Coleridge: The Critical Heritage*, 1970.

Jacobus, Mary, *Tradition and Experiment in the Lyrical Ballads (1798)*, 1976.

James, Louis, *Print and the People, 1819-1851*, 1976.

Jones, M. G., *The Charity School Movement: A Study of Eighteenth Century Puritanism in Action*, Cambridge, 1938.

——, *Hannah More*, Cambridge, 1952.

Jones, Richard Foster, *The Triumph of the English Language*, 1953.

Kemp-Ashraf, P. M., 'Thomas Spence, 1750-1814', *Essays in Honour of William Gallacher*, Life and Literature of the Working Class, Berlin, 1966.

Knight, Charles, *The Old Printer and the Λ   ʾrn Press*, 1854.

Knox, Thomas R., 'Thomas Spence: The Trumpet of Jubilee, *Past and Present*, no. 76 (1977), 75-98.

Land, Stephen K., 'Lord Monboddo and the Theory of Syntax in the Late Eighteenth Century, *Journal of the History of Ideas*, xxxvii (1976), 423-40.

——, *From Signs to Propositions: The Concept of Form in Eighteenth-Century Semantic Theory*, Longman Linguistic Library, 1974.

Laqueur, Thomas Walter, *Religion and Respectability: Sunday Schools and Working Class Culture, 1780-1850*, New Haven, 1976.

Leavis, Q. D., *Fiction and the Reading Public*, 1932.

Leonard, Sterling Adams, *The Doctrine of Correctness in English Usage, 1700-1800*, University of Wisconsin, Studies in Language and Literature, no. 25, Madison, 1929.

Locke, Don, *A Fantasy of Reason: The Life and Thought of William Godwin*, 1980.

Maccoby, Simon, *English Radicalism, 1786-1832 from Paine to Cobbett*, 1955.

Macherey, Paul, *A Theory of Literary Production*, trans. Geoffrey Wall, 1978.

McCue, Daniel, 'Daniel Isaac Eaton and Politics for the People', unpublished Ph.D dissertation, Columbia University, 1954.

——, 'The Pamphleteer Pitt's Government Couldn't Silence', *Eighteenth Century Life*, v (1978), 38-54.

MacFarland, Thomas, *Romanticism and the Forms of Ruin; Wordsworth, Coleridge, and the Modalities of Fragmentation*, Princeton, 1981.

Mayo, Robert, 'The Contemporaneity of the Lyrical Ballads', *PMLA*, lxix (1954), 486-522.

Meech, Sanford B., 'Early Application of Latin Grammar to English', *PMLA*, 1 (1935), 1012-32.

Michael, Ian, *English Grammatical Categories and the Tradition to 1800*, Cambridge, 1970.

Mitchell, Austin, 'The Association Movement', *Historical Journal*, vi (1961), 56–77.

Moorman, Mary, *William Wordsworth, a Biography*, Oxford, 1957–65, 3 vols.

More, Martha, *Mendip Annals*, ed. Arthur Roberts, 1859.

Morison, Stanley, *John Bell, 1745–1831*, Cambridge, 1930.

Neuburg, Victor, *Popular Literature, A History and Guide*, 1977.

Oberg, Barbara Bowen, 'David Hartley and the Association of Ideas', *Journal of the History of Ideas*, xxxvii (1976), 441–54.

Owen, W. J. B., *Wordsworth's Preface to Lyrical Ballads*, Copenhagen, 1957.

Parssinen, T. M., 'Thomas Spence and the Origins of English Land Nationalization', *Journal of the History of Ideas*, xxxiv (1973), 135–41.

Pearl, M. C., *William Cobbett: A Bibliographical Account of his Life and Times*, 1953.

Pendleton, Gayle Trunsdel, 'The English Pamphlet Literature of the Age of the French Revolution *Anatomized*', *Eighteenth-Century Life*, v (1978), 29–37.

Peterson, Ted, 'The Fight of William Hone for British Press Freedom', *Journalism Quarterly*, xxv (1948), 132–5.

Plant, Marjorie, *The English Book Trade: An Economic History of the Making and Sale of Books*, 1939.

Poldauf, Ivan, *On the History of Some Problems of English Grammar before 1800*, Prague Studies in English, Prague, 1948.

Prickett, Stephen, *Wordsworth and Coleridge: The Lyrical Ballads*, Studies in English Literature, no. 56, Southampton, 1975.

Prothero, Iorweth, *Artisans and Politics in Early Nineteenth-Century London: John Gast and his Times*, Folkestone, 1979.

Quinlan, Maurice J., 'Anti-Jacobin Propaganda in England, 1792–1794', *Journalism Quarterly*, xvi (1943), 12–23.

Roberts, William (ed.), *Memoirs of the Life and Correspondence of Mrs Hannah More*, 3rd edn., 1835, 3 vols.

Rolleston, F. W., *Some Account of the Conversion of the Late William Hone*, 1853.

Rollins, Richard M., *The Long Journey of Noah Webster*, Philadelphia, 1980.

——, 'Words as Social Control: Noah Webster and the Creation of the American Dictionary', *Recycling the Past*, ed. L. Zenderland, Philadelphia, 1978.

Roper, Derek, *Reviewing before the Edinburgh, 1788–1802*, 1978.

Rudkin, Olive, *Thomas Spence and his Connections*, New York, 1966.

Sambrook, James, *William Cobbett*, Rutledge Author Guides, gen. ed. B. C. Southam, 1973.

Sanford, Mrs Henry, *Thomas Poole and his Friends*, 1888, 2 vols.

Schneider, Ben Rose, *Wordsworth's Cambridge Education*, Cambridge, 1957.

Shields, Anthea, 'Thomas Spence and the English Language', *Transactions of the Philological Society*, Oxford, 1974.

Sikes, Hershel M., 'William Hone: Regency Patriot, Parodist and Pamphleteer', *Newberry Library Bulletin*, v (1961), 281–94.

Simon, Brian, *Studies in the History of Education, 1780–1870*, 1960.

Sledd, James H., and Gwin J. Kolb., *Dr. Johnson's Dictionary: Essays in the Biography of a Book*, Chicago, 1955.

Smith, J. W. Ashley, *The Birth of Modern Education: The Contribution of the Dissenting Academies, 1660–1800*, 1954.

Snyder, Alice D., *Coleridge on Logic and Learning with Selections from the Unpublished Manuscripts*, New Haven, 1929.

Spater, George, *William Cobbett: The Poor Man's Friend*, 1982, 2 vols.

Spinney, G. H., 'Cheap Repository Tracts: Hazard and Marshall Edition', *The Library*, 4th series, xx (1940), 295–340.

Spufford, Margaret, *Small Books and Pleasant Histories: Popular Fiction and its Readership in Seventeenth-Century England*, 1981.

Stephens, Alexander, *Memoirs of John Horne Tooke interspersed with Original Documents*, 1813, 2 vols.

Stone, Lawrence, 'Literacy and Education in England, 1640–1900', *Past and Present*, no. 42 (1969), 69–139.

[Thelwall, Mrs John], *The Life of John Thelwall by his Widow*, 1837.

Thompson, E. P., 'Disenchantment or Default? A Lay Sermon', *Power and Consciousness*, ed. Conor Cruise O'Brien and William Dean Vanech, 1969.

——, *The Making of the English Working Class*, New York, 1966.

——, 'Patrician Society, Plebian Culture', *Journal of Social History*, vii (1974), 382–405.

[Thompson, E. P.], 'Bliss was it in that Dawn. The Matter of Coleridge's Revolutionary Youth and How it Became Obscured', *Times Literary Supplement*, no. 3623 (1971), 929–32.

Thompson, Henry, *The Life of Hannah More with Notices of her Sisters*, 1838.

Thompson, Richard S., *Classics or Charity?: The Dilemma of Eighteenth Century Grammar Schools*, Manchester, 1971.

Tyson, Gerald, P., *Joseph Johnson: A Liberal Publisher*, Iowa City, 1979.

Vicinus, Martha, *The Industrial Muse: A Study of Nineteenth Century British Working-Class Literature*, 1974.

Ward, William S., *British Periodicals and Newspapers, 1789-1832: A Bibliography of Secondary Sources*, Lexington, 1972.

Webb, R. K., *The British Working Class Reader, 1790-1848: Literacy and Social Tension*, 1955.

——, 'Working Class Readers in Early Victorian England', *English Historical Review*, vlxv (1950), 333-477.

West, C. E., 'Lindley Murray, the Grammarian', unpublished Ph.D dissertation, Leeds University, 1953.

Wickwar, William, *The Struggle for the Freedom of the Press, 1819-1832*, 1928.

Williams, G. A., 'The Concept of "Egemonia" in the Thought of Antonio Gramsci: Some Notes in Interpretation', *Journal of the History of Ideas*, xxi (1960), 587-99.

Williams, Raymond, *Cobbett*, Past Masters, Oxford, 1983.

——, *The County and the City*, 1973.

——, *The Long Revolution*, 1965.

Willoughby, L. A., 'Coleridge as a Philologist', *Modern Language Review*, xxi (1936), 176-201.

Woodring, Carl Ray, *Politics in the Poetry of Coleridge*, Madison, 1961.

Wyld, Henry Cecil, *A History of Modern Colloquial English*, 1920.

Yarborough, Minnie, *John Horne Tooke*, New York, 1926.

Yonge, Charlotte M., Eminent Women Series, 1888.

Index